*Mythic Masks in
Self-Reflexive Poetry*

UNIVERSITY OF NORTH CAROLINA
STUDIES IN COMPARATIVE LITERATURE

Number 62

WERNER P. FRIEDERICH, *Founder*
DIANE R. LEONARD, *Editor*

Editorial Board
EDWIN L. BROWN
ALFRED G. ENGSTROM
EUGENE H. FALK
ALDO D. SCAGLIONE
JOSEPH P. STRELKA

Mythic Masks in Self-Reflexive Poetry

A STUDY OF PAN AND ORPHEUS

Dorothy Zayatz Baker

The University of North Carolina Press
Chapel Hill and London

© 1986 The University of North Carolina Press
All rights reserved
Manufactured in the United States of America

Library of Congress Cataloging-in-Publication Data

Baker, Dorothy Zayatz.
Mythic masks in self-reflexive poetry.

(University of North Carolina studies in comparative literature ; no. 62)
Bibliography: p.
Includes index.
1. Pan (Greek deity) in literature. 2. Orpheus
(Greek mythology) in literature. 3. Poets in
literature. 4. Poetry—History and criticism.
I. Title. II. Series.
PN57.P25B35   1986   809.1'9351   85-16468
ISBN 0-8078-7062-5

Contents

Preface ix

1.
Introduction and Mythology 3

2.
Early Poetic Personae 29

3.
French Parnassians and Symbolists 48

4.
Aleksandr Blok and Valerii Briusov 89

5.
An American Mythology of the Poet:
Wallace Stevens and Hart Crane 119

6.
Conclusion 147

Notes 155

Bibliography 171

Index 181

Preface

Translations of Greek and Latin poetry will appear in the text with the original poetry; the translators will be cited in the endnotes. The translations of Italian and Russian critical works and of Russian poetry are mine and will also be included in the text.

    I must first acknowledge Alfred Weber, whose seminal work in *poetologische Lyrik* provided the impetus for this study. I am happy to thank Professor Weber for generous access to his materials, for his hospitality, and for his ceaseless enthusiasm for this undertaking. Debts to one's professors can never be repaid, and I gladly acknowledge such indebtedness to Vahan D. Barooshian, John Fuegi, W. Milne Holton, and Harold J. Smith. I would especially like to thank Milne Holton for his invaluable counsel, for his encouragement, and for reading and rereading this manuscript innumerable times. Above all, I am so very grateful to Elizabeth and Daniel for their high spirits, and to Larry for his unfailing support.

*Mythic Masks in
Self-Reflexive Poetry*

Lorsqu'un homme se masque ou se revêt d'un pseudonymne, nous nous sentons défiés. Cet homme se refuse à nous. En revanche nous voulons savoir, nous entreprenons de le démasquer. Devant qui cherche-t-il à se dissimuler? Devant quel Pouvoir a-t-il peur? Quel Regard lui fait donc honte? Nous demandons derechef: comment était fait son visage, pour qu'il ait eu besoin de le dissimuler? Et une nouvelle question s'enchaîne aux précédentes: que veut dire ce nouveau visage dont il s'affuble, quelle signification donne-t-il à ses conduites masquées, quel personnage vient-il maintenant simuler, après avoir dissimulé ce qui voulait disparaître?

Jean Starobinski, L'Œil vivant

1

Introduction and Mythology

INTRODUCTION

Throughout the history of the lyric, the poet has discussed his art with his audience through the very medium of his poetry. When the poet addresses subjects such as the nature of his craft, the function of the poet, and the essence of the creative act within his poetry, he creates a distinct form of lyric poetry that Alfred Weber has termed *poetologische Lyrik*. Known in English as "self-reflexive poetry," the term denotes "alle Gedichte, die sich entweder mit dem *Dichter* (seiner Aufgabe und Funktion), mit dem *Dichten* (dem schöpferischen Prozess und seinen Wegen) oder mit dem *Werk der Dichtung* (seiner Form und seinen sprachlichen Mitteln) befassen."[1] By this most general definition, then, self-reflexive poetry is poetry mirroring and examining itself.

Although self-reflexivity has been a common feature of lyric expression since Horace's *Ars poetica*, there is a special emphasis on such introspection in modern poetry—as well as in the novel, drama, film, painting, and architecture. Weber explains the significance of this phenomenon as the poet's attempt to articulate his artistic commitment within an unlyrical world. The poet's struggle, he claims, is ultimately "ein Symptom für die extreme Belastung des schöpferischen Bewusstseins und die Isolation des Dichters in diesem technisierten Jahrhundert."[2]

Indeed, in late nineteenth- and twentieth-century poetry we find increasing emphasis on the poet, his creative role, and his position within society. Although such scrutiny is a common feature throughout the history of self-reflexive poetry, nineteenth- and twentieth-century poetry alone is characterized by the ironic self-image of the poet and the self-deprecating poetic personae that the artist himself creates.

This study focuses on the poet's scrutiny of his artistic and social roles within modern French, Russian, and American self-reflexive poetry. Within this particular lyric form, the poet wrestles with his self-conception, his artistic role, and his social identity in an effort to determine the nature and extent of his special powers, if indeed they exist at all. Moreover, he examines the importance of his work for his fellow man. In particular, this study will focus on the persona the artist creates in his effort to represent himself to his audience, especially on the mythic prototypes of Pan and Orpheus, which are frequent masks of the poet in self-reflexive verse.

Weber has shown that self-reflexive poetry, as a lyric mode, "bezeichnet einen Stoff- und Themenbereich der Lyrik, in dem von Autor zu Autor und Epoche zu Epoche stets individuelle und zeitbezogene poetologische Probleme und Überzeugungen zur Sprache gebracht wurden, in dem aber auch Ideen, Motive und Bilder feststellbar sind, die in wechelnden Kontexten mit erstaunlicher Konstanz immer wieder erscheinen."[3] The specific masks with which the poet presents himself and the conventions he chooses to describe himself are examples of motifs that, as Weber notes, appear and reappear "mit erstaunlicher Konstanz" throughout literary history.

Because the mythological figures, Pan and Orpheus, are both distinctly artists, it is not surprising that they represent two such recurring archetypes of the poet.[4] Throughout the history of lyric poetry, the artist has repeatedly invoked Pan and Orpheus as mythic prototypes. Consequently, a study of these figures, as they appear in explicitly self-reflexive poetry, affords a view of the poet's conception of his creative role and social position. As one would readily anticipate, this self-conception has hardly remained constant throughout the history of the lyric. Therefore, a historical study of these figures from their early incorporation in British, French, and Russian verse until their appearance in late nineteenth- and twentieth-century French, Russian, and American poetry reveals the dramatic transformation of Pan and Orpheus in the poet's eyes. Such a study also describes the radically changing self-conception of the modern poet.

To that end, the study begins with a brief consideration of Pan and Orpheus mythology. The object here is not mythography as such, but rather a delineation of the personality and fate of each figure in order to identify which mythic elements capture the imagination and sympathy of later poets in their attempts to describe their own artistic and social roles.

Then, a survey of the appearance of Pan and Orpheus in self-reflexive poetry from the Middle Ages to the eighteenth century shows that the poet selectively draws on the priestly, vatic identities of these figures when they are invoked as prototypes of the poet. Likewise, he systematically omits any consideration of their manic traits or the more tragic elements of the mythological tales. When conceived in this manner, Pan and Orpheus are ideal prototypes for the poet who views his role as that of a poetic priest or prophet.

The romantic period marks an era of transition in which the poet gradually abandons the pastoral, vatic image of both Pan and Orpheus and begins to confront the tragic aspects of the mythology. This development, in turn, signals the poet's reevaluation of his creative activity and his social role.

The poet's introspection is further intensified in the late-nineteenth and early-twentieth centuries when powerful mythic masks give way to self-deprecating personae. Pan and Orpheus, in symbolist and post-symbolist poetry, are clownish, maimed, or suicidal, often poetically sterile, and at times completely silent. Moreover, beginning in the nineteenth century, these mythological figures gradually assume the physical characteristics and personality of the clown—under a multitude of guises ranging from the *commedia dell'arte* Pierrot, Harlequin, and Crispin to the court jester, the *saltimbanque*, and the *pitre*. Yet the motif of the poet as clown most often retains its roots in the mythology of Pan and Orpheus. In most cases, elements of Pan and Orpheus are fused with a description of the poet as clown; in others, the poet is purely a clown figure who perhaps looks to Pan as poetic prototype. The poet as self-proclaimed fool or buffoon represents a modern literary motif that occurs with surprising regularity, transcending all cultural and linguistic barriers in both Europe and the Americas. The motif of the poet-*pitre* is one of the most important conventions used by the modern artist in his self-reflexive work. Moreover, this tragic poetic persona bears further testimony to the poet's isolation, diminished social position, and ironic self-image in modern society.

Finally, in twentieth-century American poetry, we see the gradual rejection of the self-reflexive motif of the poet-*pitre*. In its stead, the poet reaches again into ancient mythology and returns to the more vital and more positive poetic prototypes found in the Pan and Orpheus myths. Attempting to break his isolation, to reconcile himself with reality, and to reestablish his social position, the poet looks to ancient mythological prototypes, which represent for him some measure of affinity between the poet and his world.

In addition to the historical development of these mythic masks, this study presents a problem in literary influence. We begin detailed analysis of individual poems commencing with the work of the late nineteenth-century French Parnassians and symbolists, who make extensive use of Pan and Orpheus and introduce the motif of the poet as clown into their self-reflexive poetry. Subsequent examination of Russian and American poetry is limited to those self-reflexive works that in some way exhibit the influence of the earlier French Parnassians and symbolists. Thus, our work in Russian and American poetry attempts not only to study the self-reflexive nature of the specific poems, the poet's self-conception, and use of mythic masks, but also to clarify the ways in which the various poets draw on their French predecessors. Our discussion emphasizes the motifs and attitudes that ally the Russian and American poets with the French, as well as those which serve to distinguish them from their predecessors.

PAN AND ORPHEUS: THE MYTHIC TALES

Born in Arcadia of the god Hermes and Dryope, daughter of Dryops, Pan is both god and animal.[5] He is claimed to be so hideous at birth, with his hirsute face, horns, shaggy legs, and tail, that his nurse is forced to abandon him in terror. His father, Hermes, ascends Mount Olympus with the infant Pan, who serves to amuse the gods, thereby beginning his career as their clown and jester.

As a central figure of the Arcadian goat cult, Pan is a shepherd responsible for the care and fertility of the area's herds. However, he commands little respect from the Arcadians, who whip him whenever the goats fail to reproduce. Pan is a somewhat lonely figure, a shepherd piper and moonlight dancer who remains in remote caves and on hilltops, never hesitating to inspire "panic" in those who would disturb his solitude.

The first known literary characterization of Pan is the "Homeric Hymn to Pan," a fifth-century B.C. lyric that is assuredly not Homeric. The author of this hymn terms Pan νόμιον Θεὸν ἀγλαέ-Θειρον ("the pastoral God with the glorious locks"), and describes him as a charming bucolic goat-god who φρένα πᾶσιν ἔτερψε ("gave pleasure to all hearts").[6] The Arcadian Pan is the subject of many ancient Greek poets, notably Theocritus and Herodotus, but Ovid's *Metamorphoses* contains the best-known tale of Pan. It is in Ovid's story that Pan gains recognition as creator of the musical instrument, the pan-pipe. While fleeing from the amorous Pan, a nymph, Syrinx, runs to the edge of a stream and is transformed into a reed by one of her virgin sisters. Pan immediately reaches for the nymph, catches an armful of reeds, and

> Panaque cum prensam sibi iam Syringa putaret,
> corpore pro nymphae calamos tenuisse palustres,
> dumque ibi suspirat, motos in harundine ventos
> effecisse sonum tenuem similemque querenti.
> Arte nova vocisque deum dulcedine captum
> "hoc mihi concilium tecum" dixisse "manebit,"
> atque ita disparibus calamis conpagine cerae
> inter se iunctis nomen tenuisse puellae.

[Pan, when now he thought he had caught Syrinx, instead of her held naught but marsh reeds in his arms; and while he sighed in disappointment, the soft air stirring in the reeds gave forth a low and complaining sound. Touched by this wonder and charmed by the sweet tones, the god exclaimed: "This union, at least, shall I have with thee." And so the pipes, made of unequal reeds fitted together by a joining of wax, took and kept the name of the maiden.][7]

Consequently, Ovid's account is the source of Pan's reputation as creator of the pan-pipe, an instrument born of loss and used to comfort suffering as well as to charm.

However, Pan's identity as a Dionysian god must not be overlooked. Because of his animallike appearance and his amorous pursuit of many and various nymphs, Pan enjoys a well-deserved reputation as a fertility god. He takes full part in bacchanalian rites and thereby appeals to the more instinctive side of man's nature, inspiring terror or "panic" by his music. Joseph Campbell finds that Pan's orgiastic rites serve as "illustrations of that divine 'enthusiasm' that overturns the reason and releases the force of the destructive-creative dark."[8]

Furthermore, because of similar appearance, Pan is often identified with the satyrs or the Latin fauns, which are actually rougher, more lascivious creatures, and true disciples of Bacchus. Their manic "enthusiasm" is most often less than divine. W. H. Roscher explains that the confusion between Pan and the satyr figure began in antiquity. "Satyrn, Silene, Pane und Faune, all'dass lustige Völkchen, das sich nach den Anschauungen des späteren Altertums im Gefolge des Dionysos ausgelassen umhertummelt,—schon in hellenistischer Zeit verschwimmen sie in einander, und man macht zwischen ihnen keinen grossen Unterschied, ja man ist sich wirklicher Unterschiede kaum mehr bewusst."[9] Like most ancient gods, Pan is *polyonymos*, worshipped under several names. This may account for the fact that the words Pan, faun, and satyr are used almost interchangeably by many modern poets.

Finally, the Arcadian and Dionysian mythology is complemented by the very important Orphic aspect of Pan mythology. Under this guise, Pan is a prophetic figure who bears qualities that are usually considered exclusively those of Orpheus. These include the power of music to move rocks and trees and to make animals dance. Equally important is the gift of prophecy. The Orphic Pan also holds the qualities of gods greater than he, in that he is considered to be a god of creation. Considering the range of abilities of the god Pan, we should perhaps use the German mythographic term, *Allgott*, to describe this mythic figure more precisely. *Allgott* accurately reflects Pan's universal powers, and furthermore hints at the etymological confusion underlying Pan's multiple identities. As early as the *Homeric Hymns*, poets have either indulged in intentional wordplay or incorrectly understood the derivation of the word Pan to be *pan*, meaning "all," rather than *pa-on*, the "feeder" or the "grazer." The author of the "Homeric Hymn to Pan" claims, for example, "Πᾶνα δέ μιν καλέεσκον οτι φρένα πᾶσιν ἔτερψε" ("Pan [which means all] was called thus, because he gave pleasure to all hearts") (l. 46). Karl Kerényi confirms the problem of wordplay or misunderstanding: "Dass All heisst in unserer Sprache *pan* und obwohl der Name des Gottes—ausser dem gleichen Klang— nichts damit zu tun hat, wurde er später doch mit dem Weltall gleichgesetzt."[10]

Because of this fortunate confusion, the goat-god gained stature as a universal deity.

Πᾶνα καλῶ κρατερόν, νόμιον, κόσμοιο τὸ σύμπαν,
οὐρανὸν ἠδὲ θάλασσαν ἰδὲ χθόνα παμβασίλειαν
καὶ πῦρ ἀθάνατον τάδε γὰρ μέλη ἐστὶ τὰ Πανός.

[I call strong Pan, the substance of the whole, / Etherial, marine, earthly, general soul, / Immortal fire; for all the world is thine, / And all are parts of thee, O pow'r divine.][11]

This is the opening strophe of the "Orphic Hymn to Pan," one of the earliest known poems to emphasize Pan's godly, prophetic powers while modifying his Arcadian identity. The *Orphic Hymns* are a sequence of lyric tributes to the Greek gods, the collection being falsely attributed to Orpheus. Many scholars of antiquity believe that the *Hymns* were authored by Onomakritos in the fifth century B.C., but E. R. Curtius places them in the third or fourth century, written by an unknown poet in Egypt or Asia Minor. Regardless of its origin, the "Orphic Hymn to Pan" clearly depicts Pan as the overseer of the world and each of its four elements. Within this poem, Pan remains a goat-god, a musician, and a dancer, but he is also creator and sustainer of the entire universe.

αἰγομελές, βακχευτά, φιλένθεε, ἀστροδίαιτε,
αρμονίαν κόσμοιο κρεκων φιλοπαίλμονι μολπῆι
φαντασιῶν ἐπαρωγέ, φόβων ἔκπαγλε βροτείων

> [Goat-footed, horned, Bacchanalian Pan, / Fanatic pow'r, from whom the world began, / Whose various parts by thee inspir'd, combine / In endless dance and melody divine.]
> (ll. 5–8)

It is also interesting to observe that the energy that animates Pan's universe is that of song and dance. Lyric force is, then, the impetus and the goal of the world created by the god Pan.

In the final analysis, however, it is neither the historical detail of any ancient literary source nor the most reasoned or "authoritative" account of mythic material that captures the imagination of the modern artist in his contemplation of the mythological Pan; it is the rich suggestiveness of the composite Arcadian, Dionysian, and Orphic identities. The goat-god Pan is a splendid and remarkable fusion of opposites, and this, perhaps more than anything, has attracted both poet and painter throughout history. Pan is a rough "semicaperque Deus, semideusque caper" ("the God half-goat, the goat half-God"), but there are few gods more intensely human than he.[12] Few are more sensitive, seek human love more passionately, or are able to inspire man, to pacify him, or incite him more quickly than this god. As an Arcadian shepherd, Pan is forcibly an isolate by occupation; he is a cave dweller, almost a recluse, yet he is tremendously social. One has the impression that Pan is consigned to his rocks and crags almost paradoxically because of his strong identification with the human race.

Pan's gift to humanity is, of course, his music, and here another fusion of opposites presents itself. The shepherd Pan plays a coarse and primitive instrument, but is able to extract sweet, pure tones from it. And in this crudely fashioned instrument, the lonely shepherd finds solace, comfort, and true beauty. According to Ovid, Pan so firmly believes in the splendor of his music that he challenges Apollo on the lyre. Pan himself proposes a musical contest with a superior god on a superior instrument, and wins—at least in the estimation of Midas, who, although he has little taste in music, is the bona fide judge of the match.[13]

Finally, Pan's status as both god and man is provocative. Regardless of the Olympian gods' shabby treatment of this peculiar goat-god, Pan is nonetheless a divine being, and, as such, bears divine knowledge. Pan is also an earthly being, by virtue of his mother Dryope, his occupation, and his association with man. This fusion of the human and the divine in one creature has led many later Christian poets—most notably Milton—to describe Pan as a pagan prefiguration of Jesus Christ. However, the central import of this dual identity for most modern poets is that the goat-god's divinity heightens his authority as a poet and musician by asserting that in this role he is also a priest and a prophet. As mediator between god and man, Pan claims a poetic priesthood; as bearer of divine knowledge, he acts as prophet. At the same time, his humanity forces him to share in man's fate on earth, thus he is able to speak to man in a way that other gods simply cannot. And he speaks to them through his simple music, which for all its simplicity has divine powers; and in spite of his divinity, the music is created for human beings who alone can appreciate this gift.

Like Pan, Orpheus can be traced to the sixth century B.C., but no earlier, leaving the question of their relative ages unanswered.[14] Orpheus is the son of the Thracian King Oeagrus and Calliope. Although it is true that many Mediterranean and southern European peoples, especially the Macedonians, share the legend of Orpheus, the hero is clearly Thracian in origin. Roscher points out that "fast das gesamte Altertum bezeichnet Orpheus als Thraker; die Macht dieser Überlieferung spricht sich hauptsächlich darin aus, dass sämtlich Kultusstätten, welche ausserhalb Thrakiens den Orpheus in ihre Legenden und Gründungsgeschichten verwoben, diese mit der thrakischen Herkunft auszugleichen bemüht gewesen sind."[15]

Because Orpheus is an Apollonian high priest, it is not surprising that his temperament and powers resemble those of Apollo, the god who first presented Orpheus with his lyre and who brought him to favor with the other gods on Mount Olympus. Apollonian myths indicate that even animals and rocks were charmed by the high god's lyre. This intimate association with Apollo and the resulting power of Orpheus's music contribute to Horace's depiction of the hero as "sacer interpresque deorum" ("holy prophet of the gods").[16] Indeed, Orpheus is not only a poet; he also has prophetic powers, and is therefore *vates*. In this respect, Orpheus strongly resembles the god for whom he is a priest.

Furthermore, like Apollo, Orpheus is a symbol of tranquility and peace, and exerts a calming, civilizing influence on mankind. W. K. C. Guthrie notes that one of the greatest powers of the Orphic lyre is its ability to soften the hearts of the fiercest warriors and to turn their thoughts to peace.[17] In fact, in *Ars poetica*, Horace's description of the mythological hero focuses on this quality.

> Silvestris homines sacer interpresque deorum
> caedibus et victu foedo deterruit Orpheus,
> dictus ob hoc lenire tigris rabidosque leones.
>
> [While men still roamed the woods, Orpheus, holy prophet of the gods, made them shrink from bloodshed and brutal living; hence the fable that he tamed tigers and ravening lions.]
> (ll. 391–93)

The music of Orpheus, then, is influential in his society's religious and moral life; the poet Orpheus provides the means for the seer and philosopher Orpheus to guide the Thracian people. In his study, *Orphée, civilisateur de l'humanité*, Jean Coman proposes that Orpheus's ability to pacify savage animals with his music allegorically suggests his desire to control man's primitive instincts. As poet and philosopher, Orpheus uses the medium of his music to speak to man's intelligence and sensibilities. "Orphée témoigna ainsi d'une bonté infinie de coeur, et d'une supériorité et d'une gravité merveilleuse de l'intelligence qui faisait du travail le principe directeur de la vie."[18]

The best known Orphic tale, however, concerns the *katábasis*, the hero's descent into the underworld in search of his wife, Eurydice. The wife of Orpheus is an enigmatic figure in ancient literature. She is generally presumed to be a Thracian nymph, although there is no full identification of her in literary sources. In fact, the Greek authors who mention Eurydice by name are few and relatively minor.[19] It is through Roman poets—especially Ovid and Virgil—that the modern reader learns of Orpheus's marriage, which ends in tragedy. According to Ovid's *Metamorphoses*, Eurydice dies immediately following the marriage ceremony. She receives a snake bite while strolling with her bridal attendants and falls dead (Book 10, ll. 1–10). Virgil elaborates on the death by introducing an amorous shepherd, Aristaeus, who chases the bride of Orpheus until she steps on a snake and is poisoned (*Georgics*, Book 4, ll. 457–59). In any event, Orpheus so mourns the loss of his wife that he attempts to rescue her from death. Enchanting the Furies, Ixion, Cerebrus, and other guardians of Hades with the music of his lyre, Orpheus recovers Eurydice who is to follow him through the underworld back to life. Orpheus, however, violates the sole condition under which he could safely guide her to life, that he not gaze at his wife until they both safely escape the underworld.

> hic, ne deficeret, metuens, avidusque vivendi
> flexit amans oculos, et protinus illa relapsa est.
>
> [he, afraid that she might fail him, eager for sight of her, turned back his longing eyes; and instantly she slipped into the depths.] (Ovid, *Met.*, Book 10, ll. 56–57).

Interrupting his song, Orpheus turns to look at his wife and thus loses her forever.

There exist several ancient accounts that tell of Orpheus's successful rescue of Eurydice from the underworld. Euripides alludes to the victory of Orpheus in *Alcestis*, and Isocrates, too, describes the hero's power to bring the dead to life.[20] According to Peter Dronke, "these allusions show that the story of the victorious Orpheus is the archaic one, and that it predominated until the first century B.C."[21] However, following the Middle Ages, the tales of Ovid and Virgil—which were later more popular and more widely translated sources of ancient mythology—were the more influential sources of the Orphic myth. Thus, the tales of the Orphic tragedy, and not those that present a joyful ending, formed most modern conceptions of the story of Orpheus and Eurydice.

Equally evocative in Orphic mythology is the account of the *sparagmós*, the sacrificial murder of the hero. After returning from Hades alone, Orpheus is physically torn apart by the Maenads or Ciconian women. Virgil's *Georgics* attribute Orpheus's dismemberment to the Ciconian women who, angered by the hero's devotion to his dead wife, murder him in an act of nocturnal Bacchic frenzy

(Book 4, ll. 520–23). Another version based on *Metamorphoses* is offered by many scholars, most recently by Ihab Hassan in *The Dismemberment of Orpheus*.[22] According to Ovid's tale,

> . . . omnenque refugerat Orpheus
> femineam Venerem. . . .
> . . . multas tamen ardor habebat
> iungere se vati, multae doluere repulsae
> ille etiam Thracum populis fuit auctor amorem
> in teneros transferre mares citraque iuventam
> aetatis breve ver et primos carpere flores.
>
> [. . . Orpheus has shunned all love of womankind. . . .
> Still, many women felt a passion for the bard; many grieved
> for their love repulsed. He set the example for the peoples of
> Thrace of giving his love to tender boys, and enjoying the
> springtime and first flower of their youth.] (*Met.*, Book 10,
> ll. 79–85)

In his third century B.C. poem, "Erotes," Phanocles, too, describes the homosexual activity of Orpheus and even names the object of the hero's affection, the young Calais.[23] Moreover, it has been hypothesized that Orpheus deliberately allows his wife to remain in Hades in order that he might take part in the homosexual activity that became a limited feature of the Dionysian cult. A more moderate statement based on the Ovidian account might be that Orpheus turns to the young men of Thrace because his "love of womankind" is restricted to the love of his late wife. In either event, the Maenads are compelled by love and by jealousy to murder the Thracian musician.

Ovid recounts that following the *sparagmós* the Ciconian women throw Orpheus's head and lyre into the river Hebrus. The head continuing to sing without stop, both objects float down the river into the sea and eventually to the island of Lesbos. At this point, the Muses collect Orpheus's head, bury it at the foot of Mount Olympus, and place his lyre in the sky as a constellation.[24]

It is not without significance that the above tales of the Orphic *katábasis* and *sparagmós* parallel incidents in the life of the god

Dionysus. In some accounts, Dionysus succeeds in bringing his dead mother, Semele, back from Hades.[25] In addition, the Dionysus-Zagreus figure is said to be a victim of dismemberment at the hands of the Titans.[26] This duplication of events might suggest that there is a relationship of some nature between the hero Orpheus and the god Dionysus. Indeed, Orpheus is often linked to the Dionysian religion, and Dionysus is almost always associated with the later Orphic cult. Orpheus is prophetic, a *theologos,* and thus has a greater affinity with the god than with the worshippers, in traditional religious terms. In this sense, he represents the Dionysian union of god and man. Within the Dionysian rites, the worshippers are joined with the god; they are infused with his spirit and they dance with him. Ernst Cassirer describes the mood of the Dionysian rite as that which strives for "die Rückkehr in [den allgemeinen Urgrund des Lebens], die 'Ekstase,' durch die die Seele die Fesseln des Leibes und der Individualität sprengt, um sich dem Alleben wieder zu vereinen."[27] Cassirer's depiction of the Dionysian spirit would be an equally apt characterization of the spirit of Orpheus.

Contrast this philosophy and this rite with those of the disciples of Apollo. In one ritual observance, for example, Apollonian priests would climb the mountains each morning before dawn to pray and to implore their god to cause the sun to rise. Following their devotions, the sun would, of course, rise. This rite illustrates the priests' complete dependence on a god from whom they are removed and from whose world they are excluded.

From this cursory comparison of ritual, it would appear that the character of the Dionysian rite befits Orpheus, a godlike hero, more than would that of the Apollonian religion. Nevertheless, as noted earlier, Orpheus is clearly an Apollonian figure, both in musical talent and in pacific temperament. And this is the point at which the complex identity of Orpheus asserts itself.

Which ancient god did Orpheus initially serve, and for what purpose did he ultimately use his musical talents? A definitive statement on the chronology of Orpheus's alliance to Apollo and Dionysus is virtually impossible, according to most mythographers and scholars of Orphic literature. Following her study of Kern's *Orphicorum fragmenta* and examination of ancient tales and remnants of pottery and coin, Eva Kushner exclaims, "Une difficulté surgit d'emblée: celle des textes. On pressent, en effet, que la question d'Orphée, comme beaucoup d'autres, ne pourra jamais être qu'imparfaitement résolue parce que les connaissances que l'on en a aujourd'hui sont fondées sur des textes que le hasard seul a sélectionnés. Souvent, ces textes ne sont que des fragments; parfois ces fragments sont obscurs et ne livrent qu'incomplètement leur secret."[28]

Although their arguments are disputed by some classicists, the majority of mythographers—notably W. K. C. Guthrie, André Boulanger, Jean Coman, and Eva Kushner—offer various versions to the effect that Orpheus is initially an Apollonian priest who later converts to the Dionysian religion. He does this in an attempt to modify the excesses of prevailing religious practices.[29] Guthrie's outline of the Orphic religious affiliation is perhaps the most satisfying. Guthrie believes that Orpheus is a Thracian native and an established high priest of Apollo. He also asserts that much of sixth-century B.C. Greece is committed to chthonian cults, which worship demonic figures and underworld deities. Compared to the contemporary chthonian cults, the new Dionysian religion appears to be a moderate rite. Thus, in an attempt to reform the established cults, to modify their orgiastic rituals by his rational and civilizing nature, Orpheus is subsequently called upon to act as a prophet of Dionysus. Orpheus is able to assume easily this new role because he is a native of Thrace, center of the new Dionysian cult, and especially because he is already recognized for his pacifying influence as an established Apollonian priest. Thus, as a result of the influence of Orpheus and the modern Dionysian position between the chthonian and Apollonian cults, the new religion appealed to the more reasonable or sensitive worshippers and, in Guthrie's words spread "like wildfire."[30]

Regardless of the chronology of or the various hypotheses regarding Orpheus's dual alliance to two very different gods, the central theme of the hero's attachment to Apollo and Dionysus is that Orpheus never disassociates himself from either. Indeed, Orpheus emerges as the Greek hero who fuses contrary religious rites. Thus, Kushner observes that for later poets "le mythe d'Orphée représente précisément l'expression symbolique par excellence de la fusion du rêve apollinien et de l'ivresse dionysiaque, à la fois dans la musique et dans la poésie, qui, ne l'oublions pas, ne se distingue que progressivement de la musique."[31]

The issue of Orpheus's priesthood to both Apollo and Dionysus influences many scholars' views of the descent and death myths. Kushner hypothesizes that the *katábasis* is simply a symbolic expression of the passage of Orpheus from one religion to another. Orpheus, according to her argument, descends to the underworld to discover the "darker," more intuitive, and more physical secrets of the Dionysian cult. There he is initiated into the new rite. She further speculates that once Orpheus returns to assume his priesthood for Dionysus, the hero reveals secrets that he learned in the underworld. For this reason, Dionysus calls upon the Ciconian women to murder the traitorous priest. At this point, the jealous god Apollo, angered at losing his high priest to Dionysus, commands the oracular but heretical head of Orpheus to be silent. Both gods, then, share the Orphic priesthood and both share responsibility for his death, according to Kushner's version.[32]

As with the myth of Pan, the power of the Orpheus legend lies not in a definitive, composite history of the hero's life culled from fragments found in ancient literary texts. Rather, its force is found in the rich suggestion evoked by the mere outline of the major events of his life. As is the case with Pan, one of the most evocative elements of Orpheus is his ability to fuse opposites.

Orpheus's priesthood within antithetical rites is in itself a statement about the nature of poetry and the poet. In combining the ecstatic element of Dionysus with the civilizing power of Apollo, Orpheus defines the essence and power of poetry. The music of Orpheus not only makes the rocks dance and provokes men to frenzy; it is also able to persuade the soldier to lay down his weapons. The art of Orpheus is both emotive and intellectual; it is sensual and frenetic as well as philosophic and peaceful. "Le lyrisme—union du verbe et de la musique—est surtout un moyen d'action sur l'univers: c'est la force de conciliation. . . . Les différents ordres, végétal, animal, humain, divin, se retrouvent autour d'Orphée. . . . Il est au centre de la création, et dirige le choeur universel. . . . Ce pouvoir que le poète lyrique exerce sur le monde est analogue à celui du Créateur. Il le doit en effet au Dieu."[33] It is the absolute and universal creative power of the artist Orpheus that makes him such a compelling figure for later lyric poets.

Second, the ability of art to defy time and death has obsessed generations of poets. This concern is manifest in the myth of Orpheus, who was able to enter the realm of death and return alive simply by the force of his music. Furthermore, even after his death, Orpheus continues to sing. Although his head is severed from his body, then drowned and floated in a river, and finally buried, the hero's head and his oracular lyre are not silenced. True poetry transcends death.

In his interpretation of the *katábasis*, Maurice Blanchot feels that the key to this mythic material lies in the power and necessity of art: "Quand Orphée descend vers Eurydice, l'art est la puissance par laquelle s'ouvre la nuit. La nuit, par la force de l'art, l'accueille, devient l'intimité accueillante, l'entente et l'accord de la première nuit. Mais c'est vers Eurydice qu'Orphée est descendu: Eurydice est, pour lui, l'extrême que l'art puisse atteindre, elle est, sous un nom qui la dissimule et sous un voile qui la couvre, le point profondément obscur vers lequel l'art, le désir, la mort, la nuit semblent tendre. Elle est l'instant où l'essence de la nuit s'approche comme l'*autre* nuit."[34]

If such is the power of music, why was Orpheus unable to rescue his wife from the underworld? Blanchot finds that the fault lies with Orpheus, not with the experience of his creation. The hero makes two fundamental errors in his descent to Eurydice. First, Orpheus does not understand that he is able to exist in Hades only by the grace of his art. He is able to find his wife and to lead her to life only as long as he continues to play his lyre. Orpheus also fails to realize that he can approach his wife only as a symbol of the goal or object of art, "l'extrême que l'art puisse atteindre." Thus, when he turns to see Eurydice, his role as husband and lover supersedes his role as poet. He gives way to what Virgil calls *dementia* ("frenzy"), and in doing so loses access to his pure artistic ideal, represented here in the form of Eurydice. "Il n'est Orphée que dans le chant, il ne peut avoir de rapport avec Eurydice qu'au sein de l'hymne, il n'a de vie et de vérité qu'après le poème et par lui, et Eurydice ne représente rien d'autre que cette dépendance magique qui hors du chant fait de lui une ombre et ne le rend libre, vivant et souverain que dans l'espace de la mesure orphique."[35] Furthermore, Orpheus does not understand that to look upon the poetic ideal, Eurydice, is to destroy the creative process. His glance at his wife is akin to staring at the noontime sun, looking at a solar eclipse, gazing at the godhead. "Son erreur est de vouloir épuiser l'infini, de mettre un terme à l'interminable, de ne pas soutenir sans fin le mouvement même de son erreur."[36]

Charles Mauron provides another interpretation of the Orphic *katábasis* as a mythic expression of the creative process. Noting that the gaze of Orpheus strongly resembles that of Lot's wife, he suggests that creative power is in some way allied to the poet's awareness of and imaginative recreation of the past. Within the Orpheus myth, the motivation of the hero toward his wife in the underworld is clearly to recapture that which *was*—his bride and his ability to sing. Mauron creates the term *le moi orphique* to identify one's impulse to evoke the past. This, he claims, is at least a partial key to aesthetic creation; through the *moi orphique*, "la vie perdue est retrouvée (comme le temps de Proust), le chaos est réordonné par un geste psychique et une magie musicale. Une promesse de salut est acquise, sous le garant d'une beauté."[37] This is certainly the case for Orpheus. After his wife dies and he loses his ability to sing, the Thracian musician descends into Hades in an attempt to recover both. Although Orpheus is forced to leave the underworld without his wife, he returns with his powers of song, and is then able to use his art to perpetuate his memory of Eurydice.

Finally, Ihab Hassan offers an interesting explication of Orphic phenomena following both the *katábasis* and *sparagmós*. Speaking of the head and lyre that cannot be silenced and are then buried in the heavens and on earth, Hassan feels that the mythic hero no longer has control over his song. Because the ascended lyre continues to play and the buried head sings without stop, it appears that the song of Orpheus is seized by the gods to become the "music of universal harmony and eternal response." Because the hero is physically unable to sing, but sings nonetheless, the melody of Orpheus "united all opposites, and bursts there where being and nothingness seem to touch." The dismembered Orpheus is truly a prophet—much as the wild Jeremiah—who raves at the will of the gods. But he exists in this manner only because of what he was as a living man: a fusion of antithetical gods, rites, and philosophies. "The singing body of Orpheus holds, then, a contradiction—between the dumb unity of nature and the multiple voice of consciousness—that the song itself longs to overcome."[38]

Pan and Orpheus are clearly opposite in physical appearance, temperament, and fate. Orpheus is a city dweller and priest, whereas Pan is a shepherd and native to the countryside. Orpheus is recognized by the strength of his love for a single woman who, in some accounts, dies proving her devotion as his wife. Pan, however, is spurned by nearly every female figure he approaches. Orpheus is strikingly Apollonian in temperament, but Pan is a clearly Dionysian personality. In spite of these differences, however, they should be considered complementary mythic figures, primarily because of their complementary status as deity and hero. Although Orpheus, as son of a king and a muse, is not a god, he is certainly treated as one by the gods on Mount Olympus. According to the mythic tales, he is a mortal being, but he nevertheless holds magical powers, the gift of prophecy, and is privy to divine secrets. In addition, he receives gifts—most especially his lyre—from Apollo. On the other hand, Pan, who is a god by virtue of his father and is an immortal being, is never admitted to Mount Olympus. In the eyes of the gods, he is never more than a "*semicaprumque hominem*" ("the man half-goat"), and they would dismiss the final element of Alciati's identification of Pan, that he is also "*semivirumque Deum*" ("the God half-man").[39] A curious and foolish being, Pan is cheated and derided by his fellow gods.

The disparity between the gods' treatment of Pan and of Orpheus is perhaps related to the relative status of their musical instruments, the pan-pipe and the lyre. As the myth correctly suggests, the Grecian pan-pipe is a shepherd's instrument. It is constructed simply from a set of graduated tubes, usually seven in number, each resembling a simple vertical flute. The pan-pipe has no fingerholes and each individual pipe produces one note on the scale.[40] This simple instrument has the utilitarian functions of calling sheep and aiding the animals to locate their shepherd in the fog. Music historian Curt Sachs indicates, moreover, that such pipes were used exclusively for shepherding, which is to say that "they had no place in art music."[41] The more sophisticated instrument is the lyre. In Greece it is constructed from a tortoise shell or wooden body covered with animal skin as a soundboard. Two horns of an animal project from the body and serve to support a horizontal crossbar. Three to four strings are then stretched from the underside of the bowl to the crossbar, held away from the board by a bridge. In contrast to the simple pan-pipe, the lyre is considered to be "the chief, the divine instrument. . . . Being Apollon's attribute, the lyre expressed the so-called Apollonian side of Greek soul and life, wise moderation, harmonious control and mental equilibrium, while the pipes stood for the Dionysian side, for inebriation and ecstasy."[42]

The status of the two musical instruments and the very different function of their music further reinforces the curious promotion of the hero Orpheus to a godlike figure and the demotion of the god Pan to the human or bestial level. We know that Hermes, unwilling father to Pan, steals the pan-pipe from his son and presents it to Apollo as his own invention. Likewise, Hermes, original creator of the lyre, offers this instrument to Apollo, who, in turn, makes a gift of the lyre to Orpheus. Consequently, Hermes steals one instrument from his son and gives another instrument indirectly to Orpheus. Because of this intrigue, one is provoked to speculate that Hermes' role in the mythology of Pan and Orpheus is more than mere thievery and gift giving. Hermes is a god of transition, passage from one stage to the next, in particular from life to death and from death to life. Seen in this light, when Hermes steals his son's pipes and transfers the lyre via a higher god to Orpheus, is he not signalling the passage from utilitarian, purely personal music to a prophetic art? Hermes' action is a symbol of the blessing of the gods on a divine art form.

H. D. F. Kitto's theory of the promotion and demotion of deities and heroes provides a good framework for the relationship of Pan and Orpheus.[43] Kitto hypothesizes that as the various Mediterranean tribes and ethnic groups migrated and conquered others, the gods of these tribes were often altered and interchanged. The victorious ruling peoples did not always destroy or replace the deities of the conquered folk, forcing the native people to adopt a new set of foreign gods. Rather, Kitto claims that "piety and prudence" often dictated their dealings and rulings regarding religious figures; the indigenous and migrating groups would often allow the identities of comparable or compatible gods simply to merge. The peoples might also arrange a marriage between like male and female gods; or there might be a struggle for supremacy between gods with similar domains from the two religions. In this way, one cult would not merely supplant the other, but the two would be fused.

Kitto's theory may indeed shed light on the fates of Pan and Orpheus. Both figures hold virtually equivalent spheres of power as prophetic musicians, and would thus duplicate one another's roles. As a result, in the case of migrating or merging peoples, it is entirely possible that Pan and Orpheus would be identified as a single god, or that one would be promoted at the expense of the other.

The very fact that Hermes, god of a higher order, makes every attempt to suppress the music of his son, while promoting the talents of Orpheus, is testimony to Kitto's hypothesis. That the god Apollo aids Hermes in his efforts is also significant. Furthermore, there is information—albeit fragmentary—that there may also have been a struggle between the two figures. Felix Guirand briefly notes that the Pan figure in the region of Thessaly is identified as Aristaeus.[44] Aristaeus is, of course, the beekeeper/shepherd who, in Virgil's *Georgics*, chases Eurydice through a field—behavior not atypical of Pan—where she is bitten by a snake and dies. Following the death of his wife, Orpheus ceases to play and to sing. And this may have been the very object of the crafty Pan. Was he attempting to avert Orpheus's promotion and his own subsequent demise?

In any event, it is clear that with the passage of time the identities of Pan and Orpheus have converged significantly. The Orphic Pan, *Allgott*, approaches the powers of Orpheus, and the Apollonian Orpheus moves closer to the Dionysian Pan figure. The mythology, then, might be said to bear witness to the increasingly complex conception of the unique role of the poet as one who reconciles the Apollonian and Dionysian forces in man, the rational and the manic, the divine and the human, the individual and the universal.

The object of this study, however, is not to examine the nature of ancient mythology. Neither is it to proceed from the mythology itself and attempt to form a coherent tale of Pan and Orpheus from diverse, cryptic, and often contradictory mythic tales. Our goal is to examine in modern poetry those fragments of each myth that later poets extracted and often embellished in an attempt to describe their own creative and social roles.

Henri Peyre has observed that the influence of ancient texts on modern poetry is "en effet un devenir perpétuellement fluide, et non pas une donnée stable."[45] A study of the intricate matter of literary influence considers which specific Greek and Latin texts were of serious interest or in vogue in a given historical period; which had been translated, and what the popular translation brought to the text; and, of course, how the particular orientation of a specific author, period, or culture influenced perception of the ancient text. The last of the three questions is the crux of this study, and the first two will be addressed in detail in later chapters when important to the analysis of a particular work. However, before examining the poetry, a brief discussion of the translation and adaptation of Pan and Orpheus mythology is in order.

THE MYTHOLOGY:
ITS TRANSLATION AND TRANSFORMATION

There is a general concurrence that within early European literature the source material for ancient mythological tales is not Greek, but Latin.[46] Moreover, prior to the sixteenth century, information on Pan and Orpheus is primarily gleaned not from authoritative or even complete translations of the ancient texts, but from encyclopaedic sources, pictoral art, glosses in medieval manuscripts, in addition to paraphrases, interpretations, and allegories of ancient mythic material.

There appear to be three major sources of the myth of Orpheus in early European literature: various translations and allegories of the works of Ovid and Virgil, Boethius's *Consolation of Philosophy*, and a twelfth-century *lai d'Orphée*. John Block Friedman considers the sixth-century *Consolation* of Boethius to be "a primary source of the Orpheus legend for the Middle Ages."[47] The work of Boethius combines elements from both Ovid and Virgil and also offers a Christian interpretation of the mythic material. According to Friedman, "his didactic use of the legend appealed to the sensibilities of Christian readers in the sixth, seventh and eighth centuries in a way that the secular accounts of Ovid and Virgil could not, at least not until they had been properly interpreted as moral allegories."[48] This influential work was translated into French in the early fourteenth century by Peter of Paris and into English by King Alfred, and it also inspired innumerable commentaries on the *Consolation* itself.

A Breton *lai d'Orphée*, probably of twelfth-century origin, is known to have existed. Although the text of this *lai* is not extant, scholars generally concur that it most likely presented the story of Orpheus and Eurydice in fairy tale form, and that it quite possibly became one of the sources for the Middle English romance, *Sir Orfeo*.[49]

For the educated man with facility in Latin, Douglas Bush finds that Virgil "very early became a textbook."[50] The *Aeneid*, *Eclogues*, and *Georgics* were known to Medieval France and Britain, although the *Georgics*—which contains information about Orpheus—did not appear in vulgar tongues until the sixteenth century. Ovid's *Metamorphoses* was allegorized as early as 1125 by Arnulf of Orléans in his fifteen-volume *Allegoriae super Ovidii Metamorphosin*. Perhaps the most influential allegory is the anonymous *Ovide Moralisé* written in the late thirteenth or early fourteenth century. This text presents Ovid's work in couplets with elaborate allegorical appendices. Thirty-four pages—in DeBoer's edition—are devoted to the tale of Orpheus. For at least two centuries, the *Ovide Moralisé* provided the inspiration for similar adaptations of Ovid's poetry, and also furnished material for poetic composition. This Christianized text also attracted British readership and thus formed part of the English understanding of Orpheus mythology. *Ovide Moralisé* was in part supplanted by sixteenth-century translations of Ovid's text. Clément Marot published his partial translation into French in 1532. His work was completed by Habert in 1557, ten years before Arthur Golding's *Metamorphosis* appeared in Britain. Golding's was the first complete English translation of Ovid, making the Latin author available to a much wider audience than before.

Prior to the nineteenth century, poets gleaned their information on the god Pan from the same Ovidian and Virgilian paraphrases, allegories, and translations from which they learned of Orpheus. Merivale finds that "for most of the pre-Romantic Pans in English literature (and many thereafter), no Greek source need be supposed. Two stories from Ovid and a few lines from Virgil provided actions and attributes enough" to furnish the poet with material for his individual lyric representation of Pan mythology.[51] However, two additional major sources must be noted. Rabanus Maurus's *De rerum naturis* of 1023 was influential in presenting a Christianized sketch of the pagan god to the medieval world.[52] And, for a later audience, Thomas Taylor's 1787 translation of the *Orphic Hymns* introduced the omnipotent Pan, the *Allgott*, to the British Romantic poets. Merivale asserts that it is probably by way of this translation of the Greek text that "the Romantics found the Orphic Pan, the Soul of All Things, and made him a major poetic motif, which at its best became both universal and pastoral."[53]

The influence of ancient Greek and Latin texts on Russian poetry is an even more involved problem, although one with a shorter history than that within western Europe. Prior to the eighteenth century, Russian poets had relatively little access to Greek and Roman mythology. The literature of Rus was shaped by essentially three major forces: Byzantine Orthodoxy, the Mongolian invasion, and Muscovite domination.[54] Ancient western poetry and rhetoric did not form the basic principles and standards for Russian literature as they had for that of western Europe. Neither did ancient western mythology become the mythology of the Russian people, and their native mythology offers no figures truly comparable to Pan and Orpheus in the Greek tradition.[55]

Consequently, neither Pan nor Orpheus figures heavily in early Russian poetry, and both appear only after the eighteenth-century westernization program of Peter the Great. In the early eighteenth century, the Russian people were introduced to the fables of Aesop and to Ovid's *Metamorphoses* through Russian translations of these works from German texts. At the same time, there appeared *Symbala et Emblemata*, a book containing tales of ancient western mythology and drawings of Greek and Roman mythic characters. This became an "invaluable handbook for writers and artists" and was expanded and reprinted in 1788.[56] Also in the eighteenth century, a significant number of Russian poets and scholars began to travel and study in western Europe, primarily in Germany. There they became familiar with Greek and Roman mythology, again through the filter of the German culture, and then began with increasing frequency to incorporate such myths into their native poetry. Several romantic poets make limited reference to Greek and Roman mythology, although extensive use of the mythological figures, Pan and Orpheus, begins in earnest with the Russian symbolists who, according to Zoya Yur'eva, "пытались не только воскресить древнегреческий миф, но и переоценить его, переосмыслить, наполнив своим содержанием" ("attempted not only to resurrect Greek pastoral myth, but also to reevaluate it, to give it new meaning, infusing it with their themes").[57] The Russian symbolist poets view Pan and Orpheus through the additional filter of French poetry on which they model much of their work. Thus, the fabric of literary influence becomes more and more intricately woven.

Finally, to compound the complex issue of the literary history of translation and influence, Henri Peyre further notes that "l'influencé, à son tour—individu, génération, ou siècle—modifie sa conception de l'antiquité à mesure que son goût ou sa sagesse se mûrissent (ou parfois se sclérosent)."[58] And Douglas Bush further observes that "in ancient as well as later times Greek and Roman myth was not a body of fixed data but was always evolving, often confusedly and contradictorily, acquiring new embellishments and new meanings. When, for instance, the Greek writers of tragedy took up Homeric and other stories, they molded them afresh in accordance with their own dramatic, philosophical and religious ideas. And later poets have continually done likewise."[59]

Bush's assertion is especially true of complex and fertile mythic tales such as the ancient accounts of the god Pan and the hero

Orpheus. Both tales consistently spark the poetic imagination of innumerable authors from the Middle Ages to the present. Lyric poets, in particular those from the medieval period through the eighteenth century, present diverse characterizations of these mythological figures. Imaginative and sometimes novel renderings of Pan and Orpheus may often be attributed to the variety of contexts in which the early poet evokes their name. Indeed, many poets call upon these figures to assume a multitude of roles other than those of pastoral poet and prophetic musician.

A large canon of early poetry that draws on ancient mythology is devoted to adaptations of pagan gods for the Christian world.[60] Many medieval and Renaissance poets, in particular, make a concerted effort to reconcile religious conventions with the ancient literature they so admire. To do so, they are forced either to ascribe philosophies resembling Christian assumption to ancient mythic heroes, or to discredit those pagan figures who resist allegorization. Thus, many early poets distort the ancient characterizations of Pan and Orpheus, and alter them to conform with recognized Christian figures, saints, demons, pilgrims, or God himself.

The pagan god Pan, then, assumes the role of the God of a monotheistic society in many early poems.[61] He is identified specifically as Jesus Christ in such works as Milton's "On the Morning of Christ's Nativity" (stanza 8, ll. 85–90), and Spenser's *Shepheardes Calender* ("Julye," ll. 49–54, and "September," ll. 96–97). In *Le Quart Livre* (stanza 18), Rabelais attempts to concretize his identification of Pan with Jesus Christ by establishing the date of Pan's purported death as during the reign of Tiberius Caesar. On the other hand, Milton also describes the Arcadian fertility god as a member of Satan's "lusty crew" in *Paradise Regained* (Book 2, ll. 172–95), and Ronsard's *Hymne des Daimons* and Henry More's *Praeexistency of the Soul* portray him as a demonic creature.[62]

The hero Orpheus, as well, is frequently portrayed as a pagan prefiguration of Christ, most especially in the Middle Ages. The pacific Apollonian priest and reformer of the Dionysian cult is easily transformed into a hero of monotheism, such that "Orpheus-Christus" is a common portrayal of the pagan hero from the fourth century through the Middle Ages.[63]

In addition to his religious roles, the god Pan takes on a variety of political identities in lyric poetry. In one section of the *Shepheardes Calender*, Spenser's Pan becomes Henry VIII ("Aprill," ll. 50–54, 90–94); and in France, Marot identifies Pan as François I in his "Eglogue de Marot au Roy soubz les noms de Pan et Robin."[64]

Nevertheless, the goat-god is most commonly recognized exclusively as an emblem of the pastoral scene.[65] Other aspects of the ancient mythology set aside, he represents the gentle lover and shepherd piper who are essential figures of the pastoral tradition. Even in poetry written after the eighteenth century, Pan remains an element of the pastoral *genius loci*. The name of Pan is invoked for the purposes of British city-versus-country arguments in Matthew Arnold's "Lines Written in Kensington Gardens." In W. B. Yeats's "Song of the Happy Shepherd" and in Robert Frost's "Pan With Us," we find that the poets use the Pan figure as a central motif in their lamentations of the passing of the pastoral tradition.[66] Likewise, the name of Orpheus is frequently invoked as courtly lover or tragic lover, the complexity of the mythology temporarily suspended in favor of this single facet of the mythic tales.[67]

The above are limited examples of the many and varied roles into which lyric poets have forced the mythological Pan and Orpheus—with or without the blessing of the ancient literature. Such characterizations of these mythological figures have been and will continue to be the subject of many other studies. However, this investigation focuses exclusively on those poems in which Pan and Orpheus are prototypes of the poet.

2

Early Poetic Personae

Where Pan and Orpheus appear as prototypes of the poet within early self-reflexive lyric verse, these mythological figures are often curiously one-sided. Until the late eighteenth century, lyric poets focus almost exclusively on a composite Arcadian and Orphic (*Allgott*) Pan. They choose to omit discussion of Pan's manic, Dionysian identity in favor of the gentler pastoral and prophetic elements of his mythic tales. So too, early poets celebrate the pacific and prophetic Apollonian Orpheus and give little play to the Dionysian facets of the hero. Early lyric poets do so with good reason. Where the poet conceives of himself as a vatic creator, his ancient prototype or mythic persona must too evince such power. Likewise, the mythic pan-pipe and lyre must possess the prophetic gifts to which the modern poet claims to be heir.

However, consistently heroic and prophetic portrayals of Pan and Orpheus are prevalent in self-reflexive poetry only through the eighteenth century. With the romantic movement, lyric poets begin to turn to elements of failure and tragedy in the mythology of Pan and Orpheus. In addition, poets return to the manic and Dionysian aspects of the ancient musicians' identities, most especially those of Pan. The romantic poets, then, gradually abandon the earlier vatic prototypes, and with increasing frequency replace them with personae who suffer from social and political powerlessness, from a lack of credibility. These poetic figures often suffer from their own violence and social aberration as well. Most frequently, such prototypes of the poet appear to be disabled by the intense anguish that results from the very act of poetic creation.

Guillaume Crétin's fifteenth-century depiction of Pan is one of the earliest to ascribe artistic qualities to the goat-god. Crétin briefly mentions Pan in one poem as the holder—albeit not creator—of the "fleute à sept canes." However, the poet describes him more elaborately in a second poem as the "dieu Pan qui l'art tant decoras."[1] This apocryphal sketch ignores the original portrayal of Pan as an ithyphallic, almost foolish goat-god whose art was dismissed by all but an equally foolish Midas. However, Crétin's depiction celebrates both art and the artist, and an altered characterization of the goat-god contributes to this goal.

Ronsard's "Première Ode à la Fontaine Bellerie" has a similar orientation. This Pan-poet composes at his ease in a bucolic setting, confident that the entire universe will read his verse, and that the poetry will assuredly outlive the poet. Like the Pan-poet of other French Pléiade poets, especially Baïf, Ronsard's Pan is a godlike creator, capable of conferring eternal life—true life—on the subject of his verse.[2] Speaking to the Fontaine Bellerie, which was in the original text the "déesse Bellerie," Ronsard claims,

> L'Esté je dors ou repose
> Sus ton herbe, où je compose,
> Caché sous tes saules vers,
> Je ne sçay quoy, qui ta gloire
> Envoira par l'univers,
> Commandant à la Memoire
> Que tu vives par mes vers.[3]

Within the English tradition, Ben Jonson's lyric drama, *Pans Anniversarie*, goes even further in its description of an omnipotent goat-god as poet. The chorus sings a litany extolling Pan as "the best of Singers," "the best of Leaders," "the best of Hunters," and "the best of Shepherds."[4] Furthermore, he is the "Father of our peace, and pleasure" (l. 255) who through the power of his music was able to bring civilization to Arcadia.

> And come you prime Arcadians forth, that taught
> By PAN the rites of true societie,
> From his loud Musicke, all your manners wraught,
> And made your Common-wealth a harmonie.   (ll. 159–62)

In Jonson's view, Pan is far more than a vatic poet with the civilizing influence of an Orpheus; he is also creator and sustainer of mankind by virtue of his poetic power.

> PAN is our All, by him we breath, wee live,
> Wee move, we are. . . .   (ll. 191–92)

A more complex treatment of the artist is found in the work of Edmund Spenser, who invokes the mythological figure as artist's mask and mentor throughout his poetry. The early poetic sequence, *Shepheardes Calender*, presents as its hero Colin Clout, a simple pastoral piper who has taken Pan as mentor. Colin is a conventional poet-lover who, like the ancient Pan, has no pretentions about his lyric composition.

> I neuer lyst presume to *Parnasse* hyll,
> But pyping lowe in shade of lowly groue,
> I play to please my selfe, all be it ill.[5]

The poet's role and aspirations are not entirely devoid of complexity, as Clout initially would lead the reader to believe. At the close of the poem, the shepherd breaks his flute, thereby renouncing his position as piper and poet ("November," p. 101, l. 71).

David Miller returns to Pan mythology to explicate this curious turn of events and asserts that Colin finds his naive role as poet-lover simplistic. "Colin's failure in the *Calender* is precisely a failure to reenact Pan's sublimation of natural desire in the making of harmony. Instead, Colin surrenders to desire."[6] Richard Helgerson agrees that the final lines of the *Shepheardes Calender* issue "a forceful critique of the conventional poet-lover, revealing that poetry written under such a guise is solipsistic, self-indulgent, and fruitless."[7]

In his later poetry, however, Spenser continues his discussion of the nature of the poet and his poetry. He explains that to play the role of *poeta* is insufficient; the true artist must be *vates* as well. That is, those who confine their work to the *dulce*, the lighter lyrics played solely "to please my selfe," are to be considered *poetae*, whereas vatic poets explore themes of universal concern and are inspired to teach their audience about grave matters of morality, politics, and religion. Consequently, the figure of Clout is complemented in Spenser's later poetry by those of poet-priests and poet-knights—most notably Calidore of the *Faerie Queene*. Such roles also form part of Pan's identity as *Allgott* and participant in the Battle of Marathon.[8] The goat-god Pan, then, offers to Spenser the mythic model for the private, pastoral poet who is, at the same time, the public, prophetic poet. Miller observes that "the shepherd in pastoral poetry may represent a clergyman at one moment and a poet at the next, but for Spenser he comes to represent the partial identity of religious and artistic vocations."[9] Thus we find that Spenser's vision of the true poet is a composite of the pastoral and the prophetic, the shepherd and the priest or knight, *poeta* and *vates*, seemingly disparate roles reconciled in the mythology of Pan.

In early French and English poetry, the identity of the Thracian Orpheus is as ill defined as that of the Arcadian Pan. Regarding neo-Latin and French verse, Françoise Joukovsky finds that the artistic qualities of the hero Orpheus are particularly confused. "Non seulement on meconnait ses fonctions littéraires, mais on n'évoque pas les effets de ce pouvoir poétique: il est rare qu'on le montre charmant la nature."[10] Both Villon and Crétin place their Orphic poets in the company of the biblical poet and king, David, and Villon puts the pipes of Pan in the hands of Orpheus in "Double Ballade."

> Orphée, le doux ménétrier,
> jouant de flûtes et de musettes,
> par amour s'exposa au danger d'un meurtrier,
> le chien Cerbère à quatre têtes.[11]

In the work of the fourteenth-century poet, Guillaume de Machaut, we find a full history of the hero, Orpheus. "Le Confort d'Ami" includes detailed accounts of Eurydice's death, the *katábasis* and subsequent *sparagmós* of Orpheus.[12] Machaut's "Prologue" offers an abbreviated version of the Orphic myth, but provides the additional insight that music has the power to work miracles. Machaut comments that the lyre of Orpheus is capable of freeing Eurydice, and that his song can bend trees and turn rivers from their beds. The poet furthermore adds:

> Si qu'on doit croire sans doubter
> Que ce sont miracles apertes
> Que Musique fait. C'est voir, certes.[13]

The most completely developed expression of the Orphic tale in early French poetry is found in the work of Ronsard. His poem, "L'Orphée," treats at great length the effect of the Orphic lyre on other mythic figures.

> Faisant telle oraison, les âmes sont venues,
> Ainsi que gresillons, greslettes & menues,
> Pepier à l'entour de mon Luc qui sonnoit,
> Et de son chant piteux les Manes estonnoit.
> La Parque, que jamais pleurer on n'avoit veue,
> Escoutant ma chanson à pleurer fut esmue.
> Tantale n'eut soucy de sa punition,
> Sisiphe de son roc, de sa roue Ixion:
> Et dit on que long temps des fieres Eumenides,
> La face en larmoyant de pitié de paslit,
> Tant ma douce chanson le cueur leur amolit![14]

The Orphic poet evokes both an emotional and a physical response from his audience; such is the power of his song. For his audience, he draws from his peers, Olympian gods, and underworld figures; each soul who hears his music is attracted to the musician.

Joukovsky finds that Ronsard "en fait le mythe du poète, confirmant ainsi les rares intuitions de ses prédécesseurs immédiats; et ce 'vates' est l'incarnation de son propre idéal poétique, dont il prend de recueil en recueil une conscience de plus en plus nette."[15] For a concrete expression of his "poetic ideal," the *vates*, Ronsard turns to the mythic hero Orpheus. Although Ronsard admits the faults and failures of the Thracian musician—his "fureur d'amour" (l. 298) and his "faute assés pardonnable en amour" (l. 291), the French poet prefers to excuse such flaws and to emphasize the might and magic of the poetic hero. In his eyes, Orpheus is a truly exceptional being—from the moment of his birth, throughout his life, and at his death. Upon birth, the poet "avoit d'Apollon l'ame tout echaufée" (l. 6); his life is thereafter marked by the power of his song; and the gods themselves confer great honor on the poet at his death.

> Tant leur plaisoit le son d'une si douce Lyre,
> Que depuis dans le Ciel les Dieux ont fait reluire.
>
> (ll. 349–50)

Such is the power and majesty of the poet whom Ronsard selects as lyric prototype.

In seventeenth-century France, Nicolas Boileau-Despréaux attributes the organization of society to the powers of poetry, and lauds Orpheus for drawing man from his savage state into social order. For evidence of the rational and moral force of the lyric, Boileau turns to the mythology of Orpheus.

> Avant que la raison, s'expliquant par la voix,
> Eût instruit les humains, eût enseigné des lois,
> Tous les hommes suivaient la grossière nature,
> Dispersés dans les bois couraient à la pâture:
> La force tenait lieu de droit et d'équité;
> Le meurtre s'exerçait avec impunité.
> Mais du discours enfin l'harmonieuse adresse
> De ces sauvages moeurs adoucit la rudesse,
> Rassembla les humains dans les forêts épars,
> Enferma les cités de murs et de remparts,
> De l'aspect du supplice effraya l'insolence,
> Et sous l'appui des lois mit la faible innocence.
> Cet ordre fut, dit-on, le fruit des premiers vers:
> De là sont nés ces bruits reçus dans l'univers,
> Qu'aux accents dont Orphée emplit les monts de Thrace,
> Les tigres amollis dépouillaient leur audace;
> Qu'aux accords d'Amphion les pierres se mouvaient,
> Et sur les monts thébains en ordre s'élevaient.
> L'harmonie en naissant produisit ces miracles.
> Depuis le ciel en vers fit parler les oracles.[16]

Boileau considers the contemporary poet to be the heir of Orpheus and to be entrusted with his prophetic powers. Thus, he admonishes the poet to be mindful of his heritage and responsibilities when he creates a work of art because the poet is recognized as an oracle and as a spokesman of God.

Within the English tradition, lyric poets very early attribute full poetic powers to the mythological Orpheus. The Middle English romance, *Sir Orfeo*, roughly follows Virgil's outline of the Orphic myth, but casts the hero as a king and godly descendant of Pluto and Juno.[17] He is clearly a powerful figure as well as a poet, but in this Christianized version, Orfeo is also characterized by humility, charity, and dignity.[18] When Sir Orfeo loses his Lady Heurodis to a fairyland, he abandons his throne, and assumes the role of pilgrim for ten years. The romance presents its hero as a paragon of virtue, and his lyre complements his virtue. The instrument is his consolation in the wilderness and pacifies wild beasts that might otherwise harm him.

More importantly, the powers of the lyre ensure Heurodis's return to her husband. Orfeo's lyre secures his entrance to the castle where she is being held captive within the fairyland; furthermore, the lyre enchants the kidnapper-king and his court and elicits a promise from the king to return Heurodis to Orfeo. As Peter Lucas aptly remarks, the lyre "succeeds where a thousand armed men failed."[19] The final lines of *Sir Orfeo* are fitting for a fairy tale and romance, and for the medieval appraisal of poetic power.

> Now King Orfeo newe coround is,
> And his quen, Dame Heurodis,
> And lived long afterward.[20]

Orfeo, then, presents a strong image of the poet as an able and powerful figure. He is kingly and compassionate, confident and humble; he is god fearing, but has a spark of cunning. Moreover, his lyre is the vehicle through which the poet exhibits these qualities and expresses his virtue. His music not only offers consolation and entertainment, but serves as an instrument of security and justice.

The lyric power of the Orphic poet is a firmly established archetype in the English tradition. Shakespeare briefly outlines the poet's famed gift of enchantment in lyrics inserted into *Henry VIII*.

> Orpheus with his lute made trees
> And the mountain tops that freeze
>   Bow themselves when he did sing.[21]

In "The Ruines of Time," Spenser attributes even greater powers to Orpheus. Like the medieval Orfeo, Spenser's hero not only works magic with flora and fauna, but, more spectacularly, he also successfully wins Eurydice from death by the power of his song.

Motifs of the prophetic gifts and awesome abilities of the poet are not simply poetic hyperbole found exclusively in lyric expression; such confidence in the artist as arbiter of truth and messenger of divine knowledge is found also in early critical essays. Sidney's *Apologie for Poetrie*, for example, asserts that the poet alone is able to perceive that which is true and good and universal.[22] Above all men, the poet must then lead his society in this direction. Boileau, too, accords all glory to the poet, with the understanding that the true poet receives "du ciel l'influence secrète."[23]

Northrop Frye confirms this attitude in the poets of the sixteenth and seventeenth centuries. Frye argues that "the poet who sings about gods is often considered to be singing as one, or as an instrument of one. His social function is that of an inspired oracle."[24] Indeed, this bond is even stronger when the poet sings about a god or a godlike figure who is also a poet. Speaking specifically of Orpheus—but one could add the name of Pan as well—Françoise Joukovsky observes that this godlike musician had come to represent for the sixteenth-century French poets "non seulement un instrumentiste, puis le poète idéal que chacun d'entre eux rêvait d'incarner: ils reprenaient ainsi la légende à leur compte."[25] Moreover, the continual invocation of Pan and Orpheus suggests these poets' attempts to reach into the past in order to tap the power of the tradition of poetry making. In this way, the poet reaffirms his alliance with his artistic ancestry and reestablishes a continuity of poets from the sixth century B.C. to the present.

Lyric poets from the middle of the seventeenth century through the eighteenth century, however, take little interest in describing their roles in terms of Pan or Orpheus. The mythology of this period, as Douglas Bush explains, is generally confined to "travesties; mock-heroic poems; translations and paraphrases, . . . mythological allusions equally numerous and frigid."[26] In poems such as Marvell's "The Garden" and Chénier's "Les Nymphes et les satyres," for example, we find the god Pan to be simply a decorative icon on pastoral scenes.

Those poets who make brief mention of Pan and Orpheus as poets express the same vatic ideal as their predecessors. They, too, selectively draw on Pan's Orphic identity and on the prophetic powers of Orpheus, and they subdue any treatment of the limitation of poetic powers, the manic traits of each figure, or the tragedy that accounts for a significant portion of their mythology. Thus, when Lomonosov opens his political occasional poetry with an invocation to the muse, he asks that he be granted the powers of Pindar, Homer, and Orpheus.[27] And when Pan appears to a lowly shepherd in Marvell's "Clorinda and Damon," we find that the "flowry Pastures" sing praise to Pan as do the caves and fountains.[28] The exalted goat-god inspires the shepherd with song, and fills his "Oate" with full tones as well.

The romantic period marks an era of transition in self-reflexive poetry, an era in which, according to A. P. Frank, the art of *Theorie im Gedicht* is in large part supplanted by that of *Theorie als Gedicht*.[29] The former, according to Frank's definition, is the traditional *ars poetica*, a discursive (and often didactic) lyric mode. In contrast, *Theorie als Gedicht* is a mimetic lyric mode explicitly treating the theme of poetry, poetics, or the poet within its mimetic framework. René Wellek's essay, "The Poet, the Critic, the Poet-Critic," affirms that didactic, narrative self-reflexion virtually ends in the eighteenth century and becomes in the romantic period what he terms *meta-poetry*. "The 'meta-poetry,'" he finds, "is largely concerned with the self-definition of the poet and with his mission or function. It must be associated with the modern questioning of his status as seer, priest, or sage."[30]

The immediate causes of such critical introspection are many, various, and, at best, disputed. David Miller puts forth the thesis that "any time the writer's ethical (and economic) relation to his audience is not already secure within the culture he writes for, the inevitable self-consciousness of writing tends to make the project of authorship into one of self-definition."[31] Maurice Shroder agrees that "much of the concern for the plight of the artist in the nineteenth century was concentrated on a series of attempts to redefine the artist's social status and his social role."[32] Shroder argues that French poets enjoyed a parasitic alliance with the aristocracy prior to the French revolution. However, they emerged as a group *déclassé* in the wake of the revolution. Poets were then loath to ally themselves with the emerging middle class, which in turn was naturally suspicious of them. Although the poet had once been responsible for lyrics that glorify the warrior/king, describe courtly mores, and generate political statement, he turned in the nineteenth century to themes of aesthetic experience and imagination—although the popular appeal of the new orientation was highly questionable. Unclear social status and a rejection of the middle class contributed, according to Shroder, to the artist's isolation from every recognizable social group. He was ultimately left to serve the interests only of himself and his artistic peers.[33] The function of the artist in the late nineteenth century would become more purely aesthetic until proponents of *l'art pour l'art* view their role as the "preserver of the ideal in the midst of a materialistic society, to be above all an *artiste*."[34]

M. H. Abrams, on the other hand, understands this new artistic questioning as the result of scientism encroaching on the arts. The world, recently under the influence of Peacock, Bentham, Newtonian mechanics, and philosophical positivism, was suspicious of a knowledge that it could not hope to quantify. The nature of "poetic truth" was itself under question.[35] G. R. Ridge expresses a similar viewpoint in *The Hero in French Romantic Literature*.[36] He finds that the modern newspaper that emerged with the industrial revolution gradually formed the reading needs and tastes of the new industrial society.[37] The bourgeois reading public turned to prose to inform their lives, and they viewed poetry merely as a decorative and faulty version of prose, at best a handmaid, however unreliable, to science and philosophy. The poet in a democratic society is nonetheless forced to earn his living from such readers, although he holds differing views on the nature of poetry and the function of the poet. Monroe Spears agrees that the arts have lost "their utilitarian functions, which are taken over by the mass media of communication and entertainment. . . . The serious arts are driven in upon themselves and develop their proper natures under pressure; hence they become specialized, pure, advanced, extreme, austere. As they become more and more serious, intense, and uncompromising, they become more and more uninviting and incomprehensible to the public at large."[38]

A more radical, Marxist stance on this same point is assumed by Edward Reichel, who believes that the isolation of the artist in an industrial society is primarily due to the increased division of labor.[39] Reichel argues that in a world in which the mason is isolated from the carpenter, and the weaver from the tailor, the aesthete will, of course, have no means of speaking to those whose primary activity is not aesthetic. The loneliness of the poet, clutching language as his final claim to wisdom, is a product of an advanced division of society. Reichel's thesis finds support in Hugo Friedrich's description of the French symbolist poet: "Der Dichter is allein mit seiner Sprache. Hier hat er seine Heimat und seine Freiheit, um den Preis, dass man ihn ebensogut verstehen wie nicht verstehen kann."[40] This, he further claims, is merely the prototype of the modern poet in a more advanced industrial society.

Frank Kermode, too, believes in the "necessary isolation or estrangement" of the aesthete in an increasingly technological world and observes that the poet in such a world will naturally turn to antiquity for a sense of what poetry and the poet are capable of being.[41] "When, in fact, poets and aestheticians of the Image turn their attention to history, it is in search of some golden age when the prevalent mode of knowing was not positivistic and antiimaginative; when the Image, the intuited, creative reality, was habitually respected; when art was not permanently on the defensive against mechanical and systematic modes of enquiry."[42]

Regardless of the causes, the image of the artist as social victim begins to exhibit itself in the self-reflexive poetry of the romantic period. The romantic poet gradually rejects the pastoral, vatic image of Pan as well as the omnipotent role of Orpheus and attempts to deal with the tragic elements of their mythology. This development, in turn, signals the poet's reevaluation of his creative activity and his social identity.

The Pan-poet found in Keats's *Endymion* seemingly represents the traditional Arcadian conception of the goat-god found in earlier works. He is a pastoral musician and vatic creator to whom the poet cries in the fashion of a litany: "Hear us, great Pan!," "O forester divine!," "Hear us, O satyr king!"[43] Keats's poetic prototype, like that of Spenser and Ronsard, is the bearer of divine inspiration; however, in *Endymion*, Pan's poetic knowledge has a sinister edge as well, for the god is described in this manner:

> Strange ministrant of undescribed sounds,
> That come a swooning over hollow grounds,
> And wither drearily on barren moors:
> Dread opener of the mysterious doors
> Leading to universal knowledge.   (Book 1, ll. 285–289)

This fusion of the holy and the evil, of blessing and curse is echoed by Pushkin who depicts the Orphic poet as:

> Певец таинственных видений,
> Любви, мечтаний и чертей,
> Могил и рая верный житель.
>
> [Singer of mysterious visions, / Of love, dreams, and evils, / Faithful resident of the grave and paradise].[44]

Victor Hugo's discussion of poetic truth and poetic power is less complex. His poem "Pan" issues an unequivocal endorsement of the wisdom and might of aesthetic creation.

> Si l'on vous dit que l'art et que la poésie
> C'est un flux éternel de banale ambroisie,
> Que c'est le bruit, la foule, attachés à vos pas,
> . . . .
> Oh! ne le croyez pas,
> O poètes sacrés, échevelés, sublimes.[45]

However, this particular strophe is not a spontaneous tribute to artistic endeavor. Rather, it is written in response to a direct challenge from society, the impersonal "on," that poetry is merely "un flux éternel de banale ambroisie."

Hugo's later dramatic poem, "Le Satyre," portrays Pan as a clown figure—one of the first poetic clowns that will appear in abundance in symbolist and post-symbolist poetry. The satyr-clown attempts to climb Mount Olympus to prove the power of his music. However, the gods initially ignore the rough, clumsy goat whom they do not even recognize. They call him a "pauvre paysan" and describe Pan as "cornu, boiteux, difforme."[46] But then Pan sings, plays his pipes, and finally reaches for the divine lyre, which he also plays majestically. While singing, the poet grows larger than Titan and the lyre expands to gigantic proportion until the goat-god cries, "Place à Tout! Je suis Pan; Jupiter! à genoux" (p. 430, l. 8). The poet emerges victorious from the contest dramatized in "Le Satyre," but again the goal of Hugo's Pan was to prove his worth to an audience who initially found him foolish.

Victor Hugo's "Le Poëte dans les Révolutions" offers an equally dramatic argument regarding the social status of the poet, who is described in the inscription as a "vox clamabat in deserto" (p. 291). The poem is written in the form of a dialogue between the artist and his society. The poet would like to be compared to the Greek Orpheus, an artist who spoke to his fellow man and fought for all humanity. However, he is contradicted by the voice of the world, who questions and even ridicules such comparison.

> Insensé! quel orgueil t'entraîne?
> De quel droit viens-tu dans l'arène
> Juger sans avoir combattu?   (ll. 25–27)

The Orphic poet attempts a rebuttal, presenting himself as an "être prédestiné, ayant reçu de Dieu la mission de civiliser les hommes et de leur montrer de loin, malgré leurs sarcasmes, leurs persécutions même, l'avenir meilleur dont il a la vision."[47] Although the world recalls the status and abilities of the poet in times past, it rejects the idea that contemporary poets hold such powers.

> On dit que jadis le poëte,
> Chantant des jours encor lointains,
> Savait à la terre inquiète
> Révéler ses futurs destins.
> Mais toi, que peux-tu pour le monde?
> Tu partages sa nuit profonde;
> Le ciel se voile et veut punir;

> Les lyres n'ont plus de prophète,
> Et la Muse, aveugle et muette,
> Ne sait plus rien de l'avenir! (ll. 61–70)

The poet has clearly lost his vatic identity, and even his Muse is debased in the eyes of the world. Although the Orphic *apologia pro vita sua* is strong, his society remains deaf to his claims.

The distinction between poetic powers of the past and those of the present is treated also in Shelley's "Orpheus." The poem's narrator recalls that at one time Orpheus "gently sang of high and heavenly themes."[48] His early song was nourished by "ambrosial food" and was compared to a clear brook feeding its banks, reflecting both sun and moon. However, after the death of Eurydice and that of the hero, the music of Orpheus is much different. It rises from a murky stream that stagnates in a barren field. This body of water reflects no light, but produces a noxious gas, "a pale mist, / like aereal gossamer, / Whose breath destroys all life" (ll. 20–21). Although the Orphic lyre would once cause all nature to dance, the present song kills the worm, veils the rocks, and thrashes the weary trees. Indeed, the power of Orpheus is a deadly force.

The simple dichotomy between the song of joy and the song of pain is complicated by the response of the chorus to the brutal rhythm and sinister tone of the hero's music. "What wondrous song is that?" they inquire (l. 35). Regardless of the tragic source of his song, the music of Orpheus is nonetheless poetry. The inherent truth and value of the creative product redeems the grief and anger that inspired the creation.

> Thus the tempestuous torrent of his grief
> Is clothed in sweetest sounds and varying words
> Of poesy. . . . (ll. 81–83)

Anger is thus a valid source of artistic invention for the Orphic poet.

Although earlier poets claim to have found consolation in their art, there is no such creative ecstasy for Shelley's Orpheus. Upon his return from Hades, his "deep and fearful melody" (l. 55) sung in isolation affords him only a means of expressing his grief. Nevertheless, the agony of Orpheus—once sublimated in art—brings pleasure to the chorus and to nature, although it cannot comfort the artist.

Like Hugo's "Le Satyre," Shelley's "Hymn of Pan" draws on Ovid's account of the Midas story of a mythological framework (p. 43). "Hymn of Pan" was written for the opening scene of Mary Shelley's verse play, *Midas*, and is counterpointed within the play by his "Hymn of Apollo."

Opening the debate on the relative merit of their poetry, Apollo identifies his role as musician.

> I am the eye with which the Universe
>   Beholds itself and knows itself divine;
> All harmony of instrument or verse,
>   All prophecy, all medicine is mine,
> All light of art or nature;—to my song
> Victory and praise in its own right belong.   (ll. 31–36)

The god's poetic themes are abstractions—Knowledge, Divinity, Virtue, Truth—and his verse focuses exclusively on the ideal. The goat-god Pan, however, speaks of human experience in his poetry. He treats those themes that are most important to mankind and that form the most intimate elements of man's life.

> I sang of the dancing stars,
>   I sang of the daedal Earth,
> And of Heaven—and the giant wars,
>   And Love, and Death and Birth.   (ll. 25–28)

For Shelley, the lyre of Apollo represents the voice of the god, an "otherworldly wisdom," and the pipes of Pan symbolize the voice of the true poet.[49] Pan is both god and animal; he has the wisdom of a god, but he is bound to the earth and thus can speak to man and move him by his verse.

Moreover, the god Pan has known the special joys and terrible fears of man. And this is the basis of the tension within the "Hymn of Pan." Pan reveals that he had once assumed the role of a vatic poet. As such, he addressed issues of universal concern; he sang of nature and of man's triumphs. When he sang, every being on earth was silent. However, the final eight lines of the "Hymn" indicate that both Pan's poetry and the audience's response to his poetry have changed. The goat-god recounts how songs of joy turned into songs of suffering when he embraced the nymph-reed.

> And then I changed my pipings,—
> Singing how down the vale of Maenalus
> I pursued a maiden and clasped a reed.
> Gods and men, we are all deluded thus!
> It breaks in our bosom and then we bleed.   (ll. 29-33)

The reed is his own musical instrument, but it is a cruel one that pierces his chest, making him bleed and then producing only sorrowful tones.

The reed is also a nymph whom he desired and could not possess. Like all gods and men, he is wounded by her rejection. However, Pan's frustrated sexuality is sublimated in song, just as the nymph is transformed into a reed. And this song is his sweetest because his nymph-reed wounded him so deeply.

However, Pan's audience scarcely reacts to his song. Tmolus cannot comprehend the tragedy of the poet's song for age "has frozen his blood." Likewise, Apollo cannot fully appreciate human longing or is envious of such emotion. Thus, at the close of "Hymn of Pan," the goat-god tells his most compelling and most revealing tale to an audience who is incapable of sharing the sorrow of such "sweet pipings."

In his dramatic poem, "Pan and Luna," Robert Browning also refutes the Virgilian claim that Pan spontaneously created song after song with ease and serenity. According to Virgil's account, Pan sang suddenly and beautifully while courting a nymph who followed him willingly. Browning, however, maintains that the source of Pan's song was not his joy in attaining love, but the pain of rejection.

Furthermore, Browning's Pan is not the charming, pastoral creature previously envisioned. He is not Shelley's sweet piper, struggling with the discovery of his innocent sexuality. Rather, he is more akin to Hugo's satyr. Browning describes the goat-god as a "rough red Pan," "half-god half-brute" who lays a devious trap for a pure and childlike Maid-Moon.[50] Upon the entrapment, Pan's treatment of his victim becomes increasingly loathsome.

> So did Girl-moon, by just her attribute
> Of unmatched modesty betrayed, lie trapped,
> Bruised to the breast of Pan, half-god half-brute,

> Raked by his bristly boar-sword while he lapped
> —Never say, kissed her! that were to pollute
> Love's language—which moreover proves unapt
> To tell how she recoiled—as who finds thorns
> Where she sought flowers—when, feeling, she touched—
>   horns! (ll. 81–89)

Browning has removed the elements of innocence and primitive sexuality from the character of the fertility god, and has replaced them with the half-brute's violent sexual aggression.

Each Pan-poet—the ancient and the modern—reaps what he sows. In "Pan and Luna," the seed of Virgil's Pan falls to the ground bringing forth flower and song from the soil. For the modern Pan, "rock's the song-soil rather" (l. 111). Rock can give life to no flower and produces only pine trees which sway with Pan's song and serve to snare yet other Luna-nymphs.

Browning explains within the context of "Pan and Luna" that he has no desire merely to retell the ancient mythic tale of the Arcadian goat-god.

> . . . The myth
> Explain who may! Let all else go, I keep
> —As of a ruin just a monolith—
> Thus much, one verse of five words, each a boon:
> Arcadia, night, a cloud, Pan, and the moon. (ll. 100–104)

The poet has isolated the basic elements of the ancient mythology that prove to be most evocative for him. With these five elements he is then able to create a personal mythology of the poet to supersede the ancient mythology of the ancient poet.

Given this freedom with the Virgilian account, Browning creates a portrait of the artist as social anomaly, a "half-god half-brute" (l. 83). Furthermore, the creative product of such an artist is far from the poetry that the traditional norms of beauty might prescribe.

So, too, the Pan of Elizabeth Browning is an asocial beast. The voice of the poet in "A Musical Instrument" asks,

> What was he doing, the great god Pan,
>   Down in the reeds by the river?
> Spreading ruin and scattering ban.[51]

Browning's Pan, like many others, is well able to sing and pipe sweetly, to revive dead flowers and even fix the sun at eternal noon. However, he is able to do so only after he has cropped and deformed a beautiful reed until it is but a "poor dry empty thing" (l. 23).

In "A Musical Instrument," Pan situates himself at the very place where life is most abundant and where vegetation is thickest and most lush. There, at the bank of the river, Pan proceeds to destroy life. The lilies wilt when he appears; dragonflies flee; and Pan crops the reeds that grow near the water. Browning then describes in minute detail how the goat-god "hack'd and hew'd" the fresh reed (l. 15). He cut into it, notched it, and "drew the pith, like the heart of a man" (l. 21). Finally, once the reed is unrecognizable as a living plant, the cruel beast laughs and plays his tortured instrument.

Much like Shelley's "Orpheus" and "Hymn of Pan," "A Musical Instrument" reveals that the poet's pain and cruelty give way to the purest music.

> Sweet, sweet, sweet, O Pan!
>   Piercing sweet by the river!
> Blinding sweet, O great god Pan!
> The sun on the hill forgot to die,
> And the lilies revived, and the dragon-fly
>   Came back to dream on the river.   (ll. 31–36)

Although Pan has initially disturbed the order of nature and has actually destroyed elements of nature, his music reorders the chaos he imposed. In fact, Pan's pipe enhances nature and gives it greater beauty than it possessed in its virgin state. The sun will not set; the dragonflies are now able to dream; nature has a heightened glory because of the artifice of music and the artificial reordering of nature.

In the final strophe, however, Browning reminds us that the artist is "yet half a beast" (l. 37). Regardless of the splendor of his creative product, he is nonetheless marked by his cruelty and his perversion of natural elements.

> The true gods sigh for the cost and pain—
> For the reed which grows nevermore again
>   As a reed with the reeds of the river.   (ll. 40–42)

The "true gods" clearly do not count Pan among them. Browning does not tell us if the gods even hear the poet's music; they are thinking only of the one reed that has been cut and dried. And for this transgression of nature, the "true gods" consider the artist Pan a lesser being.

The nineteenth-century Pan and Orpheus of Hugo, Shelley, and the Brownings are more complex and often coarser versions of the poetic personae of earlier poets. Shelley's Orpheus is embittered and inhuman; Hugo's Orphic poet is told that he is powerless. Similarly, Hugo's Pan wages a futile fight for recognition, and Robert Browning's Pan-poet is vile, lascivious, and unworthy of a place in society. As the poet's personae, Pan and Orpheus are tortured beings. Like their ancient prototypes, their song springs from suffering and denial; their loneliness and their isolation as well as their deprivation of sexual power are channelled into aesthetic energy. The resulting poetry, however, is as little comfort to the modern poet as it was to the mythological Pan and Orpheus.

In the poetry of the late nineteenth and early twentieth centuries, the artist's critical introspection becomes even more acute. His degenerating social status and diminished self-esteem are more forcefully presented within his verse. And self-deprecating irony becomes a common feature of self-reflexive poetry. Correspondingly, the poetic prototypes of Pan and Orpheus are further transformed to become grotesque, sexually impotent, poetically sterile, and pitiful shades of what they once were.

3

French Parnassians and Symbolists

Post-romantic French poetry witnesses the increasing appearance of the artist-hero within self-reflexive literature. Moreover, discussions of aesthetic values, examination of the artistic temperament, and evaluation of the creative experience are among the most prominent themes in late nineteenth-century French poetry. Noting this phenomenon, R. P. Blackmur argues that at this point in literary history "the subject of the artist and the sensibility of the artist began to be the heroic subject and the heroic sensibility which best expressed society itself."[1] Although it is true that the artist is prominent in the literature of this period, the artist-hero is hardly heroic in the classical sense of the term. He commands neither the respect nor the admiration of his society. In fact, the conflict between the sensibilities of the artist and those of his society—and not the concurrence of aesthetic values—is the common refrain of late nineteenth-century literature. Contrary to Blackmur's conclusions, the interests and values of the artist-hero rarely express those of the society at this time. When George R. Ridge states that the "aesthetes of *l'art pour l'art* are firmly grounded in a social context," he also asserts that "indeed, they turn to art because they abhor their wretched society. It is *ugly* in the full meaning of the word. Sin, vice, perversion are traits they can tolerate, even admire for their artificiality, but not vulgarity and ugliness. The aesthete, like any other hero-type, acts in response to his society. In this case, it is an ugly, decadent society. He withdraws from it in disgust, but the very withdrawal, let it be stressed, is assuredly a form of response."[2]

Critical essays of the period would support Ridge's observations, for many literary figures of the time firmly disavow any form of alliance between the poet and a reading public. Théophile Gautier insists that his poetry should serve to "épater le bourgeois" and Mallarmé's first critical essay, "Hérésies artistiques: l'art pour tous," reveals his scorn for the "masse" and the "foule."[3] Indeed Paul Valéry later observes that if there exists any quality common to the many and disparate symbolist poets, it is their desire to be "étranger à l'esthétique" and to "dédaigner la conquête du grand public."[4] We need only recall the title of the novel that served as aesthetic touchstone and presented a popular prototype of the artist—Huysmans's *A Rebours*. Literature of this period would reverse the traditional aesthetics, oppose the expected in art, and run counter to established social values. For Gautier and his symbolist heirs, true art is disinterested and has no pretensions of social, moral, or political significance. "Il n'y a de vraiment beau que ce qui ne peut servir à rien; tout ce qui est utile est laid."[5] Art is *causa sui*, justifies its own existence, and exists independent of whatever the social structure might be. In the wake of the Third Empire and in the face of an increasingly democratic society, the Parnassian and symbolist poets created and flaunted an anachronistic aristocratic ideal of art in an attempt to replace the lost reality of an exalted and vatic poetic identity.

Second, a study of the ancient motifs and mythic personae that the symbolist poet uses to depict himself within self-reflexive poetry speaks to the contrary of Blackmur's thesis. In the poetry of this period we find continued use of Pan and Orpheus as poetic personae. However, the mythic prototypes of the French symbolists are not at all the vatic personae of their pre-romantic predecessors.

In the poetry of Laforgue and Mallarmé, we find that the self-reflexive Pan desires only to escape the isolation of his poetic craft within a sensual world. As prototype of the artist, the French symbolists' Pan finds his aesthetic concerns to be sterile and his devotion to his Muse confining. Consequently, he refuses to repress his social nature any longer. The Pan-poets of Laforgue and Mallarmé, then, attempt to abandon their art and, in its stead, to explore their humanity through sexuality.

The symbolists' Orpheus, too, has undergone a radical transformation. Nerval's Orphic El Desdichado, a lutenist who descends into the underworld for his wife, attempts to compromise his artistic identity with his emotional and physical life. At the same time, Mallarmé's Orphic poet, Igitur, would deny himself a life for the sake of artistic purity. Running to one of two extremes, the poet as Orpheus attempts to deny his art and replace it with a full sensual life, or to deny himself a personal identity and live exclusively for the Muse.

In addition to the mythological poetic prototypes, Pan and Orpheus, new poetic personae emerge as important motifs in nineteenth-century French poetry. In his self-reflexive work, the French symbolist poet frequently presents himself as a *pitre* ("clown") or as the *commedia*'s Pierrot. Yet, although these figures are startling representations of the poet, they are not radically different from the French symbolists' personae of Pan and Orpheus. That is, the self-reflexive image of the poet as *pitre* or Pierrot contains distinct elements of the earlier mythological prototypes.

Indeed, the manic activity of the nineteenth-century French Pan is often indistinguishable from that of another prototype, the *pitre*. Mallarmé's poet-*pitre* of "Le Pitre châtié" confronts the same conflict as the earlier Pan-poets and makes the same choices in confrontation with his artistry. He, too, betrays himself and his poetry and runs from his Muse toward sensuality. Pan and the poet-*pitre* are virtually identical poetic prototypes in that they play out the same tragic scenes within self-reflexive poetry. Both suffer from their bondage to poetry; they seek to resolve their conflict with bacchanalian activity; ultimately both meet with identical fates and begin their struggles once again.

Many French poets looking for expression of their creative identity find the figure of Pierrot to be compelling. The figure of Pierrot is a stock character from the Italian *commedia dell'arte*, well known throughout Europe by the end of the eighteenth century. Pierrot is traditionally identified by his stark white face framed by a black skullcap. He wears a loose white smock that is often decorated with large dark buttons or pom-poms running down the front.[6] An unassertive and bumbling lackey, Pierrot is further recognized by his self-effacing demeanor. Much of his role in comic improvisation revolves around his painful, undeclared love for Colombine. Finally, this *commedia* valet—unlike most others—is distinguished by his sensitivity and his virtue.

In the seventeenth and eighteenth centuries, the character of Pierrot was popularized in France by a variety of actors, including Dujardin and Hamoche, who were considered among his best interpreters. Pierrot achieved his widest fame in the nineteenth century because of the efforts of Deburau and the Funambulists. Today, wide recognition of the comic character can be attributed to the paintings of Rouault and Picasso and to Godard's *Pierrot le Fou*. However, since the eighteenth century, the French clown has been known most generally through the song, "Au Clair de la lune," written in 1712 by Pierrot impressario Hamoche:

> Au clair de la lune
> Mon ami Pierrot
> Prête-moi ta plume
> Pour écrire un mot.
>
> Ma chandelle est morte
> Je n'ai plus de feu,
> Ouvre-moi ta porte
> Pour l'amour de Dieu.
>
> Au clair de la lune
> Pierrot répondit:
> Je n'ai pas de plume
> Je suis dans mon lit.
>
> Va chez la voisine,
> Je crois qu'elle y est
> Car dans sa cuisine
> On bat le briquet.

The character of Pierrot is particularly endearing and remarkable because he is a virtuous figure within the *commedia dell'arte*. In his case, his fortitude and humility are his only protection against a harsh society, for Pierrot's central role in the *commedia* is that of a scapegoat. Furthermore, he plays this role not only for his fellow actors but for the audience as well. Kay Dick describes the *commedia* figure in this manner:

> He was the one who stood just below the stage and opened his mouth to produce some witticism, the meaning of which was lost, because simultaneously a more attractive and cruder personality towered over him on the stage and nullified Pierrot's feeble attempt at self-expression.
>
> He was the ever-available target for mockery and scorn and suffered not only from the contemptuous kicks and insults heaped on him by the grander members of his family, but was forced to submit to much baiting from the audience whose play in this was almost a convention. . . . A poor zany, wretched in appearance, inadequately covered in cast-off clothes, having nothing of his own, disciplined to submit to the forceful nature of those whose destiny was enough to provoke a stream of pitiless and intemperate abuse.[7]

Thus, as a result of his miserable plight, Pierrot was forced to develop the virtues of fortitude and meek dignity in self-preservation. George Sand also finds that Pierrot has retained from his pitiful origins a sense of the "spiritual poverty of mankind," that is, a recognition of the ignorance and venality of the society about him.[8] These particular qualities and aspects of the clown's wisdom have endeared him to the artist from the Renaissance through the twentieth century. In addition, such virtue and insight prove to be especially important for the nineteenth-century French artist when he looks to Pierrot as poetic persona.

In her study of Pierrot, Pauline Heurre finds that the clown represents the modern poetic identity precisely because of his integrity, his fortitude when faced with adversity, and especially his honesty; that of all the *commedia* figures, Pierrot is the most noble, at least in his intentions.[9] Although it is true that the nineteenth-century poet-Pierrot is a noble innocent, his innocence is somewhat *détourné*. His white blouse is often smudged and ragged, hands stuffed into torn pockets; he appears more experienced and more worldly wise.

In contrast to the bacchanalian Pan and the poet-*pitre*, the poet as Pierrot concerns himself exclusively with the absolute purity of his art. In order to fulfill his artistic aspirations, he eschews all social contact. In the works of Laforgue and Verlaine, the poet masks himself, remains apart from society and virtually escapes from life so as not to sully his poetic ideal. Much like the early Italian character, the poet as Pierrot in modern France only suffers from his contact with his fellow man. Despite the impoverished and often tragic circumstances of his life, he nonetheless is remarkable in his ability to retain artistic dignity. Verlaine's Pierrot is a ghost of a poet who has lost every means of communication with his society. Still, he preserves his ideal of artistic purity. Laforgue's many poet-Pierrots are somnambulant "rêveurs lunaires" who have forsaken shabby reality in quest of the moon's sterile purity.

Poet-*pitre* or poet-Pierrot, the image of the poet as clown in a variety of stock types and styles is a central motif in the self-reflexive poetry of late nineteenth-century France. Wallace Fowlie, too, has noted the poet's "reincarnation" in the symbolist period as a clown and *voyou*.[10] Jean Starobinski also observes that "depuis le romantisme . . . le bouffon, le saltimbanque et le clown ont été les images hyperboliques et volontairement déformantes que les artistes se sont plus à donner d'eux-mêmes et de la condition de l'art."[11] He further asserts that

> il s'agit là d'un autoportrait travesti, dont la portée ne se limite pas à la caricature sarcastique ou douloureuse. Musset se dessinant sous les traits de Fantasio; Flaubert déclarant: *Le fond de ma nature est, quoi qu'on dise, le saltimbanque;* . . . Jarry, au moment de mourir, s'identifiant à sa créature parodique: *Le père Ubu va essayer de dormir;* Joyce déclarant *Je ne suis qu'un clown irlandais, a great joker at the universe;* Rouault multipliant son autoportrait sous les fards de Pierrot ou des clowns tragiques; Picasso au milieu de son inépuisable réserve de costumes et de masques; Henry Miller méditant *sur le clown qu'il est, qu'il a toujours été*.[12]

Consider the triple significance of the clown—under whatever guise—as the poet's symbol of his fate.[13] First, the clown is socially and physically abnormal. He lives apart from society, but at the mercy of society, on the fringe of humanity. More often than not, clowns have no home; they are vagabonds, destined to wander like the Jews and the gypsies. Furthermore, they are frequently characterized by a physical deformity: hunchbacks, midgets, fat men with eyes that whirl, ears that wiggle, or noses that squeak, paste-faced, double-jointed novelties. And, if a clown has no naturally grotesque feature, he will immediately assume at least one, a large red nose, pointed ears, long feet, an immense belly. Recognized more by his maimed physique than by what he says or does, a clown is not a true human being. He is a freak, both socially and physically.

Second, a clown is an actor by trade. As such, he bears no responsibility for his words and actions, which are purportedly dictated by an anonymous "other." He assumes a false identity and, in doing so, hides his own. Wearing a mask or a thick layer of makeup, he camouflages truth; the clown either sports an exaggerated grin to hide his pain from the world (and the world's pain from an unknowing world) or he wears an elaborate frown to disguise his mockery of self and others.

Finally, self-mockery guides much of the clown's play and antics. He trips over his own feet, and then puzzles at what could have possibly caused his fall; he is repeatedly the victim of traps and ruses; he fails to understand when a woman means "no" and is then thrilled when she slaps him. Any attention whatsoever—jeers, tomatoes from the audience, or the back of a woman's hand—is translated as a sign of affection. The clown plays tricks on few people but himself and laughs mainly at his own foolishness, his body and his self. Speaking specifically of the clown as persona of the poet, R. W. B. Lewis confirms that "in the world's view, he is a laughable entertainer; in his own view, he has a voice of sadness, even despair, muffled behind his clownish make-up."[14]

In this respect, and in many others, Pierrot and the modern clown resemble the ancient Pan. Just as Pierrot and other clowns are the objects of abuse—their audience's and their fellow clowns'—so too was the ancient Pan whom the gods scorned and his own nurse found repulsive. The Arcadian people, too, maligned their god as the source of agrarian ills. However, neither Pan nor the modern clown completes his role as the traditional *pharmakos* as outlined by Northrop Frye; neither is actually banished from his residence because he is deemed unfit to live in a society.[15] Instead, each figure is fated to live on the fringe of his society and at times to be an isolate. Because of his role as shepherd, Pan lives apart from the Arcadians and remote even from other shepherds. Pierrot travels from town to town, as do the modern *pitres*. The *commedia* figure voyages not in the company of his troupe, but tags behind them, caring for the dogs that accompany the theatrical group. And, as such, Pierrot, like Pan, is a shepherd of sorts. Pan and the clown figures live somewhat apart from their communities, but neither is driven from his people. In this way, society can attribute fault to Pan and the *pitre* and blame them for general misrule. And society can also profit from their merry making and their wisdom.

Regardless of the exact characterization of the poetic persona—Pan, *pitre*, Orpheus or Pierrot—the French symbolists' artistic prototypes share many important qualities and experience identical problems. Each poet figure is an outcast in his society or understands himself to be an alien among his fellow men. Mallarmé's Igitur, faun, and *pitre châtié* cannot find a place for themselves within their world, and Laforgue's Pierrots perceive their world to be a cultural void, a lunar vacuum. Many of the symbolists' personae are incapable lovers, among them the Pan figures of Mallarmé and Laforgue and the Orphic El Desdichado of Nerval. Nonetheless, these poets are expressers of self, in particular the Pan and *pitre* of Mallarmé and the Pierrot of Laforgue. They are also truth tellers. Mallarmé's Orphic Igitur is committed to the pursuit of universal truth, and Verlaine's Pierrot is persecuted for his revelation of truth through his poetry. Therefore, because he is alienated from his society and because he is compelled nonetheless to speak to his society, the poet must assume a disguise in order to communicate the truth. The French symbolist poetic persona, then, is a clownish Pan, a bizarre lunar Pierrot, a depersonalized Orpheus, each mask symbolizing the poet's ironic role in modern society.

Within the French literary tradition, Théophile Gautier's "Bûchers et Tombeaux" begins the transformation of the gentle god Pan into a decadent poet-*pitre*. Gautier's Pan is declared dead, as are the pastoral idylls he has come to represent. Nonetheless, Pan shows himself to the world in the form of a skeleton rising from the coffin. In this role, he is the sole remnant of the art of antiquity, a concrete art described in Gautier's Parnassian manifesto, "L'Art."

Despite his decaying form, the skeletal Pan "se fait voir" and he does so intending to "épater le bourgeois."

> Il pousse à la danse macabre
> L'empereur, le pape, et le roi,
> Et de son cheval qui se cabre
> Jette bas le preux plein d'effroi;
>
> Il entre chez la courtisane
> Et fait des mines au miroir,
> Du malade il boit la tisane,
> De l'avare ouvre le tiroir.[16]

Pan, the last remaining true artist, serves only to shock, to posture and to play the fool in a world of bourgeois, Christian art forms. He not only makes a mockery of traditional values, represented here by the emperor, the pope, and the king, but he also laughs at the antisocial elements that have virtually become social establishments. For example, he visits a prostitute, but only for the purpose of making faces in her mirror. He does so not only to mimic her precious poses and gestures, but also to strike out at the institution of the *courtisane*, which caters to a higher social class of customer than does the *prostituée*. The Pan-skeleton further asserts that this *courtisane* is so unappealing that he has less interest in her than in the antics that her mirror provokes. This poetic scenario reinforces Ridge's view that the late nineteenth-century poet might revel in common vice, but he will not tolerate the ugliness and vulgarity that accompanies such vice within bourgeois society.

However, in the final strophes of "Bûchers et Tombeaux" Pan is discovered for what he is. He plays the role of the comedian, but he is a "comédien que le ver mord"; Pan is not only a mask for the poet, but a "masque sans joues"; he is a fool who mocks his society, while also playing "le mélodrame de la Mort" (ll. 93–96).

Nevertheless, because the poem is a true poetic manifesto, "Bûchers et Tombeaux" offers a resolution to the death and decay, the horrible masquerade of Pan. After he recognizes the pitiful role he has been forced to play, both art and the artist experience a form of baptism by fire, and then await rebirth. The skeleton, dead and dried by "la foule priée" (l. 73), will burn with the image of a Christian god. From this fire, art will be purified, returning to "les sources du beau" (l. 106).

> Reviens, reviens, bel art antique,
> De ton paros étincelant
> Couvrir ce squelette gothique;
> Dévore-le, bûcher brûlant! (ll. 97–100)

The self-reflexive poetry of Jules Laforgue differs radically from that of Gautier in that it does not take the form of an artistic manifesto and therefore does not express ideals of artistic achievement in terms of what is real or even possible. Rather, Laforgue argues much less optimistically for the creation of a pure art form and emphasizes instead the irreconcilable split between the world of reality and the world of art. Thus, Laforgue treats the lot of the poet as an inevitable, inescapable, universal condition that the poet can at best realize, yet must realize in order to survive.

Between 1882 and 1886, Laforgue created three self-reflexive works describing the plight of the artist, *Les Complaintes, L'Imitation de Notre-Dame la Lune*, and a sequence of short stories entitled *Moralités légendaires*. Both lyric works focus on the artist as Pierrot, and one of the *Moralités*, "Pan et la Syrinx," recounts a tale of a poet who is Pan. It is not surprising that Laforgue's Pierrot and his Pan resemble each other markedly; they follow similar artistic paths and encounter identical poetic obstacles.

The Pierrot of Laforgue's lyric poetry is a unique version of the *commedia* clown. First of all, he is not only one clown, but a number of clowns, *les* Pierrots who speak in "Locutions *des* Pierrots." Warren Ramsey notes that the plural Pierrots allow Laforgue to "gain a greater degree of ironic detachment" from his poetic persona.[17] Signalling the poet's fragmented identity, Laforgue shifts from *ils* to *il* and even *je* with little apparent distinction between the pronouns and the clown or clowns to whom he refers. This linguistic confusion reinforces the impact of the multiple, almost schizoid, clown identities, which include a lord, a lover, a French poet, and an actor.

Yet each Pierrot is clothed and masked in the same traditional *commedia* garb—of a sort.

> Une face inberbe au cold-cream,
> Un air d'hydrocéphale asperge.

> Les yeux sont noyés de l'opium
> De l'indulgence universelle,
> La bouche clownesque ensorcèle
> Comme un singulier géranium.
>
> . . . .
>
> Campant leur cône enfariné
> Sur le noir serre-tête en soie,
> Ils font rire leur patte d'oie
> Et froncent en trèfle leur nez.[18]

These are "dandys de la Lune" and "parias blancs" who aspire to be legendary, but ultimately die of "chronique orphelinisme" (sec. 2, l. 13; sec. 4, l. 16; and "Locutions," sec. 12, l. 6). The poet-*pitre* in the lyric sequence resembles a sleepwalker, someone attempting activity without being fully conscious of reality. But this is not the full import of Pierrot's demeanor. Laforgue's poet is so fully aware of his world and so sensitive to its forces that he is repelled by it. Consequently, he is compelled to insulate himself from the world in the interest of self-preservation. He suffers from the solitude of his fate, but realizes that he cannot survive otherwise.

The Pierrot whose dramatic soliloquy forms "Les Locutions des Pierrots" lives

> Entre les Edens de mes vers
> Et la province de mes pères.   (sec. 15, ll. 7–8)

The world in which the Pierrots live is "pauvre" and "charlatan." To live between an impoverished reality and a poetic Eden is to exist in a form of limbo. Furthermore, his limbo appears to be a world "à rebours." "Tiens! l'Univers / Est à l'envers," Pierrot cries,

> Où commence, où finit l'humaine
> Ou la divine dignité?
> Jonglons avec les entités,

> Pierrot s'agite et Tout le mène!
> Laissez faire, laissez passer;
> Laisser passer, et laissez faire:
> Le semblable, c'est le contraire.
> ("Complainte de Lord Pierrot," ll. 27–28, 37–43)

Throughout both sequences, Laforgue's poet grapples with great and difficult questions; he contemplates the absolutes of infinity and nothingness, the ideal and the qualities of true art. However, a world in which "le semblable, c'est le contraire" allows him no conclusions.

The clowns' response is to live "la vie impossible" (l. 46) in an artistic limbo that barely seems more desirable than the world they reject.

> Au clair de la lune,
> Mon ami Pierrot,
> Filons en costume,
> Présider là-haut!
> Ma cervelle est morte.
> Que le Christ l'emporte!
> Béons à la Lune,
> La bouche en zéro. (ll. 1–8)

This macabre version of the traditional tune is our introduction to the poet Pierrot and forms the first strophe of "Complainte de Lord Pierrot." We learn that the Pierrots are all lunar beings. They worship the anti-sun, the celestial body that pretends to be the sun, but neither gives nor sustains life, and commands no power of its own. From this impotent body, the artists claim to receive sustenance and poetic inspiration. At the same time, the Pierrots understand that "La Lune est stérile," but they court her nonetheless, and beg,

> Vends-moi donc une bonne fois
> La raison d'être de Ton Sexe!
> ("Locutions des Pierrots," sec. 3, ll. 11–12)

The moon, of course, has no sex and grants the Pierrots no satisfaction or consolation. It leads them only into a series of "nuits blanches" ensuring their solitude with neither physical gratification nor poetic inspiration. In A. G. Lehmann's explication of Pierrot's lunar world, the clown is "an *absence* from the object world which he observes . . . to the precise extent that world is rendered in terms of lunar beauty. Pierrot is dissolved; the world instead takes on the significance of his costume, pallid face, hesitancy, hopelessness."[19]

In the final strophes of "Locutions des Pierrots" the god Pan appears to the clown in the form of a poet-mentor who sings his advice. The mythological Pan serves not only as sage, but also as an ancient prototype of the modern poet Pierrot. He, too, sought the affection of cold, virginal creatures, but learned that he could be fertile and creative only when he holds a sterile, inanimate object, that is, his flute. Consequently, Pan's terse message is harsh advice.

"Meurs, quand tout vit à tes dépens;
"Mais entre nous, va, qui perd gagne!"
                    ("Locutions des Pierrots," sec. 15, ll. 11–12)

These are severe words, but appropriate for the artist in a world of contradictions and unfulfilled desire. These are the sentiments of an older poet—here a prefiguration of the Pierrot—who fully recognizes his status in a world in which "la semblable, c'est le contraire."

However sage, Pan's counsel offers little consolation to Pierrot, who appears to be defeated at the close of "Locutions." He simply wanders through yet another "nuit blanche" (sec. 3, l. 1) against the backdrop of the stark lunar landscape. Somewhat haggard and poetically impotent, Pierrot is now mute, "la bouche en zéro" (sec. 16, l. 7). He does, however, retain his dreams of the "Lunes d'atan" and the "Edens de mes vers"—both ideals of poetic experience that will later torment the Pan and Orpheus of Mallarmé (sec. 16, l. 11; sec. 15, l. 7).

Laforgue's *Moralités légendaires* is a sequence of short stories, each presenting similar themes of creative conflict and artistic sterility. And, in each tale, the artist assumes a different persona—Hamlet, Salomé, Lohengrin, and others—to describe his plight. The poet-Pan in the *Moralités* provides an interesting analogue to the Pierrot in Laforgue's poetic sequences. Pan is victimized by the same venal world that causes the Pierrots to suffer, and, like the poet-*pitres*, he makes the same artistic choices, which begin in sensuality and end in sterility.

The narration of "Pan et la Syrinx ou l'invention de la flûte à sept tuyaux" begins with demythology. We learn that Pan was never the ithyphallic fertility god that tradition claims; in fact, he has dreamed, but never loved. And "ses rêves lui ont encore plus vidé le coeur."[20] In reality, as it is presented by the story, Pan is a cerebral being. Like the Pierrots, he lives in isolation, in a vacuum between the world and his poetic ideal, but never touching either.

In an attempt to break his solitude, Pan courts the nymph, Syrinx. However, she, like Notre-Dame la Lune, is sterile, rejecting all sensual experience, living exclusively for an artistic ideal: "Je suis une âme esthétique trempée sept fois dans l'eau glacée de la fontaine Castalie chère aux chastes Muses; je suis la plus fidèle des compagnes de Diane . . ." (p. 169). Although she spurns him as a lover, the nymph leaves Pan with a resolution to his dilemma as an artist and a social being. Before transforming herself into a pan-pipe, a "flûte à sept tuyaux," she explains, "Vous voyez bien, vous-même; il n'y a que l'art; l'art c'est le désir perpétué . . ." (p. 183).[21] The artist's lot, as Syrinx explains, is exactly that which Pan endures, caught between reality and the ideal. He is locked in a state of unfulfilled desire, creating and recreating his fantasies. This, he now learns, is the essential condition of artistic creation, a state that he himself had described in lyric form earlier in the tale.

> Mon corps a mal à sa belle âme.
> Ma belle âme a mal à son corps,
> Voilà des nuits et des nuits que je brame,
> Et je ne vois rien venir encor.   (p. 160)

As in any true *moralité*, Pan is finally rewarded for his trials. First, he receives moral assurance in the form of the nymph's advice, and then he witnesses a concrete demonstration of his artistic worth. The poet-Pan is finally allowed to possess his Syrinx—not as a physical being, a nymph, but in the form of a seven-piped flute, a new, more complex, and more subtle instrument than he has ever played before. The pipe represents not only Pan's physical possession of a symbol of the nymph and a higher level of artistic achievement, but it is also a musical tool designed to "perpétuer le désir." When Pan plays his Syrinx, he no longer recalls if the nymph existed in reality or only in his dreams. This distinction is no longer important to Pan because, through the power of his flute, he is able to recreate the nymph and his desire for her. "Il reprend sa flûte à sept tuyaux, sa flûte talisman, âme de Syrinx sur ses lèvres. Et, comme dans un si beau soir de l'Age Pastoral, il est permis de se répéter . . ." (p. 187). Mythologically, this is the most crucial passage of the story. The modern poet-Pan consciously picks up his pipes, knowing that he does so expressly to recreate his desires. Like the ancient Greeks who hear the souls of men in wind and in music, Pan recognizes that to breathe into a pipe is to breathe life into one's desires, in this case, to create the soul of Syrinx. So, too, did Orpheus use the power of music to restore the memory of his wife, and to perpetuate his desire for her. Equally crucial is the modern Pan's understanding that such poetic power is his exclusive right and has been his privilege since "l'Age Pastoral." When he sings and plays, he lays claim to a poetic heritage and reenacts the mythic ritual that firmly establishes the poet in his society.

According to Joseph Campbell's theory of the function of mythology, this mythic consciousness situates man within history and within his society. Furthermore, without mythic consciousness, he cannot have a sense of his role in society.[22] Within the context of "Pan et la Syrinx," however, the Pan-poet never finds a sense of his social role; he remains isolated from reality and receives his notion of the poetic role only from the past. And this past appears to be rather removed from his reality; it is a golden age, "un si beau soir de l'Age Pastoral," a hazy dream in the distant past (p. 187).

After receiving his flute, Pan recognizes that he is not a "halluciné" as he once feared. However, he continues to trot about "comme un fou" calling out his nonsensical cry, "Hoyotoho!" (pp. 188–89). He is as much a clown as the Pierrots of the "Locutions" and "Notre-Dame." But, unlike the poet-Pierrots, he has found a method of evading reality and of satisfying himself artistically. "Heureusement, et désormais, il lui suffit, dans ces vilaines heures, de tirer une gamme nostalgique de sa Syrinx à sept tuyaux, pour se remettre, la tête haute, les yeux larges et tout unis, vers l'Idéal, notre maître à tous" (p. 189). Although this method does not ally him with society and actually forces greater distance between the artist and the world, it does afford the poet a glimpse of his artistic ideal.

Paul Verlaine's "Pierrot" appears to be written in direct response to Jules Laforgue's two self-reflexive poetic sequences. The entire poem is a description of the poet as Pierrot who once was, but is no longer a "rêveur lunaire." Furthermore, Verlaine's verse portrays a dramatically degenerate form of the Pierrot found in Laforgue.

> Ce n'est plus le rêveur du vieil air
> Qui riait aux aïeux dans les dessus de porte;
> Sa gaîté, comme sa chandelle, hélas! est morte,
> Et son spectre aujourd'hui nous hante, mince et clair.
>
> Et voici que parmi l'effroi d'un long éclair
> Sa pâle blouse a l'air, au vent froid qui l'emporte,
> D'un linceul, et sa bouche est béante, de sorte
> Qu'il semble hurler sous les morsures du ver.
>
> Avec le bruit d'un vol d'oiseaux de nuit qui passe,
> Ses manches blanches font vaguement par l'espace
> Des signes fous auxquels personne ne répond.
>
> Ses yeux sont deux grands trous où rampe du phosphore
> Et la farine rend plus effroyable encore
> Sa face exsangue au nez pointu de moribond.[23]

Were it not for the tattered remnants of traditional Pierrot garb, the blouse and white sleeves, the flour-white face, and the "chandelle" from "Au Clair de la lune," we would be unable to identify this figure as Pierrot. Our recognition is reinforced by echoes of Laforgue's poet-Pierrot, the gaping mouth and cold winds of a lunar landscape.[24] This Pierrot, however, most closely resembles a decaying cadaver or a scarecrow, arms flapping in the breeze. He does not even approximate the skeletal Pan of Gautier's "Bûchers et Tombeaux," so still and horrible is he.

"Pierrot" is more than simple visual horror. The poem con-

French Parnassians and Symbolists / 63

tains several important statements on the role of the artist. First, we note that despite the grotesque features of the clown, he is unable to attract an audience. The final lines of the third strophe indicate that Pierrot's arms, covered with scraps of his blouse, make "des signes fous auxquels personne ne répond." His gestures are signs that an audience cannot decipher, and his circus act has no meaning for them. Thus, Pierrot plays out his part without spectators because his role and his act are incomprehensible to the modern world.

However, in the final line of the first strophe, we learn that there exist a limited number of people who comprehend the words of the poet and respond to his song. "Son spectre aujourd'hui nous hante," claims the poem's narrator. The ghost of Pierrot speaks, first of all, to Léon Valade, a personal friend of Verlaine and fellow poet to whom the poem is dedicated. More generally, he speaks to all fellow poets who recognize their fate in his gruesome death. The creative world realizes that it has no true audience, and that it speaks only to fellow artists. The symbiosis of the poetic community is their only possible form of existence, but it is also their death, as the corpse of Pierrot indicates. This argument is again brought forth at the conclusion of the poem at which time Pierrot's complexion is described as "exsangue." The choice of adjective is especially noteworthy as *exsangue* is also commonly used to describe a work of literature that has no life, no muscle (*Robert*, "vidé de force, de substance"). The fate of art, then, follows the fate of the artist.

"Pierrot" is not an isolated poem in the work of Verlaine; several of his self-reflexive lyrics treat the role of the poet with the same stark irreverence. In the collection *Parallèlement*, there are several. "Pierrot Gamin" opens with a firm assertion that the Pan-poet of the pastoral tradition is dead.

> Ce n'est pas Pierrot en herbe
> Non plus que Pierrot en gerbe,
> C'est Pierrot, Pierrot, Pierrot.
> Pierrot gamin, Pierrot gosse,
> Le cerneau hors de la cosse,
> C'est Pierrot, Pierrot, Pierrot!   (p. 374, ll. 1–6)

The gentle, musical, pastoral poet no longer exists and has been replaced by a "poète-grimacier," a midget dandy with the "subtil génie / De sa malice infinie" (ll. 10–12). Verlaine is explicit about the significance of the decadent, malicious clown.

> Grandis, car c'est la coutume,
> Cube ta riche amertume,
> Exagère ta gaieté,
> Caricature, auréole,
> La grimace et le symbole
> De notre simplicité! (ll. 31–36)

The mask of the poet has become transparent. He is a pained and bitter fellow, disguising his bitterness with a frozen, exaggerated grin. A true clown.

But a closer examination reveals that the grin is actually a grimace—a word that is repeated twice in "Pierrot Gamin" (ll. 12 and 35). This is the resolution of the two opening sets of clues that clash throughout the poem. On one hand, Pierrot is described in endearing terms as an innocent, but daring boy. He is a "gamin," a "gosse," "mignon"; he is a "frère" and a "camarade" (ll. 4, 8, 25). This is the gentle schoolboy Pierrot as depicted in the popular sketches of Adolphe Wilette in the 1880s and 1890s.[25] At the same time, Verlaine's description is laced with a rough, almost sinister portrayal of the clown. This characterization is evoked by the "éclair d'acier" in his eyes, the "lèvres rouge-de-blessure" and the "rictus fins" (ll. 9, 13, 15). A *gamin* would have lips reddened by pilfered strawberries, not lips that are bruised and bloodied. The opposing images are reconciled in the figure of Pierrot, a clown who conceals his private identity behind a public mask. The grimace behind the grin and the bitterness behind the gaiety are revealed simultaneously in the final lines as the symbol of the poet's condition.

We find the same juxtaposition of opposites in "Caprice." The poet within the poem is described as a "faux pauvre et faux riche," "tour à tour souple drôle et monsieur somptueux" (ll. 1, 4). And, without being identified as a specific clown, such as Pierrot or Harlequin, this poet is, nevertheless, a poet-*pitre*.

> Ton habit a toujours quelque détail blagueur.
>
> Un bouton manque. Un fil dépasse. D'où venue
> Cette tache—ah ça, malvenue ou bienvenue? (ll. 6–8)

The first two of four strophes build a sequence of seemingly contradictory images. The poet-*pitre* laughs and cries simultaneously; his tie is both well and poorly knotted, his shoes both shined and dull.

The final two strophes, then, resolve the conflict which the initial two prepared. Yes, the poet is a vagabond. But he is so only because he dares to speak the truth. "Gueux, mais pas comme ça, l'homme vrai, le seul vrai" (l. 13). In fact, according to Ovid's account of the Orpheus myth, complete truth is a necessary condition of poetic speech. The Thracian hero was permitted to descend to the underworld "si licet et falsi positis ambagibus oris / vera loqui sinitis" ["if it is lawful and if you permit me to lay aside all false and doubtful speech / and tell the simple truth"] (*Met.*, Book 10, ll. 19–20). Only then is he able to work the magic of his music.

Verlaine plainly outlines the fate of those whose language is "vrai" and who live as poets. He predicts their salvation, but also laments their lives on earth as "petits sacrés coeurs de Jésus plus lamentables," "coeurs plus blessés qu'une cible," and "pauvres coeurs mal tombés, trop bons et très fiers" (ll. 19–22). There is naturally a bitter side to the poet. His lips reveal the irony of his existence, and he curses both the poets whose language is not "vrai" ("Poète, va, si ton langage n'est pas vrai," l. 14) and the society that refuses to recognize him. And, for the true poet, Verlaine offers one small piece of advice: "Meurs sauvé, meurs de faim pourtant le moins possible" (l. 24). The ironic implication of his advice is that a poet of integrity cannot enjoy both self-respect and social acceptance. Salvation and acclaim are mutually exclusive for the poet.

Several of the clown figures in the poetry of Paul Verlaine are neither as ill fated as the clown figure in "Pierrot" nor as sinister as "Pierrot Gamin." In fact, when one initially thinks of the Pierrot figure in Verlaine's lyric verse, one instinctively recalls the collection, *Fêtes galantes*, in which a number of the *commedia dell'arte* characters as well as later stock figures gather to recreate a world of fantasy, a "fête foraine." Poems such as "Pantomine" and "Fantoches" (pp. 83, 90) describe a world of simple pleasures and of sorrows that are never more than momentary melancholy. Even the verses of love lost are light in tone and, like the others, are composed largely of rich rimes in octo- and decasyllables with strong caesuras. However, behind the backdrop of folkloric innocence, Jean Starobinski sees a tragic motivation for such poetry.

> Le monde du cirque et de la fête foraine représentait, dans l'atmosphère charbonneuse d'une société en voie d'industrialization, un îlot chatoyant de merveilleux, un morceau demeuré intact du pays d'enfance, un domaine où la spontanéité vitale, l'illusion, les prodiges simples de l'adresse ou de la maladresse mêlaient leurs séductions pour le spectateur lassé de la monotonie des tâches de la vie serieuse.[26]

Starobinski argues, then, that only in the artificial world of complete fantasy can the poet's inventive spirit feel free.

Many of the self-reflexive themes expressed in the work of Laforgue and Verlaine are further explored by Stéphane Mallarmé. Indeed, it would not be an exaggeration to state that the majority of Mallarmé's poetry is explicitly self-reflexive. Sonnets such as "Salut," "Eventail," and "Une dentelle s'abolit" describe the act of creation, and numerous works offer homage to poets, painters, and musicians whom Mallarmé particularly admired—Poe, Baudelaire, Gautier, Verlaine, Whistler, Wagner, and even a fictional character, Huysmans's des Esseintes. However, most of Mallarmé's self-reflexive work is not of praise, but of tragedy and treats not the joys of creation, but the agony of poetic sterility. "Renouveau," "Angoisse," "Las de l'amer repos," "Tristesse d'été," "Soupir," and "Le vierge, le vivace et le bel aujourd'hui," each repeat the theme of the poet's boredom, his frustration with his society, and his inability to create. "Je veux délaisser l'Art vorace d'un pays / Cruel," cries the poet in "Las de l'amer repos" (ll. 11–12). In this and in other poems, he searches for a poetic ideal symbolized by "l'azur." But the Mallarméan poet ultimately laments, "J'ai beau tirer le câble à sonner l'Idéal" ("Le Sonneur," l. 10). He finds that his society, his audience, is a mere "bétail ahuri des humains" ("Le Guignon," l. 1) and that neither he nor his work has any place among them.

It is not surprising, then, that the poet's personae within such self-reflexive lyrics are hopelessly tragic figures—"des mendieurs d'azur" in "Le Guignon," the suicidal bell ringer of "Le Sonneur," "le poète impuissant" in "L'Azur," yet another beggar in "Aumône," and "le hagard musicien" of "Petit Air II." Like many of his contemporaries, Mallarmé also chooses modern expressions of the classical figures, Pan and Orpheus, to act as poetic personae within his lyrics. "L'Après-midi d'un faune," composed between 1865 and 1877, presents the poet as a clownish Pan, a tragic hero whom the Mallarmé scholar, Harold Smith, goes so far as to call an antihero. During the same period, Mallarmé also begins his enigmatic *Igitur*, a lengthy lyric composition in which the poet reenacts the Orphic *katábasis* in an attempt to discover "la poésie pure." And, like Gautier, Laforgue, and Verlaine, Mallarmé presents himself as the poet-*pitre* within his self-reflexive works. "Le Pitre châtié," written between 1864 and the late 1880s, introduces the theme of the dichotomy between art and reality and prepares the way for a more profound treatment of this idea in "L'Après-midi d'un faune." In all three works, Mallarmé continues the theme sung by earlier French symbolists—that of the modern poet's firm isolation from his society.

Many critical studies of "Le Pitre châtié" concentrate exclusively on the early version, which was written in 1864. Because of syntactic complexity and condensed, obscure imagery, the final version is ignored by critics such as Russell King.[27] Wallace Fowlie, however, rightly feels that it is incorrect to rely solely on the earlier poem simply because of its relative clarity.[28] One might even argue that the two versions are actually different poems. For these reasons, we will examine the two poems separately. Each sheds distinct light on the identity of the modern poet as depicted by Mallarmé.

The early "Pitre châtié" is a sonnet in which the poet addresses his Muse.[29] However, this is the extent of the classical structure of the poem, for the traditional relationship between the lyric poet and his Muse has been radically altered. By classical standards, Mallarmé's poet would appear to be grossly disrespectful to his goddess Muse in that he addresses her in the familiar, second person. Comparing the poet's stance in this poem with the traditional manner of addressing the Muse, Francesco Piselli argues that "la familiarità con la Musa (expressa in *ton* pitre, *notre* baraque) prende una fumosità chiusa e volgare; la lampada poetica soffoca" ("the familiarity with the Muse—expressed in *ton* pitre, *notre* baraque—establishes a stuffy and vulgar arrogance; the poetic lamp is smothered").[30]

Furthermore, the poet himself is not the classic gentleman of letters who aspires to serve his Muse faithfully. Rather, he is a discontented clown who attempts to escape his poetic servitude. Identified first in the title of the poem, the artist is a *pitre*, the choice of diction being particularly significant in its pejorative connotation. A *pitre* is a lowly carnival clown who has little share in the tradition of the great *commedia* clowns, Harlequin and Pierrot. Moreover, within his diminished arena he is not even a main attraction, but merely a hawker, an inferior sideshow buffoon who serves to draw passersby into the tent.

The poet-*pitre*'s invocation to his Muse does not end in the first strophes. The entire poem is addressed to her and takes the form of a confession, an explanation for his infidelity to art. The poet confesses that he has pledged himself to a woman other than his Muse; he then crawls through the theater window and escapes. Within the real world, the clown discovers his true senses, but there he also loses his creative identity. After removing his clown garb, the poet swims in an invigorating, icy pool, his stage makeup washing away. In this exposed condition, the clown's genius ceases to exist. He cannot create or even exist outside the artificial environment of the carnival, particularly in a habitat that is so completely alien to him.

The series of oppositions upon which the poem is constructed conveys the significance of the poet-*pitre*'s flight. The clown forsakes his Muse for a mistress. The tyranny of the Muse is subsequently contrasted with the freedom the clown experiences with his new love. Exchanging artifice for reality, the clown chooses spontaneous, physical sensation and rejects the tawdry acting that was his life. His lover's eyes are described as pure lakes, unlike the smoky atmosphere of the theater. Swimming in the lakes of a woman's eyes, the poet is reborn; he is fresh, clean, and naked, no longer covered with soot and greasepaint.

We recall that the *pitre* was initially attracted to the clear blue color of his lover's eyes, the color suggesting *l'azur*, poetic purity. However, once the poet dives into these lakes of sensuality in search of his artistic ideal, the water freezes about him and thus indicates the creative sterility of such physical sensation. Although he believed that such freedom would produce artistic fecundity, the poet finally recognizes that his art is possible only within the environment of illusion and artifice. "Cette crasse était tout le génie!" (l. 14). Harold Smith finds that through the series of juxtaposed oppositions in "Le Pitre châtié" "the point of the parable is clear. The artist must renounce life to recreate it in art. The hero cannot be both naked and clothed, artist and lover, actor and natural being. The actor is caught in a dilemma. He can neither rival nature in his art nor escape his role to become a purely natural man. Art ('cette crasse') is both a barrier and sole means of access to the sky."[31] Furthermore, once the poet applies his grotesque greasepaint and sets himself and his art apart from his world and its reality, he has done so irrevocably.

The final version of "Le Pitre châtié" minimizes the element of love that motivates the 1864 draft. The eyes in the finished poem are those of a tragic clown, weeping with the desire to be someone other than a foolish actor. To escape his role as a "histrion," the vulgar comic actor cuts a hole in the circus tent and flees the Muse who guides his every word.

From the opening strophe, the poem is informed by metaphors of baptism. The poet-*pitre* prays for a rebirth—not in the spirit but in the flesh. He rejects his role as Hamlet, a cerebral being caught in intellectual stasis, and searches for spontaneous, physical experience. And so the clown dives into the lake of his sorrow and desire, to undergo a baptism of the senses.

However, the traitor-poet is punished with failure in his attempt to abandon art for reality. He is as pitiful a swimmer as he is a Shakespearean actor and goes through the motions of swimming in fits and starts. With each stroke, with each attempt to break from illusion and to assert the power of the artist in reality, he sinks further in the waves. Once naked in the elements, the clown becomes a victim of his desire. The waves prove to be too strong for his weak limbs, accustomed only to artistic simulation of physical motion. The noon sun beats on the white body, once exposed only to soft stage lamps. Ultimately, the lake of sensuality is transformed into a glacier of sterility ("l'eau perfide des glaciers"), and the poet-*pitre* drowns and freezes in the "rance nuit de la peau" (ll. 12, 14).

It is not until the final moment before drowning that the poet fully understands that this baptism and rebirth are impossible for him. The clown has already been anointed with greasepaint, baptised as a poet, actor, creator of artifice. His makeup was his initiation ("c'était tout mon sacre," l. 13) into the rite of a god of illusion, and, because of that mark on his soul, he simply cannot exist outside of his world of the imagination. Neither can he return to introduce reality into the ideal. It is in this light that Piselli understands the central theme of "Le Pitre châtié." "Anche questo è un esito della concezione di caduta; posto che l'essere mondano sia l'opposto dell'Assoluto, che il Réel sia radicalmente inferiore all'Idéal, il poetare sarà un truccare la realtà, il fingere un Beau che è irrimediabilmente lontano. Tale impegno è logorante e soffocante, consistendo in una servitù senza premi al tirannico dovere poetico; allora il poeta tenta di prendere il mondo come va, nella sua ingenua freschezza, e riesche anche ad acquistarla: ma non è più poeta." [This is a consequence of the idea of the fall; assuming that the worldly condition were the opposite of the Absolute, that the Real were radically inferior to the Ideal, then to be a poet would be to disguise reality, to counterfeit a Beauty that is irremediably beyond reach. Such an undertaking is wearing and stifling, amounting to bondage without reward to tyrannical poetic duty; then the poet attempts to accept the world as it is, in its natural freshness, and even manages to acquire this (freshness): but he is no longer a poet.][32]

The rupture in "Le Pitre châtié" between the real and the ideal, sensuality and artistic creation, nature and art, is further explored in Mallarmé's most celebrated work, "L'Après-midi d'un faune." This self-reflexive poem is a portrayal of the artist divorced from his world. In this work, Mallarmé identifies the poet not as a clown or *pitre*, but as the mythological Pan. The faun in this poem is a bacchanalian figure, but falsely so. He would gladly take his pleasure with various nymphs, with wine in the noon sun, but he cannot.

Mallarmé's faun is so removed from physical reality that he finds true sensation only in reverie and in his artistic recreation of such reverie. In fact, he is artistically impotent within reality—under the Sicilian sun with real women and true wine—and finds that he can create only in the shadow, dreaming of nymphs he might possess, blowing into empty grape skins like a flute. L'*impuissance littéraire*—"poetic impotence"—is a central theme of "L'Après-midi d'un faune" and will become a major motif in twentieth-century self-reflexive poetry. Just as Pan's sterility is a constant fear and taunt in Arcadian mythology, so is Mallarmé's faun tormented with physical impotence and poetic sterility. Forced to scrutinize his artistic activity in the face of an unlyrical world, the poet will inevitably question his very ability to create.

"L'Après-midi d'un faune" begins *in medias res*. The faun wakes from his noon nap with hazy recollections of sexual experience with two rosy nymphs. However, he cannot recall if this occurred in his dreams or in actuality. "Aimai-je un rêve?" the faun asks and immediately replies, "hélas! que bien seul je m'offrais / Pour triomphe la faute idéale de roses" (ll. 5, 8–9). This statement, built on contradictory elements, forms the nucleus of the eclogue and serves as a crystalline expression of the faun's conflict. "Hélas!" the Pan-poet laments when he realizes that he was indeed alone in his pleasure, only dreaming of possessing the nymphs. The faun regrets that what he thought was his first sexual encounter never actually took place, except in the sterility of his mind and his desires. In the same breath, however, the poet proclaims that the experience was nonetheless a triumph. Moreover, it was a triumph precisely because it was not real. The nymphs' submission to the faun was ideal, that is, conceived and guided solely by the artist's sensibilities and subconscious desires. Harold Smith remarks that "the phrase 'la faute idéale de roses' recalls the famous 'l'absente de tous bouquets' or the preference of the lover-poet of 'Mes bouquins fermés . . .' for the 'sein brûlé' as opposed to the real, succulent flesh."[33] Each of the three expressions asserts the supremacy of imagined, created experience over experience that is subject to the whims and constraints of reality. The one flower that does not exist represents for Mallarmé the infinite possibility of all flowers and the perfection of one ideal blossom. Similarly, the "faute idéale" becomes the synthesis of all that the Pan-poet might desire and imagine possible when he first approaches a nymph.

When the faun begins to awaken from his dream, his first inclination is to perpetuate his memory of the nymphs, to prolong the sensation, and to sublimate it through artistic recreation. He does so because he is an artist bound to the ideal. "Ces nymphes, je les veux perpétuer" (l. 1). Both R. J. Austin and R. G. Cohn remark that the construction of this sentence is particularly suggestive.[34] The natural word order would be "Je veux les perpétuer." However, the syntax of Mallarmé's line gives the reader the indication that the sentence might end before the infinitive and consequently creates the anticipation of an expression of sexual desire. The final verb eliminates this possibility and contradicts the reader's initial expectation by asserting something very different. The poet does not claim to desire the nymphs; rather, he would like to recreate the memory of his illusory experience with them. Much like Laforgue's Pan in *Moralités légendaires*, Mallarmé's faun is forced to sublimate in art what he might desire in reality.

The faun does this in two distinct fashions that nevertheless proceed toward one end. First, he calls upon his artistic memory to recreate, prolong, and even inflate the events and sensations of his dream ("réfléchissons"; "regonflons des SOUVENIRS"). He admits that the senses he draws on for this renewed experience are not physical but poetic. The women, he realizes, are purely a function of his "sens fabuleux," that is, his fictive, imaginative senses (not marvelous or fabulous senses, as some have asserted). In fact, the faun's physical senses are not at all aroused in the intense heat of the Sicilian sun. He is aware only of the one breeze that is created by his breath running through his flute, "le visible et serein souffle artificiel / De l'inspiration, qui regagne le ciel" (ll. 24–25). Again, it is the artistic memory and creative forces—and not the natural elements—that inspire Mallarmé's faun.

Second, the Pan-poet invokes the *genius loci*, attempting to tap this artistic font for confirmation of the experience that his poetic memory recalled. "O bords siciliens d'un calme marécage," he implores, "CONTEZ" (ll. 26, 28). The verb *conter* means to recount an event, a story, but it also holds the additional connotation of an imaginative rendering of the story, and it sometimes implies that the teller is actually fabricating the entire tale. In any case, the imaginative element of artistic creation of the event emerges once again.

Because of his repeated attempts at a poetic sublimation of the sexual experience that he cannot enjoy in reality, the faun might be understood as an artistic hero. Indeed, R. J. Austin considers "L'Après-midi d'un faune" to be an expression of the triumph of the artistic sensibility over the baser, physical impulses.[35] And, although Wallace Fowlie emphasizes the conflict between these forces in the poem, he too determines that the faun is ultimately "more intoxicated by his art than by his adventure."[36] However, the faun's attempts at poetic creation are only attempts, and they never become completed acts of creation. Although he directs his energy toward art, in each instance the faun doubts the value of his creativity and ultimately rejects his art, propelling himself instead in the direction of sensuality. For this reason, Harold Smith finds that "the subject of the poem is not the triumph but the defeat of art, the defeat of the Faun-musician by the Faun-lover. If the poem represents the victory of art, the victory is that of the poet and not the persona. Mallarmé triumphs as creator of the poem, while his hero abandons his chaste art and succumbs to the forces of life, time and nature."[37] Although the majority of Mallarmé critics find that this work is structured on a counterpointed pattern of physical loss rechannelled into artistic sublimation, the movement of "L'Après-midi d'un faune" is more complex. The faun first abandons his art in search of the nymphs. Losing his nymphs, he then attempts poetic recreation of his experience. However, the faun ultimately rejects his artistic sublimation and rushes once again toward sensuality. The poet, then, vacillates between two urges, finally moving from artifice toward spontaneous, physical experience.

Although the Faun-lover defeats the Faun-musician, the lover is not a complete victor. There, too, Pan fails. He never actually takes physical possession of his nymphs and, in fact, fears punishment for simply desiring Venus. Like the *pitre châtié*, the Pan-poet is marked as an artist and therefore cannot deny his life's mission, his poetic priesthood. Neither can he be happy outside of his vocation.

Lines 33 to 37 present a condensed illustration of the conflict between the artist and the man.

> Inerte, tout brûle dans l'heure fauve
> Sans marquer par quel art ensemble détala
> Trop d'hymen souhaité de qui cherche le *la*:
> Alors m'éveillerai-je à la ferveur première,
> Lys! et l'un de vous tous pour l'ingénuité.

Noon is described here as an animallike hour, a time of intense physicality. Both motionless and burning, this bestial hour marks the poet's rush toward sexuality and entices him to desire too much physical gratification ("trop d'hymen," l. 38). The artist who seeks "le *la*," the extreme purity of his music, should not be concerned with impure desires. Sexuality, reality in general, must not be allowed to encroach on the exclusive nature of his craft; sensuality must not sully the purity of his commitment. Consequently, when the poet awakens from his first sexual dream, he regrets to find that he is still a virgin, a lily. He is "droit et seul" (l. 40), harboring desires that he, as poet, cannot consummate.

The faun then notices what appear to be teeth marks on his chest, and he admits his hope that this is a sign that he did indeed rape a nymph. However, he soon realizes that the bite is a raw, perverse form of the *Küssenmuse*. Pan's love bite may actually be a wound inflicted by his pipes. Much as the mythological goat-god was pierced by the reeds when he chased Syrinx to the river side, Mallarmé's faun, too, is bruised by his instrument just at the point when he most desires his nymphs. Smith explains that the wound—be it by the Muse or by the pipes—is a "symbol of the fatality that makes the Faun an artist, that inspires a fatal love for the absolute."[38] Mallarmé's faun, like the *pitre châtié*, has been baptised and marked as poet. As a result, he cannot escape his artistic role for physical freedom. Nor, it seems, can he be satisfied with poetic sublimation of sensuality.

The Pan-poet is a faltering disciple of the absolute and repeatedly denies the power and beauty of his art. His musical attempt at recreating the nymphs is described in devastating terms as "une sonore, vaine et monotone ligne" (l. 56). And, after the faun dares to make this admission, he speaks even more directly about his role as musician. The faun asks that his pipes return to the lake's shore and grow again as wild reeds, as if he never played them and never lost his nymphs on their account.

> Tâche donc, instrument des fuites, ô maligne
> Syrinx de refleurir aux lacs où tu m'attends!
> Moi, de ma rumeur fier, je vais parler longtemps
> Des déesses; et par d'idolâtres peintures,
> A leur ombre enlever encore des ceintures:
> Ainsi, quand des raisins j'ai sucé la clarté,
> Pour bannir un regret par ma feinte écarté,
> Rieur, j'élève au ciel d'été la grappe vide
> Et, soufflant dans ses peaux lumineuses, avide
> D'ivresse, jusqu'au soir je regarde au travers.   (ll. 57–66)

After having abandoned his flute, the Pan-poet finds solace in bacchanalian revelry. The emphatic "moi" at the opening of line fifty-nine asserts the rupture between self and music. The personification of the pan-pipes as a separate, alien entity further reinforces this emotional separation between the faun and his art.

The poet will no longer sing, yet he drunkenly blows into empty grape skins like a flute. This image finds a parallel earlier in the poem when Pan asks that his experience with the nymphs be inflated ("regonflons des SOUVENIRS," l. 67) into poetry. Having lost his confidence with both the nymphs and his poetry, the faun now returns to a substitute form of satisfaction—solitary, Dionysian sensation. He thus inflates grape skins as he once wished to inflate experience into lyric expression.

Mallarmé extends this imagery later in the eclogue when the faun further describes his newly kindled passion (ll. 98–109). A ripe pomegranate bursts in its maturity and Mount Etna explodes at the moment that Pan imagines taking the goddess Venus. The poem reaches its crescendo with a flow of sweetness and ashes, blood and lava, metamorphic expressions of the physical gratification he has so long desired. However, once again, the faun is interrupted at the very moment of satisfaction. His physical attempts are ruptured just as abruptly as each of his artistic trials. Like the *pitre châtié*, although the faun has rejected his art, he is forever an artist and must be punished for his transgression. The punishment in this case is fashioned for the faun's particular crime, desiring both artistic and physical life. Thus, in the final strophes, the faun finds that his words have been silenced and his body made heavy: "l'âme / De paroles vacante et ce corps alourdi" (ll. 111–112).

"L'Après-midi d'un faune" thus ends in negation. The faun is sterile—poetically empty and physically exhausted. The setting is silent and dark. The final line, nevertheless, indicates clearly that the struggle has not ended for Mallarmé's faun. The poet announces that he is leaving the intense sun of his desire and will return to the shadow, the place of potential artistic creation. However, he goes there in search of the two rosy nymphs. He finds himself, then, in the same position as in the opening lines of the poem. The cycle of irreconcilable opposition recommences.

The Pan-poet's conflicting passions for art and life are dramatically underscored by their ironic interplay. Harold Smith notes that the faun's dilemma is that "the artist must refuse life in order to create. Paradoxically, to possess the nymphs the Faun must refuse them. He [has] lifted the forbidden veil and lost the very vision that he sought to grasp."[39] Mallarmé's artist discovers that he cannot create unless he completely rejects the natural impulses of his life. At the same time, he finds that nature is unsatisfying unless he inflates or sublimates it through artistic recreation. In essence, the faun must continually reject his world in order to engage his artistic senses.

Mallarmé continues his struggle with his poetic identity and further argues this problem in his later, more hermetic poetry. Abandoning the use of the faun and the clown as poetic personae, Mallarmé turns in later works to the mythological Orpheus to describe the role of the artist. However, Mallarmé is not the first French symbolist poet to explore this myth in self-reflexive verse.[40] Many do, most notably Gérard de Nerval, whose "El Desdichado" is a tragic study of the Orphic poet.[41]

"El Desdichado," the opening work in *Les Chimères*, is an overtly self-reflexive poem. John Kneller describes the sonnet as a study of the poet's *moira*, his lot in life as prescribed by the gods.[42] Indeed, the artist's fate is captured in the very title of the poem, "El Desdichado" meaning the disconsolate, the unfortunate. Albert Gérard agrees that "le *desdichado* n'est pas un homme quelconque: c'est un poète, un artiste. Et nous constaterons par la suite que le thème central qui unifie le sonnet est celui de la relation entre l'art et la souffrance et de la conquête de la souffrance et de la mort par la puissance imaginative de l'art."[43]

The sonnet's sorrowful title is reinforced by a stark opening line, "Je suis le Ténébreux,—le Veuf,—l'Inconsolé."[44] The intensity and specificity of the definite articles, both Spanish and French, force the reader to recognize that the poem does not comment exclusively on the poetic persona of Nerval, or on that of the nineteenth-century French artist. Rather, it represents the fate of each and every poet throughout history. Nerval indicates as much by the diversity of his imagery, the historical and geographic scope of his references within the poem. In addition, he draws on ancient motifs as well as medieval symbols and lore.[45] His poetic persona plays both lute and lyre. Furthermore, the setting of the poem is never specified, although El Desdichado refers to his life in Greece, Italy, France, and Spain. In this manner, Nerval's sonnet spans both time and place, as does its broad depiction of the tragic poet.[46]

El Desdichado is presented as a direct descendant of Orpheus. We cannot claim that he is the mythological figure himself because he refers to his musical instrument as "la lyre d'Orphée," the lyre of another individual. Nonetheless, as Gérard's analysis indicates, the poet resembles Orpheus in his talent and in his suffering. He is a model of the failed Orpheus. After two attempts to retrieve his wife, the hero in Nerval's sonnet is alone and his Eurydice remains dead. Moreover, like the lyre of the mythological hero, his lute is memorialized as a constellation. However, the modern poet's instrument refuses to shine from the heavens because it is composed of black stars. And the poet sings only of melancholy.

The Orphic poet in Nerval's sonnet poses the same question that Mallarmé's Pan asks in "L'Après-midi d'un faune." "Suis-je Amour ou Phébus? . . . Lusignan ou Biron?" (l. 9). Am I a lover, a man, an emotional and physical being; or am I an exclusively cerebral and aesthetic being? Although this question creates a context for expression of the poet's dilemma, it is a purely rhetorical device; the query is answered in the very next line. El Desdichado is neither Eros nor Phoebus-Apollo; he is a poet.

> Mon front est rouge encor du baiser de la Reine;
> J'ai rêvé dans la Grotte où nage la Sirene. . . .   (ll. 10–11)

Like the faun and the *pitre châtié,* Nerval's poet is literally stigmatized as an artist. He has received the *Küssenmuse* and will carry her stigmata with him forever. Because of the Muse's claim to his loyalty and devotion, the poet finds that he cannot function as a normal man. When he finds himself in the grotto of the siren, he is not tempted as every other man has been. He resists her seduction because he can only dream, but not act in her presence. As a poet, he is compelled to construct more fantastic fictions and to imagine more perfect forms of beauty, even while being confronted by the fatal Sirens. This admission on the part of El Desdichado is the answer to his question about his identity.

Although the mythological motifs have been altered, Nerval's poetic persona mirrors the Pan-poets of Laforgue and Mallarmé. Within the self-reflexive lyrics of these three poets, both Pan and Orpheus have been forced to choose between their humanity and their artistry. They are isolated by their dissatisfaction with the world and its offerings. At the same time, they are frustrated by their inability to realize the perfection they imagined they would find in their art. Both figures attempt to find satisfaction—or at least a measure of consolation—in the world with women, Pan with his nymphs and Orpheus with Eurydice, but when their attempts fail, their only solace is the song that springs from their failure. These poets are left to sublimate their sorrows in their art.

Thus, the poet's human failure is a certain measure of his artistic victory, for his lyric expression is his one true triumph. El Desdichado claims,

> . . . j'ai deux fois vainqueur traversé l'Achéron:
> Modulant tour à tour sur la lyre d'Orphée
> Les soupirs de la Sainte et les cris de la Fée.   (ll. 12–14)

Despite his defeat in reclaiming his wife, the Orphic poet nonetheless emerges from the underworld victorious. He is a victor precisely because of the song that his descent engenders. The poetic mandate to transform such suffering into song gives value to the pain of *katábasis*. Albeit tragic, the descent is truly successful because of the poetry it engenders.

A decade after Nerval's creation of "El Desdichado," Mallarmé depicts the modern poet as Orpheus in his *Igitur*, a lyric work that many critics agree is the poet's most enigmatic. The fact that the poem is an unfinished composition compounds the mystery and confusion surrounding the work. However, when one considers *Igitur* in the framework of the entire body of Mallarmé's work, it becomes clear that this poem shares a central theme with many of his earlier lyric compositions, such as "Salut," "Las de l'amer repos," "Une dentelle s'abolit," and "Ses purs ongles" as well as "Le Pitre châtié" and "L'Après-midi d'un faune." The poet's cry of conflict seen in these earlier works is echoed once again in *Igitur*: "Ici: Névrose, ennui (ou Absolu!)."[47] The dichotomy between the man and the artist is again expressed as a conflict between the exalted man as a failed, compromised artist and the pure artist as a man alienated from his society.

At the time of *Igitur*'s composition, Mallarmé claimed in a letter to Henri Cazalis that he had conquered his difficulty with his identity and his *impuissance littéraire*—"poetic impotence." Moreover, he attributed his resolution to a new poem, *Igitur*. "Je te dirai un seul mot de mon travail que je te porterai l'été prochain: c'est un conte, par lequel je veux terrasser le vieux monstre de l'Impuissance. . . . S'il est fait (le conte), je suis guéri; *simila similibus*."[48] The figure of the poet within the new work is also moved to "terrasser le vieux monstre de l'Impuissance." This is the character of Igitur, Mallarmé's Orphic poet.

In their attempts to describe this poetic persona, the major critics refer to Igitur as a Christ figure, as Hamlet, a clown, a priest, and an alchemist. However, without identifying him explicitly as Orpheus, all agree that his development within the poem parallels the Orphic *katábasis*. Igitur, whose sole desire is to create a work of absolute beauty, a *magnum opus*, descends to an underworld as a necessary prelude to this creation. The poem, *Igitur*, is the chronicle of the poet's descent.

Much like Nerval's El Desdichado, Mallarmé's Igitur lacks a fully articulated, specific identity. Indeed, Mallarmé's poet is marked by his willed rejection of a personality. The entire movement of the poem, *Igitur*, is a gradual but total effacement of personality, a shedding of individual experience. This negation of self, concurrent with a vision of past poetic masters, allows Igitur to become a universal poet and to seek pure, universal forms of poetry. In this sense as well, the figure of Igitur is reminiscent of El Desdichado because Nerval's poet, too, has little specific characterization and, at the same time, assumes the identities of all poets from the medieval troubadours to the modern lyricists.

Both figures of the poet—Mallarmé's and Nerval's—most strongly resemble their ancient prototype, Orpheus. The depersonalization of the artist is a central element that allies Igitur, in particular, with the Greek hero. Orpheus, too, is able to mask his identity and to disassociate himself from the living because of the power of his music. Orpheus's art so charms the gatekeepers of Hades that he succeeds in entering the underworld as if he were dead and rightly belonged there. In other words, through the power of his music, Orpheus is able to abnegate his identity and thereby enter the underworld in search of perfect beauty.

Unlike the mythological hero, however, Igitur does not play a lyre; he plays no musical instrument as far as the reader knows. He is neither god nor hero, and the reader assumes that he has no wife who meets a tragic end, because he is still a young boy. Although the skeletal biographies of Orpheus and Igitur are completely dissimilar, Igitur is nonetheless an Orphic poet in terms of the essence of the Orphic myth. Igitur, like his ancient predecessor, dissolves his identity and enters an underworld in hopes of discovering poetic beauty. Once he claims the discovery of such beauty, Igitur, like Orpheus, knows that this power will enable him to defy mortality.

One of the major critical difficulties with Mallarmé's poem is that the reader holds little specific information about the character of Igitur. Basically, we know only his name, and the name is somewhat enigmatic. The word *igitur*, a Latin conjunction meaning "therefore," is recognized most familiarly from the Biblical account of creation, "Igitur perfecti sunt coeli et terra" ("Therefore the heavens and the earth were finished"). Thus, the word *igitur*, evokes the most awesome and miraculous act of creation, the first act of divine creation. Igitur is the creative man as well, challenged to model his creative activity after the first act of creation, and entrusted with a pure world to shape and build as best he can.

In addition, Gardner Davies finds that "le nom Igitur évoque, d'ailleurs, une dialectique plutôt qu'un personnage."[49] The poem bears this out, for Igitur is a young boy whose gradual development into a man and an artist is based on argumentation and opposition rather than on tradition. Igitur is said to be a product of his race ("le passé compris de sa race qui pèse sur lui," p. 54), but he nevertheless defines himself in contrast to his ancestors. Ultimately, he evolves into the final term of the Hegelian dialectic, the synthesis, the *igitur*. Mallarmé refers to the Hegelian concepts of negation and synthesis in his correspondence with Henri Cazalis: "C'est t'apprendre que je suis maintenant impersonnel et non plus Stéphane que tu as connu,—mais une aptitude qu'a l'Univers spirituel à se voir et à se développer, à travers ce qui fut moi. . . . Ainsi je viens, à l'heure de la Synthèse, de délimiter l'oeuvre qui sera l'image de ce développement. Trois poèmes en vers, dont *Hérodiade* est l'Ouverture, . . . et quatre poèmes en prose, sur la conception spirituelle du Néant."[50] *Igitur* and *Un Coup de dés* are two of the four prose poems to which Mallarmé refers in this letter, and *Igitur* expresses most clearly the synthetic argumentation that led the poet to "une aptitude" of the poet's universal mission. Moreover, as Davies posits, the character of Igitur appears to embody the very synthesis of which the poet speaks in his correspondence.

Igitur is described in direct opposition to Mallarmé's earlier poetic prototypes. He differs radically from figures such as the *faune* and the *pitre châtié*, who are obsessed with their sense of self and their physicality. When faced with the conflict of "névrose, ennui (ou Absolu!)," both of the earlier figures flee their Muse. They refuse the terrifying challenge of pure poetry and choose instead the anxious pursuit of physical experience. In contrast with the earlier poetic personae, the boy Igitur rejects his physicality, "la sensation de fini" (p. 54), and finds escape in the impersonal.

In the opening sections of *Igitur*, the poet is described as the embodiment of "neutralité" (p. 37). He then displays "indifférence" and evinces "nulle émotion" until at the close of the second section we understand the full extent of Igitur's quest for depersonalization:

". . . je vais m'oublier . . . et me dissoudre en moi. . . .
L'heure a sonné pour moi de partir, la pureté de la glace s'établira, sans ce personnage, vision de moi—mais il emportera la lumière!—la nuit!" (pp. 50–51).

The poet has dissolved his identity to the point that the mirror no longer reflects his visage, an image used repeatedly throughout the poetic sequence.

Once Igitur has negated his individuality, his perceptions become universal. Rejecting the finite, he becomes conscious of the infinite. D. J. Mossop has accurately described Mallarmé's theory of the impersonality of the poet as seen in the character of Igitur. "The pure poet is the one who has identified himself with his pure self by transcending finite personality, reduced for the purpose to 'néant.' . . . The pure poet must make himself as representative as possible of the sum of human intelligences and sensibilities throughout the ages. The 'one' must negate his 'one-ness' by transcending it and becoming the 'many-in-one.'"[51] Thus, Igitur's personal development within the poem is paralleled by the development of his poetic powers. The Orphic poet attempts to transcend chance, time, and "ennui." Freeing art from these constraints, he will then be able to create his "Grand Oeuvre," which encompasses the opposing elements—"l'Absolu," "l'Infini," "la Clarté," and "l'Idée."

Just as Igitur seeks universality by negating his individuality, so too he seeks his *Grand Oeuvre* by erasing any trace of the only book he knows, the ancient "grimoire." Igitur reveals his intentions in the introduction to the poetic sequence.

Quand les souffles de ses ancêtres veulent souffler la bougie, (grâce à laquelle peut-être subsistent les caractères du grimoire)—il dit 'Pas encore!'
Lui-même à la fin, quand les bruits auront disparu, tirera une preuve de quelque chose de grand (pas d'astres? le

hasard annulé?) de ce simple fait qu'il peut causer l'ombre en soufflant sur la lumière—(p. 35).

The ritual with the single candle is evocative of eastern religious rites, which provide the reader with insight into Igitur's symbolic gesture. In the Buddhist tradition there is a basic meditation in which one blows out a candle, recalls that a candle was once present; but because of the transient nature of human perception, one also knows that it is no longer possible to perceive the candle. Thus one attempts to determine what is now in the place of the lighted candle. Darkness, of course, invites unlimited suggestion. The power of suppressed or negated sensation, introduced in the poem's opening lines and explored further in this passage, is a concept central to *Igitur*. It is also the very principle that Mallarmé evokes in his earlier metaphors of "la page blanche" and "l'absente de tous bouquets." Likewise, the book in a darkened room, the book that cannot be read, is infinitely more suggestive than a singular, finite work that exists and can be read. The poet, Igitur, releases the power of the work through its negation—blowing out the candle—which will engender the infinite possibilities for his *Grand Oeuvre*.

However, before purifying the process of poetic creation, the poet must prepare and purify himself. He first waits for midnight to strike, and when it does, the hour announces, "J'étais l'heure qui doit me rendre pur" (p. 41). This statement contains a past tense, a present tense, and an implied future; it appears to have no meaning outside of the continuing present. This is the nature of midnight itself, which is neither yesterday nor tomorrow, but only the present. The eternal present of midnight, "le rêve pur d'un minuit" (p. 40), controls the poem from this moment forward. At the end of this sequence, at the completion of the action, it will still be midnight. Time and its constraints no longer exist for Igitur.

"Il se sépare du temps indéfini et il est" (p. 55). Once released from time, Igitur truly exists and is thus able to begin his descent. At the very outset, the poet begins his personal negation; he witnesses his own death and entombment and actually hears the door to his grave close behind him. However, because Igitur lives in an eternal present, the tomb continues to close with each step he takes. The sealing of the tomb takes on the rhythm of his heart, each beat signifying not the continuation of life, but death.

After his identity is negated, Igitur prepares to assume the role of poet. The sound of the tomb door, the beating of his heart now become "le frottement familier et continu d'un âge supérieur" (p. 45). On his descent, Igitur passes and pays homage to the dust-covered tombs of past poets. Moreover, he carefully covers himself with their dust "pour que l'ombre dernière se mirât en son propre soi, . . . pour qu'elle se voie, elle, pure, l'Ombre . . ." (p. 45). As a result of this ritual anointment with ashes, Igitur becomes not only a poet, but also "the synthesis of all the pure selves that have preceded him."[52]

At this point, Igitur has negated both time and space. He has eliminated his self and is living in an eternal present with the collective experience of all past poets.[53] As poet, Igitur must now attempt creation of his *Grand Oeuvre*. However, this work must reflect "l'Absolu," the infinite possibilities of poetry, and must not be merely a finite example of poetry that is written subject to chance and the whims of time and location. Mossop finds that "the same ideal of purity (or multiplicity-in-unity) that the poet must try to realize in himself had, according to Mallarmé's theory, to be reflected in the content of his poetry."[54] To realize this ideal, Igitur must abolish chance—that element which reduces infinity to the finite within reality. "Hasard," which is the antithesis of "l'Absolu," is a function of the condition of time. Chance depends upon a future tense that, in the eternal present of this poem, no longer exists. Having already destroyed the element of time, Igitur is nevertheless charged with the task of eliminating the entire concept of "le Hasard."

Toward this end, a tripartite ritual ensues. Igitur first shakes a pair of dice, symbol of the concept of chance. Second, the poet closes the sorcerer's book. Finally, the poet extinguishes the candle, leaving both dice and book in complete darkness. Because the reader never learns the result of Igitur's roll, Mallarmé critics often postulate that he threw a seven or a twelve composed of double sixes (the latter having been jotted in the margin of an early draft). The answer must be both. In a single throw, Igitur is able to roll all possible combinations of a pair of dice because by blowing out the candle, "il réduit le hasard à *l'Infini*" (p. 62). More important, however, is the sorcerer's book, the *grimoire*, that also becomes, in Mossop's terms, "multiplicity-in-unity." Once it dissolves in the darkness, the volume becomes an absolute, the infinite possibilities of poetry, "l'absente de tous bouquets."

Through this ritual, the poet effectively returns to the *igitur* of Genesis 2:1 when the world had not been touched by man and was open to the limitless possibilities of man's work on the earth. A new poetic universe is Igitur's to understand and to shape.

However, Igitur's *grimoire* has not actually been transformed into what Mallarmé would call his *Grand Oeuvre*. The obscured *grimoire* nonetheless symbolizes the ideal of pure poetry and the existence—both actual and potential—of a universal work of poetry. In his commentary on the late poetry of Mallarmé, Walter Strauss notes that "any one poet can create only a fragment of The Book, but a fragment that implies and invokes the existence of The Book."[55] No one finite poem, not *Igitur*, and not *Un Coup de dés* as critics have postulated, can serve as Mallarmé's dream of the *Grand Oeuvre*. Nevertheless, each poem must reflect and decipher one small image of the immense *grimoire*.

In the closing strophe, Igitur takes his place in the stars and thus makes a final Orphic gesture. Just as the ancient hero's lyre is immortalized as a constellation, so too does Igitur take his place with the stars. However, once again the condition of the modern poet demands that the ancient mythological tale be altered. Unlike the Orphic lyre, Igitur does not shine brightly from the heavens for all eternity. Rather, the modern poet makes his bed "sur les cendres des astres" (p. 63), and in doing so reaffirms his poetic depersonalization.

In his study of Mallarmé, Walter Strauss makes use of a novel, *Le Soleil des morts*, written in 1897 by Camille Mauclair, a friend of Mallarmé.[56] The novel's author has asserted that the life of his central character, Calixte Armel, represents an intellectual biography of Mallarmé. In support of the novelist's claim, Strauss notes an anagram of the poet's name in the name of the character (supplemented by the "ix" of the "Sonnet allégorique de lui-même").

Strauss focuses on a passage from the novel which presents the poet as an Orphic figure:

> On peut se tromper en religion . . . pas en art. Aussi est-ce une vocation terrible et exclusive, qui veut tout l'homme et ne permet pas l'erreur; il faut y entrer sans tourner la tête pour voir quelque joie secondaire, comme fit Orphée notre maître, qui perdit Eurydice, image de son âme, pour n'avoir pas eu la patience de ne la contempler qu'en pleine lumière. Notre lumière à nous, c'est la gloire. Et, si nous ne voulons pas qu'Eurydice meure et que la gloire soit, selon l'expression fatale, 'le soleil des morts'—il nous faut fermer à jamais les yeux au soleil de la vie ordinaire. . . . Le *credo* de l'artiste moderne, c'est le silence.[57]

This passage from *Le Soleil des morts* could conceivably be a statement by Mallarmé's Orphic poet, Igitur. Unlike the earlier poetic prototypes, the *faune* and the *pitre châtié*, Igitur is able to renounce every form of "joie secondaire" and devote himself to his art. By descending the staircase and calling for his personal death, the poet rejects the "soleil de la vie ordinaire." Thus, when he extinguishes all light, he is then able to create his glory, the light of true poetry—"notre lumière à nous." The *credo* of the modern artist, then, as witnessed by Stéphane Mallarmé, is retreat, isolation, depersonalization, estrangement from the world, and ultimately silence.

The Orphic personae of Nerval and Mallarmé are much like the French symbolist portrayals of the artist as Pan, Pierrot, and the poet-*pitre* in this respect. Each of the figures experiences alienation from society at the very moment when he attempts intimate communication with that society, that is, when he approaches artistic creation. Thus, Laforgue's mute Pierrots wander expressionless in a lunar vacuum, silenced by the discovery that they are unable to speak to their fellow man. Mallarmé's faun also cannot express himself adequately when confronted by the physical world and by other beings, in particular by women. Outcasts from their society, these figures are like the Orphic Igitur who must perform a suicide rite before he is able to create. Estranged from his society, the poet is forced either to assume a disguise or to negate his personal identity before he can bring his lyric creation to the world.

Because he is disenfranchised from a community, the poet flounders in a dilemma of self-definition. If his is a mission of self-expression and of declaiming the truth, but he has no audience, then his identity as poet has little meaning. His self-conception as poet disintegrates. The poet then has no choice but to portray himself as a mute, a depersonalized individual, a corpse hanging in the wind, and as an alien in a cultural void.

4

Aleksandr Blok and Valerii Briusov

The Russian poetic self-conception as expressed in early twentieth-century self-reflexive verse is remarkably similar to the self-image of the French symbolists. Moreover, Russian poets such as Aleksandr Blok and Valerii Briusov pursue lines of self-questioning and self-doubt that are reminiscent of the French. The same can be said of the mythic figures and poetic clowns as personae within Russian poetry of this period. However, this observation is not unexpected because the roots of Russian symbolism are firmly planted in the French symbolist tradition. When the Russian symbolist movement began several decades after the French movement, the Slavic poets found models in Laforgue, Gautier, and Verlaine, among others.

The Russian debt to French symbolism is well documented, particularly by Georgette Donchin's *The Influence of French Symbolism on Russian Poetry*.[1] Russian acquaintance with French symbolism began as early as 1887 with K. K. Arsen'ev's discussion of decadence in his article, "Содержание и форма в новейшей русской поэзии" ("Form and Content in the Newest Russian Poetry"), which appeared in *Вестник Европы*. Equally important was Z. Vengerova's "Поэты символисты во Франций" ("Symbolist Poets in France"), which appeared in an 1892 issue of the same journal. These accounts were followed by Dmitrii Merezhkovskii's 1893 pamphlet, *О причинах упадка и о новых течениях современной русской литературы* (*On the Causes of Decadence and on the New Trends in Contemporary Russian Literature*). Such theoretical discussions on the western literary movement were complemented by a number of collections of French symbolist poetry translated into the Russian language. These include several pamphlets translated by the poet Valerii Briusov, the earliest being his translations of 1909, *Французские лирики в XIXв* (*Nineteenth-Century French Poetry*). In any case, it is clear that every major Russian symbolist poet had, at the very least, a superficial awareness of French symbolist theory and poetry.

In addition to adopting their central poetic tenets and techniques, Russian symbolists also emulated the European concept of the poet. This is understandable in light of the evidence that many of the early Russian studies of French symbolism focus as much on the poets as on the poetry. Such articles discuss the упадочничество ("decadence") of the western poets as much as the ways in which such qualities might reveal themselves in the French poetry. Joan Grossman finds that Russian poets at the turn of the century found their models in both western literature and reality—Huysmans's Des Esseintes, Poe's Rodrick Usher, and Poe himself, as well as Baudelaire and Verlaine. Grossman further asserts that "something other than literary emulation obviously was involved. The point of such emulation was self-definition."[2]

Like their French counterparts, the Russian symbolists defined themselves by negation. They were united in a common protest against the stale literature of their immediate predecessors, by a revolt against the *taedium vitae,* and by a common disgust for the bourgeois cultural values of their contemporaries. Victor Erlich remarks that for the Russian poet "symbolism was as much a stance as it was a style. By the end of the century the cleavage between the artist and his society—which had set in during the Romantic age—seems complete and irrevocable. Under the aegis of the New Sensibility the estrangement from the bourgeois becomes the poet's essential characteristic, a badge of distinction, an article of faith."[3] Because of their similar attitude toward their role within society, one might rightly expect that the Russian poets of this period would define and present themselves in their self-reflexive verse in much the same way that their French models had done a decade earlier.

The poetic prototypes in the work of Aleksandr Blok are comprised of a variety of clown figures, most frequently Harlequin and an unnamed poet-*pitre*. And, like the poetic clowns of Mallarmé,

Blok's self-reflexive clowns court the world's favor, but with little success. Much like the *pitre châtié*, they learn that to do so is to compromise one's poetic ideals and, in effect, to betray one's artistry. Furthermore, Blok's Harlequin and his poet-*pitre* derive little joy from their contact with their fellow man and bury themselves further in agonized introspection.

Briusov's Orphic poet, like that of Mallarmé, resists any alliance with his society—be it the ancient Maenads and their orgiastic rites or the modern world and its technology. Likewise, the Pan figure in Briusov's self-reflexive poetry attempts to escape an unlyrical twentieth-century Russia and to reestablish contact with his ancient artistic past. Pan's modern songs are only those of lamentation and regret for the past. Briusov's Pan, then, is the antithesis of Mallarmé's faun and Laforgue's Pan in that the Russian figure resists his society while he clings to his artistic commitment.

Aleksandr Blok, one of the most important Russian symbolist poets, is noted for the tragic persona he assumes within his verse. In "Masks and Doubles in Blok's Early Poetry," Lucy Vogel finds that "among the characteristic features of Blok's lyrics is the protean nature of his lyrical 'I'. . . . Indeed, Blok never seems more like himself than when he wears a mask."[4] Considering the pervasive influence of French poetry on the early Russian symbolists, we are not surprised to discover the poet-*pitre* among Blok's many poetic masks. Blok's lyric poetry from 1901 until 1906 presents the reader with the full cast of *commedia* figures from Pierrot and Colombine to Harlequin.

Although Blok's clowns are fully articulated *commedia* personages in both name and dress, they depart radically from their Italian prototypes in manner and spirit. First, because they are products of the twentieth-century imagination, Blok's characters, like those of Laforgue and Mallarmé, lack the innocence of the Italian comic figures. Blok cannot draw exclusively on naive farce and *comique de gestes* and injects modern cynicism and irony in their stead. Second, because the *commedia* of the western European tradition is foreign to Slavic folklore, Blok's clowns more closely approximate the rather sober fools of the Russian tradition.

Ewa Thompson first recognized that there exists in the Slavic tradition no clown of the type that appears so frequently in western literature.[5] The figures of the *commedia dell'arte* never made their way into early Slavic folklore as they did into other major western folklores. These stock characters made their appearance in Russian literature in the late nineteenth century and then only via modern French literature. Compared with early European clowns from Pantalone to Till Eulenspiegel, the clowns of Russian folk literature have little to offer. Thompson states emphatically that "in Russia the buffoon and the clever fool tradition did not develop. . . . One observes a relative absence of Eulenspiegels and buffoons."[6] However, this is not to say that the Slavic folk tradition has no archetypal clownish or bizarre figures whatsoever. The Russian culture has, Thompson explains, a history of "holy fools" (дурачок, юродивый, блаженный, странник), which begins as early as the pre-Mongol era and continues through the Soviet period.[7]

The holy fools known as юродивые were acutely moral and humanitarian souls whose religious ideals and moral integrity distinguished them from their fellow men. Furthermore, they were said to possess powers of clairvoyance and to receive revelations from the deity. However, such men were not only holy, but were also foolish because they feigned madness for the purpose of inspiring religious or moral fervor in others. Despite their madness—be it real or contrived—the юродивые were respected figures in the Russian folk tradition and gained the admiration and devotion of men from the very highest and the very lowest social ranks. Thompson further notes that when the юродивые, or God's fools, commented in a bold or forthright manner on topics of political significance, they enjoyed complete immunity from reprisals. No man—including Ivan the Great and Boris Godunov—dared to harm a holy fool for speaking his mind. To the contrary, their wisdom was valued so highly that men of every social status vied to lodge the юродивый in their homes. However, the fool made no permanent home in any one man's dwelling, for he was a wanderer who traveled to share his wisdom with all men.

In this respect, the юродивый resembles another variation of the holy fool known as the странник. This fool, like the юродивый, is characterized by his religious and personal asceticism. The странник, too, received revelations from the deity and was revered for his prophetic powers. However, this fool did not pretend to be mad, rather he wandered and lived in perpetual insecurity for God's sake.

Both the юродивый and the странник are found at the level of the folk tale, and their modern counterpart in more sophisticated, authored literature is a synthesis of the two. The modern Russian holy fool is an archetype created by the fusion of the юродивый and the странник. Ewa Thompson delineates the modern character of the holy fool:

> Il folle sacro stilizzato, quindi, possiede certe caratteristiche dei *jurodivye* e degli *stranniki*. Appartiene decisamente a una minoranza, e se distingue da coloro che appartengono a "questo mondo". Ha una personalità epifanica, il suo sviluppo spirituale è segnato da rapidi cambiamenti, che risultano da illuminazioni improvvise, piuttosto che da graduali transizioni. E ridicolizzato da "questo mondo", come Pierre alla *soirée* Anna Pavlovna, come Zhivago, che irrita il padre di Marina con il suo comportamento umile, come Raskol'nikov, mentre esegue il suo fallito tentativo di riconciliazione con l'umanità, baciando la terra dopo una pubblica confessione di assassinio. . . . Per contrapporsi a questa realtà, il folle riccore a un comportamento scandaloso, al vagabondaggio fisico, o a forme di ricerca spirituale meno visibili, come l'introspezione. . . . In tutti i casi, i folli sacri stilizzati sono privi di vanità e di gretto egoismo, ciò li rende cari al narratore che, di solito, ne parla con approvazione.
>
> [The stylized holy fool, then, possesses certain characteristics of the *iurodivyi* and the *stranniki*. He decidedly belongs to a minority, and is distinct from those who belong to "this world." He has a prophetic personality and his spiritual growth is marked by rapid change which results from sudden enlightenment rather than from gradual transition. He is ridiculed by "this world," such as Pierre at the *soirée* of Anna Pavlovna, as Zhivago who irritates Marina's father by his humble behavior, as Raskolnikov, while he carries out his unsuccessful attempt to reconcile himself with humanity, kisses the earth after a public confession of the murder. . . . In his opposition to reality, the fool resorts to shocking behavior, to

physical wandering, or to a form of spiritual inquiry which is less obvious, such as introspection. . . . In each case, the stylized holy fools are lacking in vanity and in narrow-minded egoism, qualities which endear them to the narrator who usually speaks about them with approval.]⁸

The western reader would find that the Slavic holy fool bears a significant resemblance to the fool in Elizabethan drama. The audience or reader not only laughs at such fools and sympathizes with them, but also gleans sage counsel from them. Their wisdom sets them apart from the *commedia* figures, their counterparts in later European literature, and most other European fools. Such figures command little respect, and then mainly for their cunning and trickery, and very rarely for their wisdom. On the other hand, Enid Welsford finds that Shakespeare's fools—such as Puck, Jacques, and Lear's fool—are highly respected in the western tradition. The Elizabethan court fool is not "a mere butt or fool to the normal members of the community, but his detachment enables him to be their critic. The laughter becomes more subtle. It is no longer caused by the mere juxtaposition of normal and abnormal; it is caused by the incongruity of the servant being in reality stronger than the master, the madman wiser than the man of sense. Shakespeare's fools are detached critics of society."⁹ As social critic, the Elizabethan court fool—like the Russian юродивый—remains immune in the midst of fierce political battles. The British fool assumes this privilege after he adorns himself in motley and takes up his bauble. Welsford's description of the Shakespearean fool characterizes much of the role of the Russian holy fool as well.

The poet-*pitres* of Aleksandr Blok appear to be a synthesis of western European and Russian fool archetypes. Although they are identified as Pierrot and Harlequin and are dressed according to the prototypes of the Italian *commedia*, Blok's poetic clowns succeed in incorporating critical elements of the Slavic fool and the Elizabethan fool in motley. In Blok's self-reflexive poetry, there is a blending of traditions—without compromising the native Russian motif—to express the Russian poetic identity of the early twentieth century.

"Двойник" ("The Double") contains one of Blok's clearest expressions of his poetic self-conception. The poem opens in the heroic fashion, with an invocation and dedication to the Muse. However, in Blok's lyric, the Muse is Colombine and the poet is Harlequin.

> Вот моя песня—тебе, Коломбина.
> Зто—угрюмых созвездий печать:
> Только в наряде шута-Арлекина
> Песни такие умею слагать.

> [Here is my song—for you, Colombine. / It is a sign of the gloomy constellations. / Only in the clothes of the clown-Harlequin / Am I able to compose such songs.][10]

In the opening strophe, the poet announces that his is a poem of great importance; it was conceived in the heavens. We also learn that the poet must disguise himself in order to create such verse. Moreover, Blok's poet-*pitre* is compelled to reveal the truth within his verse. However, before doing so, he must don the clothes of a fool. In this respect, Blok's Harlequin resembles the юродивый who lives and acts like a madman as he preaches and prophesies. Even more striking is the similarity between the шут-Арлекин and the Elizabethan fool who must bedeck himself in motley and carry his bauble to speak the truth without reprisal. Both Blok's poet-*pitre* and Shakespeare's court fool must signal their approach with bells to warn those who may fear their truth.

The body of "Двойник" is a description of the poet's special disguise as a *pitre*. And, like Laforgue's multiple Pierrots, Blok's poet, the шут-Арлекин, is actually two men, two clowns.

> Двое—мы тащимся вдоль по базару,
> Оба—в звенящем наряде шутов.
> Зй, полюбуйтесь на глупую пару,
> Слушайте звон удалых бубенцов!
>
> . . . .
>
> В смертном весельи—мы два Арлекина—
> Юный и старый—сплелись, обнялись!

[The two of us—we trail through the market, / Both of us—in clanging clown outfits. / Hey, take a look at this foolish pair, / Listen to the sound of the bold bells! / . . . In death-like joy—we are two Harlequins— / One young, one old—interlaced, embraced!] (ll. 5–8, 31–32)

The two are different to the point of being opposites. The old man appears to be senile and crippled; the young fellow has gay and cunning eyes. The old man smiles; the young one trembles. The young Harlequin cries, "Мне скучно! Мне душно!" ("'I am bored! I am suffocating!'") (l. 19), and the old man attempts to calm him. But both are Harlequin and both are one and the same man.

The двойник, the double identity, is consistent with the stock type of the Italian Arlecchino, who is a chameleonic valet.[11] Unlike Pierrot with his whiteface makeup, Harlequin hides his identity only by a black half-mask, which he often removes to reveal himself or to exchange one disguise for another. This protean quality is one of the central comic elements of Arlecchino's character. Blok's poet-двойник draws on this quality as well.

First, the clown is clearly the stock character of Harlequin. He is identified as such by name, by association with Colombine, and by his costume. The early *commedia* figure is recognized primarily by an outfit fashioned of irregular, diamond-shaped patches of various colors. He also sports a felt cap with fur tail, the black half-mask, and carries a wooden sword. Blok's clown, too, is described as wearing "пестрый наряд" ("multi-colored clothes") (l. 26). In addition, both the Italian Arlecchino and the Russian шут-Арлекин double as hunchbacks.

Second, the hunchbacked figure in "Двойник"—the older double of the young clown—represents a radically different clown figure. When the young Harlequin exchanges his traditional disguise for that of the old man, he assumes the role of the Elizabethan court fool. The old man is deformed, as were many of the court fools, and he carries both bauble and bells. Blok's fool is distinct from the young Harlequin in that he is patient and understanding. Although he appears to be senile, he is wise and shares his wisdom with his young companion. At the same time, he is a mocker and a true spectacle. Together, the шут-Арлекин and the figure of the court fool–юродивый form Blok's poetic identity.

Under both guises, the poet has the same problem, one that he shares with Paul Verlaine's "Pierrot." He can neither attract the attention of the passersby with his outlandish clothes, nor can he receive their kind treatment as a fellow man.

О, если только заметят, заметят,
Взглянут в глаза мне за пестрый наряд!

[Oh, if they would only notice, notice, / And for my multicolored clothes, look into my eyes!] (ll. 25–26)

His lot, as he describes it, is to be ignored by society. The people milling in the marketplace, those sitting on the park bench, and passersby on the street do not flock to the poet-*pitre*, the modern юродивый. To the contrary, they look at him "равнодушно" ("with indifference") (l. 17). Although the court fool wears his motley to signal that he is a truth bearer, and the юродивый exhibits his madness to inspire others with his fervor, the effect of the modern poet's absurd disguise is nil. "Кто," the poet cries, "удостоит нас взора?" ("Who would favor us with a look?") (l. 13). Society overlooks his poetry and his wisdom just as it overlooks him.

The dual postures of the двойник allow Blok to objectify and divide the poet's creative role and social status. On one hand, the двойник is a sage. He is a court fool who alone has insight into his society, and he is a юродивый who exists only to guide his fellow man with his moral counsel. On the other hand, this sensitive creature must be insulated from a crude society that remains indifferent to his virtue and wisdom. For this reason, within the poem he literally stands behind a double who appears to be more callous to his public (ll. 11 and 24). Like the multiple identities of a true Arlecchino, one mask is superimposed over another. The young Harlequin protects the older sage from a world that belittles and rejects his concern for its members.

Blok's manipulation of pronouns in the final strophe is highly significant and illustrates the very problem treated in the poem. In the first eight strophes, before the reader is made aware of the dual identity of the poet-*pitre*, the speaker, Harlequin, addresses his reader in the first person—"Я трепещу," "Мне душно!" "Я - Арлекин" ("I am trembling," "I am suffocating!" "I am Harlequin") (ll. 18, 19, 24). The poet-*pitre* does not initially reveal his dual identity. Consequently, his alter-persona, the old man, is described in the third person, his physical location clearly demarcated as behind or at the side of the young Harlequin. In the early stanzas, he claims merely to be accompanied by the old man and furthermore asks, "Кто угадает, что мы с ним—вдвоем?" ("Who would guess that we are together?") (l. 14).

However, once the admission of identity is made in line 31, the я and the он (the *I* and the *he*) become мы (*we*), and the two physically embrace. Moreover, in the following line, the pronouns again shift to an objective third person denoting both the young and old clowns. After he is revealed, the speaker objectifies his words, drawing away from his exposed identity as if in self-defense. Just as the poet initially confided that he must wear the Harlequin garb to objectify himself sufficiently before composing his song, so must he later use this linguistic device to distance himself from a hurtful audience.

At the same time that Blok shifts from first to third person in line 32, he also introduces a second person pronoun in a deliberate fashion, thereby drawing the reader into the poem. He begins with an imperative in line 33, followed by a second person reflexive pronoun used for emphasis ("О, разделите! Вы видите сами." ["Oh, make the distinction! You can see for yourself."] [l. 33]). The вы can certainly not refer to the Muse, Colombine, who is addressed in the first strophe, because the speaker uses the familiar ты form when speaking to her. The reader, then, must recognize himself as one of the passersby in the marketplace. He is responsible for the двойник, the doubling of the poet.

Finally, the use of an imperative implies the existence of a specific speaker, no longer the young Harlequin who is now denoted by an objective third person. The speaker, at this point, is the revealed двойник, the fused double identity that is distinct from either young or old Harlequin. After the two clown figures are drawn into the light of Colombine's window, they become one. After they have access to the Muse and are removed from the marketplace, the two are transformed into one poet. Representing both day and night to the poet, Colombine is his Muse in the traditional sense; she binds him to her and nourishes him with her inspiration.

However, the obligation of the poet—like that of the Russian юродивый—is to impart such revelation to his fellow man. Thus, the sight of Colombine forces the poet to return to his public. Although each confrontation with society is painful, the artist is obliged by virtue of his mandate from the Muse to speak to his society. Thus, the poem begins again as the poet-*pitre* cries,

> . . . О, люди! О, звери!
> Будьте, как дети. Поймите меня.
>
> [. . . Oh, people! Oh, beasts! / Be like children. Understand me.] (ll. 39–40)

Pan and Orpheus are said to have wielded miraculous power over man and animal; they pacified man, tranquilized beasts and even caused the trees and rocks to dance. The modern poet, however, recognizes that he no longer holds such powers. He is reduced to appealing for simple understanding from man and animal.

The tone of the двойник's plea is not weak or suppliant. Rather, the final line is reminiscent of the admonition of Jesus Christ: "Unless you turn and become like children, you will never enter the kingdom of heaven" (Matthew 18:3). That is, unless you trust this man as a child might and recognize his special powers without fully understanding them, you will not benefit from his mission. This is the essence of the plea of Blok's poet-Harlequin. Much like Jesus Christ and the prophetic юродивый, the twentieth-century poet-*pitre* chooses not to appeal to the rational side of man; instead he speaks to his innocence and his faith. In this manner, the Harlequin asks to retain the position of earlier prophets and poets, to be respected as a man and to be distinguished as a seer.

"Я был весь в пестрых лоскутьях" ("I was all in multi-colored rags"), a poem written two months before "Двойник," paints an equally vivid portrait of the poet-*pitre* meeting his audience (p. 196). Again, the artist is disguised as Harlequin in red and white costume. Yet, he has exchanged the traditional black half-mask for grotesque makeup, and he appears to bait his audience while entertaining them.

> Я был весь в пестрых лоскутьях,
> Белый, красный, в безобразной маске.
> Хохотал и кривлялся на распутьях,
> И рассказывал шуточные сказки.
>
> [I was all in multi-colored rags, / White, red, in a hideous mask. / I laughed and made faces at the crossroads. / And recounted foolish stories.] (ll. 1–4)

The poet recounts his stories in the manner of the Old Testament prophets. His tales are long, loud, and rather incoherent; they tell of strange and mysterious people and events. Like the mad юродивый, the teller raves, drawing out his account in an exaggerated fashion.

But the poet's audience wants no part of him. Its members smirk, feign illness, and finally cry, "Довольно!" ("Enough!") (l. 12). The Harlequin's tales are outside of his society's range of experience—they speak "О стариках, и о странах без названья, / И о девушке с глазами ребенка." ("Of old men and of countries without names, / And of a girl with the eyes of a child.") (ll. 7–8). These are elements that the audience cannot comprehend. The people, therefore, reject such tales.

The poem exists at the will of those who hear it, and when the hearers no longer wish to hear the poem, it comes to an end at their command. Although the poem issues from the poet, it lives independently of him and is critically dependent on the reader, the audience. It begins at the reader's wish and it dies when he tires of it.

Another of Blok's Harlequin-poets faces a similar situation in "Свет в окошке шатался" ("Light quivered through the small window") (p. 157). Again the poet faces an audience that ultimately rejects his gift of a poem.

In this work, Harlequin leaves a masked ball and goes into the street to whisper to the night. There he is joined by a woman for whom he creates a poem. However, he does so not in the traditional fashion by reciting or singing; rather, he draws a wooden sword, the classic prop of Harlequin, and writes a letter with the sword. The act of creation by means of a weapon is a mighty and impressive display, one that presumably would startle and enchant any woman, any audience. This woman, however, only pretends to be amazed at his art. Recognizing her pretense, the poet leaves her.

In a study of French symbolism, Warren Ramsey observes that "if the poet happens to be a romantic, even a late-blooming and ironical one, the misunderstanding between the sexes may stand for other apprehensions, the one between the poet and society, for example."[12] This appears to be the case with Blok's Harlequin. The poet-*pitre*'s meeting with the woman was to have been his moment of truth, an unveiling of the clown's identity and power. The poet had removed himself from the masked crowd composed of mere buffoons. He, on the other hand, is identified as the more distinguished Harlequin, and the distinction between such clown figures is clearly drawn out within the poem. The buffoons band together in a masquerade, concealing their foolery with a costume of lies. The poet-*pitre* literally stands apart from this group. He leaves the ball, descends into the darkness of the street to speak softly and to reveal his true nature. While the revelers are physically trembling under their grand costumes, the poet sheds his mask of weakness to reveal his creative power, his sword.

However, both Harlequin and his poem are ultimately rejected. The final strophe depicts the poet standing in "у задумчивой двери" ("a pensive doorway"), laughing. And, Harlequin again afixes a grinning mask to conceal his poetic identity.

After writing this poem, Blok sent a copy to Zinaida Gippius with the following commentary: "Пока что разрежаю мою сгущенную молниеносную атмосферу жестокой арлекинадой, которой стихотворное выражение и посылаю Вам." ("Meanwhile I thin out my dense, lightning-filled atmosphere with a cruel harlequinade, the expression of which I am sending you.")[13] The pain and complexity of his poetic identity being too difficult to treat directly, Blok chose a comic persona and the ironic mode to reveal the plight of the creative man. The tragic experience of Harlequin and Pierrot, masked by their comic appearance and antics, are paralleled by the painful artistic identity of Blok's poet and his clownish demeanor. The comic personae from the *commedia dell'arte* allow the poet to distance himself from his tragic role, and thus "thin out" the experience for the purpose of lyric expression and exposition.

In "В час, когда пьянеют нарциссы" ("At the hour when the narcissi get drunk"), Blok again identifies the poet as a clown (p. 233).

> Я, паяц, у блестящей рампы
> Возникаю в открытый люк.
> Это—бездна смотрит сквозь лампы—
> Ненасытно-жадный паук.
>
> [I, a clown, under the brilliant lights / Rise from the trap door. / There—the abyss peering through the lamps—/Is a grasping-greedy spider.) (ll. 9–12)

The artist is not a respected actor who walks out to center stage to greet a receptive audience; once more he is a buffoon who crawls onto the stage from a hatchway. Furthermore, he is terrified of the bestial audience that he will be unable to control.[14] The poet, then, makes every attempt to captivate the crowd in the sole fashion they will understand—he makes faces, dances, and rings bells as a vaudeville star or jester might.

The poem ends as one "нежный друг" ("sweet friend") in the wings recognizes the tragedy of his comic stance, and weeps.

> И, пока пьянеют нарциссы,
> Я кривляюсь, крутясь и звеня . . .
> Но в тени последней кулисы
> Кто-то плачет, жалея меня.
>
> [And while the narcissi get drunk, / I make faces, spin, and ring . . . / But in the shadow of the far coulisse / Someone cries, pitying me.] (ll. 13–16)

Like the god Pan, this poet-*pitre* rightly belongs with the drunken flowers and the smell of the earth. However, he plays instead the role of a pitiful fool who makes the ignorant masses laugh, while the knowing few cry.[15]

Finally, the 1906 poem, "Балаган" ("Buffoonery") attempts to put an end to the poet's masquerade by conducting funeral services for his buffoonery (p. 325). At this funeral appears a wan Harlequin who is said to be surprisingly "еще бледней, чем лик Пьеро" ("even paler than the face of Pierrot") (l. 6). Colombine, too, attends, but hides the *commedia* costumes she has sewn.

Addressing his fellow artists, the poet asks that they correct their craft with truth (l. 10). The implication is that the poet must refuse the role of poet-*pitre*, shed the comic garb, and bare his true identity. Only in doing so will he be able to create. In this way, he will also pave the way for a healthier art form, presumably one for which the poet would be able to command a more sensitive readership.

> Актеры, правьте ремесло,
> Чтобы от истины ходячей
> Всем стало больно и светло!

[Actors, correct the craft, / So that from the truth / All will become painful and light!] (ll. 10–12)

Unfortunately, the poem, "Балаган," is where Blok's thoughts on this matter begin and end. His later poetry and drama both present a series of comic personae and doubles that continue to speak the poet's despair in his creative identity.

Lucy Vogel rightly observes that many of the techniques employed in Blok's lyric work are the same that will be developed later in theater by the absurd dramatists. "Blok makes the agony of his divided hero more vivid by conveying it through comic effects. In the absurd world where doubles meet and interact, where discourse is not communication and where borders between the fantastic and factual, comic and tragic are blurred, one is not likely to find coherence of meaning or a logical sequence of events. The conventions of lyrical poetry combine with those of the theater of the absurd—incongruities, exaggerations, distortions, masks."[16] Although she refers only directly to the poem, "Двойник," Vogel's argument is applicable to all of Blok's self-reflexive poetry in which the poet appears in comic garb. Blok's Harlequins and Pierrots are all victims of intricate doubling and are caught in an unending cycle of assuming and removing their masks in the self-conscious manner that anticipates the characters of Pirandello (especially those of *Enrico IV* and *Cos'è, se vi pare*). The clowns are desperately alone, yet they prance and play as do Beckett's Vladimir and Estragon:

> Vladimir: C'est vrai, nous sommes intarissables.
> Estragon: C'est pour ne pas penser.
> Vladimir: Nous avons des excuses.
> Estragon: C'est pour ne pas entendre.
> Vladimir: Nous avons nos raisons.[17]

The old and young Harlequins in "Двойник" might well have a similar exchange. They, too, appear to chatter so as to avoid reflection. They, too, have their reasons for doing so. They bicker, cry, and comfort each other as do the pairs in *En attendant Godot*.

The absurd vision of the poet's role in modern society also characterized the self-reflexive poetry of Blok's symbolist counterparts in France—in particular the lyrics of Jules Laforgue. Laforgue's poet-*pitre*, we recall, is another victim of multiple identities, all under the guise of Pierrot. The poet figures of Laforgue and Blok are especially similar in that they are most often found alone—trapped under a spotlight on stage, having run away from a party, or galavanting in solitude across a lunar landscape. Even in the midst of the market, they are alone simply because they are unable to speak to those around them. Their audiences laugh, yawn, or passively dismiss them because there exists no means of communication to unite the poet and his society.

In his self-reflexive poetry written between 1890 and 1920, Valerii Briusov, too, reveals an urgent concern for the artist's relationship to his society, his human identity, and his poetic powers. Indeed, Briusov addresses the very questions that Mallarmé poses in "Le Pitre châtié" and "L'Après-midi d'un faune." This he does through the personae of Orpheus and Pan. Briusov's poetic personae repeatedly focus on the role of individual experience in the poet's life and ask what part the world can play in his art when the demands of his craft are so consuming. Danylo Struk's study of Briusov's poetry draws attention to the theme of the poet's escape from the modern world.[18] Within Briusov's lyric work, modern society and modern technology are viewed as a corruptive force on the art of the poet. Thus, the artist is compelled to retreat from his society if his work is to flourish. Unlike the Mallarmean Pan figures who attempt an anguished life as both man and artist, Briusov's Pan-poets recognize that they must deny themselves the attractions of the world and direct their exclusive attention to the service of their Muse. And like Mallarmé's Orphic poet Igitur, Briusov's modern Orpheus instinctively realizes his singular role as artist, although his unique devotion to this vocation often falters.

Briusov's account of the poet Orpheus opens with the *katábasis*. "Орфей и Эвридика" ("Orpheus and Eurydice") takes place as the mythic hero attempts to lead his wife from the underworld, and the poem is structured in the form of a dialogue between Orpheus and his wife. For his version of this dramatic event, Briusov breaks through the romantic, apocryphal, but highly popular versions of Orpheus mythology and returns to Ovid's *Metamorphoses* as a source for his poem. Consequently, Briusov focuses not on the power of love and the might of poetry, but on the failure of Orpheus to accomplish what he intended in spite of his love and his music.

According to Ovid's tale, Orpheus loses his wife because he doubts her willingness to follow him back to life.

> hic, ne deficeret, metuens, avidusque vivendi
> flexit amans oculos, et protinus illa relapsa est.
>
> [he, afraid that she might fail him, eager for sight of her, turned back his longing eyes; and instantly she slipped into the depths.][19]

In "Орфей и Эвридика" Briusov isolates the fear that Ovid describes. He concentrates on Eurydice's inability to leave the underworld and Orpheus's painful realization of his failure.

From the very beginning of the poem, Eurydice warns her husband that she cannot envision leaving the underworld. When urged upward, she repeats,

> Я не смею, я не смею,
> Мой супруг, мой друг, мой брат!
>
> [I dare not, I dare not, / My husband, my friend, my brother!][20]

Refusing to heed her words, Orpheus is convinced only of the power of his love and the force of his music. And he replies,

Я, заклявший лирой—бога,
Песней жизнь в тебя вдохну!

[I, who with the lyre entranced—the gods, / Will breathe life into you with a song!] (ll. 19–20)

The hero's convictions are sadly unfounded. Although his music is capable of arousing man, calming beasts, charming the keepers of hell, and entrancing the gods, it is nonetheless unable to inspire the dead. Therefore, Eurydice neither recalls his love nor is moved by his song.

Сердце—мертво, грудь—недвижна.
. . . .
Помню сны, - но непостижна,
Друг мой бедный, речь твоя.

[My heart is dead, my breast still. / I recall dreams, but your words, / My poor friend, are incomprehensible.]
(ll. 29, 31–32)

Orpheus refuses to submit to reality until his wife fades behind him and he is left with the echo of her voice. Only then does Orpheus turn to look at Eurydice, for he finally realizes that he will never win her regardless of his divine song. His music fails to compel her toward him and toward life, and so he turns for a final gaze at his lost wife. With this tragic gesture, the hero ultimately recognizes the impotence of his music. Briusov's modern Orphic poet is a victim of the myth that art is omnipotent, that it can even conquer death. However, when he tests that myth within reality, he finds that he is left with loneliness and disillusionment with his art.

The Orphic tale is continued in Briusov's "Орфей" ("Orpheus"), which begins at the point when the hero returns after losing his wife a second time (vol. 3, p. 280). Like "Орфей и Эвридика" this poem is faithful to Ovid's account of the ancient myth in preserving the elements of tragedy and violence in Orpheus's return to the living. After his voyage to the underworld, Orpheus is stunned and silent, according to Ovid. "Cura dolorque animi lacrimaeque alimenta fuere" ("Care, anguish of soul, and tears were his nourishment") (*Met.*, Book 10, l. 75). Briusov's Orpheus is also "изнывая и немея" ("dejected and silent") (l. 3), and as in Ovid, Orpheus is fatally stoned upon his return.

In the opening four strophes of Briusov's poem, Orpheus is greeted by the Maenads. They are wild, half-clothed, and crazed, and they attempt to erase with bacchanalian revelry the hero's memories of the *katábasis* and his dreams of Eurydice. The following four strophes present their persuasive appeal to the poet by which they attempt to involve him in the rites of Dionysus. The Maenads claim that their society has conquered death through the mysteries of wine. Conquering death is, of course, the sole feat that Orpheus has failed to accomplish with the power of his art. Thus, the women ask him to take their god as his god.

However, Orpheus does not respond directly to their arguments. And so they appeal to him through his song and thereby attempt to entice his involvement with them:

> Ударь, певец, в живые струны
> И буйство жизни повторяй!

> [Strike, singer, the living strings / And repeat the violence of life!] (ll. 19–20)

Refusing to sing about the "буйство жизни" ("violence of life"), Orpheus instead gathers the Maenads for a song about Eurydice and the *katábasis*. The audience is offended by songs of truth and of peace, songs that express sentiments so foreign to their experience. As a result, they simply and quickly murder the singer.

> Но песню заглушают крики . . .
> Уж—камни в яростных руках.
> И пал певец с улыбкой ясной.

> [But cries are drowning the song . . . / Stones—already in enraged hands. / And the singer with the serene smile fell.] (ll. 39–41)

They stone Orpheus to death and continue their frenzy as before.

The central events recounted in "Орфей" follow closely the Ovidian account of the Orphic *sparagmós*.

> . . . et Bacchei ululatus
> obstrepuere sono citharae, tum denique saxa
> non exauditi rubuerunt sanguine vatis.
>
> [And howlings of the Bacchanals drowned / the lyre's sound; and then at last the stones / were reddened with the blood of the bard / whose voice they could not hear.] (*Met.*, Book 10, ll. 17–19)

However faithful Briusov remains to the outline of Ovid's tale, he nonetheless changes the motivation for the murder of Orpheus. Ovid intimates that the Thracian women murdered the hero out of jealousy for his devotion to Eurydice. Briusov's poem reveals yet another reason for the *sparagmós*—the alienation of the artist from his society because of his artistic veracity.

"Орфей" presents to the reader a clear dichotomy between Orpheus and the Maenads. They are "опьянённы и безумны" ("drunken and crazed") and he is "исполнен веры" ("filled with truth") (ll. 9, 35). They claim to discover the secrets of life "в сладострастном бреде" ("in voluptuous delirium"), whereas Orpheus finds truth in his "вещая лира" ("prophetic lyre") (ll. 31, 49).

Briusov also explains that the Thracian women are like panthers; they are wild, bestial, and unable to be subdued by music. But Orpheus has just returned from the underworld, where he learned of his divine powers and his humanity. He now realizes the force of his music over the living and, at the same time, is compelled to recognize the painful limitations of his power. As Briusov indicates in "Орфей и Эвридика," Orpheus learns that neither human love nor divine poetry can conquer death. The hero, then, breaks the spell of his music with a willful, human act when he turns to gaze at his wife. Thus, when the hero returns from the underworld, he returns with a recognition of the awesome magic of his music, but also with a sense of personal humility.

As such, Orpheus, the musician, is an alien in the Dionysian society as described by Briusov and Ovid. His music is sacred, and their lives and art are profane. He is both divine and human, whereas they are bestial. Most important, when confronted with truth and prophecy, his audience can react only with violence. "Буйство жизни" ("the violence of life") (l. 20) is the basis of their culture—not the truth and reason that guide the poet Orpheus. In his reworking of the Ovidian tale, then, Briusov creates a radically polarized structure. Within this framework, the modern poet emerges as an alien and unwelcome voice in a violent and uncivilized world.

In a later work, "Ученик Орфея" ("Student of Orpheus"), Briusov brings the tale of Orpheus directly into the twentieth century by characterizing the modern poet as heir and apprentice to the mythological hero (vol. 3, p. 10). Furthermore, the plight of the modern student is analogous to that of his ancient mentor. "Ученик Орфея" can be seen as a parallel poem to "Орфей" in that the ancient and modern poets experience identical difficulties in their creative roles.

Speaking in the first person, the young poet opens the work with a celebration of the pastoral poet and of bucolic lyrics, a tribute to the beauty and power of poetry. He himself claims to listen for verses in the sea and for rhythms in the wind, "метр тех своих живых баллад" ("meters such as his living ballads") (l. 10). Furthermore, not only does the student lay claim to his identity as a poet, he also declares himself to be a disciple of the mythological Orpheus and aspires to share the magical powers of the ancient poet.

> Орфей, сын бога, мой учитель,
> Меж тигров так когда-то пел . . .
> Я с песней в адову обитель,
> Как он, сошел бы, горд и смел.
>
> [Orpheus, son of god, my teacher, / Among tigers once was singing . . . / Like him, with song I would descend / To the hellish place, proud and brave.] (ll. 29–32)

Thus, the fledgling poet embraces all joys and sorrows of the pastoral tradition as he seeks his own poetic inspiration in nature and searches for guidance from the poet Orpheus.

However, in the second three strophes, the tone of the young poet changes dramatically, and we find that he is frustrated in his creative work by modern society itself.

> . . . гремя, звеня, стуча,
> Играет Город в жизнь . . .
>
> [. . . thundering, ringing, beating, / The City plays in life . . .] (ll. 14–15)

The city is personified as a forceful villain that has invaded life and destroyed its natural order. The industrial world and the noise of a rushing metropolis have replaced the pastoral era and the world of the mythological Orpheus. As a result, the modern poet is forced to compromise his ideal with reality, to incorporate technology into nature.

> Гудки авто, звонки трамвая,
> Стук, топот, ропот, бег колес,—
> В поэмы страсти, в песни мая
> Вливали смутный лепет грез.
>
> Все звуки жизни и природы
> Я облекать в размер привык:
> Плеск речек, гром, свист непогоды,
> Треск ружей, баррикадный крик.
>
> [Auto horns, trolley clangs, / Noise, tramping, rumble, wheels spinning,— / In poems of passion, in songs of May, / They infuse the dim bubble of dreams. /
>
> Every sound of life and nature / I am accustomed to shaping in meter: / Lapping of the river, thunder, the whistle of inclement weather, / The crack of rifles, a barricade cry.] (ll. 17–24)

The student of Orpheus has curiously set the idea of "жизнь" ("life") in opposition to the concept of "природа" ("nature"). Modern life finds its rhythms in rifles and in machines. Nature, however, produces "поэмы страсти" ("poems of passion") and "песни мая" ("songs of May") (l. 19) in gentler cadences. It appears that life is a corrupting force of modern society, twisting a world that was once innocent. Moreover, the rhythms and sounds of this modern world seem to have obliterated those of nature.

Having established such a dichotomy for the modern poet, Briusov introduces the tragic aspect of the Orphic myth to complete the analogy between the ancient poet and his modern heir. When the young poet compares himself to his mentor, he does not fail to recall the Orphic *sparagmós*.

> Но диким криком гимн Менады
> Покрыли, сбили лавр венца;
> Взвив тирсы, рвали без пощады
> Грудь в ад сходившего певца.
>
> Так мне ль осилить взвизг трамвайный,
> Моторов вопль, рев толп людских?
> Жду, на какой строфе случайной
> Я, с жизнью, оборву свой стих.

[But with wild shouts the Maenads drowned / The hymn, tore down the wreath of laurel; / Having raised the thyrsus, they rent without mercy / The breast of the singer who had descended into hell. /

Thus am I to overcome the tramway screech, / The wail of engines, the bellow of the crowd? / I wait at any random stanza; / With life I will interrupt my verse.] (ll. 33–40)

Briusov has transformed Ovid's Maenads into the combined ills of modern life, the city, mechanization, and war. Just as these frenzied women drowned the song of the earlier poet, so these elements of modern life make lyric poetry virtually impossible for the disciple of Orpheus. Thus the modern poet's intimate identification with Orpheus is further reinforced by their common alienation from their societies. We recall from Briusov's "Орфей" that the ancient audience demanded art that would speak to "буйство жизни" ("the violence of life") (l. 20). Because the musician spoke only truth and would not subvert the nature of his music by acquiescing to their demands, both he and his art were forced to die. The violent, disturbing images of modern society in "Ученик Орфея" serve the same function as the Maenads in the earlier lyric and in Ovid's tale. They clash with the artist's conception of his creative world and force him to compromise either his life or his art.

However, the modern poet in "Ученик Орфея" is not the hero that his ancient teacher was. He equivocates in the face of his society and chooses compromise over martyrdom. The poet admits in the sixth strophe that he has grown accustomed to compromising poetic ideals.

Все звуки жизни и природы
Я облекать в размер привык.

[Every sound of life and nature / I am accustomed to shaping in meter.] (ll. 21–22)

He allows both nature and the city, quietude and violence, images of pastoral life and of war to confront one another within his poetry. He does so because society demands this of him, because this curious juxtaposition of contradictory elements is precisely the nature of modern life. However, in doing so, the poet breaks with the Orphic tradition of adhering to the holy, the eternal, and the true within one's art, even at the price of one's life, as witnessed in "Орфей."

Consequently, when comparing himself to his mentor, the poet must stop short of total identification with the ancient musician. Thus, in light of the artist's equivocation, the young poet's self-description in the final three strophes emerges as a confession of weakness and as a student's admission of failure before his master.

Я с песней в адову обитель,
Как он, *сошел бы*, горд и смел.

[Like him, with song I *would descend* / To the hellish place, proud and brave.] (Emphasis mine) (ll. 31–32)

I would endure the terror of Hades, he claims, I would test my poetic mettle, I would be honest and brave, were it not for the unyielding pressure of the modern world. The young poet constructs an analogy that, he feels, explains why he cannot fulfill his poetic promise. "Я сошел бы . . .," the poet insists in the eighth strophe, but in the lines that immediately follow, he asks the reader to recall the dismemberment of his ancient mentor. The Maenads crushed Orpheus. They rent his laurel wreath and raised in its place the thyrsus of Dionysus. Therefore, how might the modern poet protect himself against the violent, corruptive elements of his society? If the great Orpheus could not survive as poet in his world, the young poet certainly cannot hope to persevere. "Так мне ль осилить . . .?" ("Thus am I to overcome . . .?") (l. 37).

After setting up the analogy in the eighth and ninth strophes and then posing his question in the tenth, the young poet concedes his inability to follow perfectly the example of his martyred mentor. He admits that he has succumbed to "life"—as opposed to allying himself with "nature"—and that "с жизнью" ("together with life") (l. 40), he will be unable to produce poetry that might please his teacher. The pastoral imagery of the opening three strophes, which is then interspersed with images of modernity in the next three strophes, is entirely missing from the final lines. The poet's alliance with modern society, its industrialization, and its cities forces him to break with the Orphic tradition. Thus, in the final line, the poet concedes, "Я, с жизнью, оборву свой стих" ("With life I will interrupt my verse") (l. 40).

The figure of Pan as poet enjoys a fate no gentler than that of Orpheus or his twentieth-century pupil in the poetry of Briusov. He, too, is victimized by the corruption of the modern world and the disintegration of poetry in an industrialized society. Drawing on the figure of Pan as an exclusively pastoral poet, Briusov is able to express forcefully the dichotomy between a pure, bucolic environment and modern life, which is characterized by rapid change and industrialization.

Briusov's initial two portraits of the mythological Pan are traditional characterizations of an innocent pastoral piper. The 1914 poem, "Вечерний Пан" ("Evening Pan") depicts the goat-god as a simple and joyous lyricist who gives praise to the heavens for his solitude and peace (vol. 2, p. 116). "Снова сумрак" ("Dusk once again") of 1920 again presents the god in his bucolic setting, this time with a vigorous Slavic orientation (vol. 3, p. 413). The rocky ledges and caves of ancient Arcadia are replaced in Briusov's poem by grassy fields and the pine trees of Russia. Nonetheless, as in "Вечерний Пан," the character of Pan remains faithful to ancient lore.

> Вот он, царь земных веселий,
> Древний бог, великий Пан!
>
> [There he is, the king of earthly joys, / The ancient god, the great Pan!] (ll. 7–8)

In two lyric poems written in 1923, Briusov's depictions of the poet as Pan are altered dramatically when the god appears under conditions radically different from those described in the Greek mythological tales. In "Зимой" ("In Winter") and "Лесная Тьма" ("Forest Gloom"), Briusov again lifts the goat-god out of ancient Greece and transports him into the Soviet Union (vol. 3, pp. 180–81). The poet then examines the role of Pan in his new contemporary setting and considers Pan's ability to sing and chant, as well as his capacity for mere survival under his altered conditions.

The setting of "Зимой" ("In Winter") is the antithesis of Pan's ancient sun-bleached rocks and caves. Briusov now situates the poet in the middle of a Russian winter; the native herbs and flowers have died and been replaced by a hard frost sealing the earth. It is night. There is no moon. The only sounds we hear are those of the wind, moaning and crying. Finally, Pan appears against a backdrop littered with decaying corpses.

The images of desolation and waste are reinforced by a desperate, staccato rhythm and pounding alliteration, which are particularly harsh in the Russian language.

> Плачь, Ночь! Зима, плачь, плачь, здесь, там,
> По травам, трапам, тронам, трупам,
> По тропам плачь, плачь по цветам!
> Скуп свет; нет лун. Плачь, Ночь, по трудным
> Дням! . . .
>
> [Weep, Night! Winter, weep, weep, here, there, / For the grasses, the escape hatches, the thrones, and the bodies, / For pathways weep, weep for the flowers! / Dim light, no moon. Weep, Night, for hard / Days! . . .] (ll. 10–14)

The composite image is one of terror and disaster—be it of the ascendancy of Stalin, as suggested by the date of the poem, or of the rapid encroachment of modernization on primitive and innocent life, represented here by mint and caraway.

In either case, Briusov issues a call for lamentation. Дувун ("The Wind") is to blow the horn. The Night is to cry out. Both personifications of nature will appeal on behalf of what was, but no longer exists. And, in the final strophe, the role of the poet is articulated:

> . . . стон из туч, стон с суши к струйным
> Снам, Панов плач по всем гробам.
> Пой в строки! в строфы! строем струнным
> На память мяты по тропам!
>
> [. . . a groan from the clouds, a groan from the land in flowing / Dreams, a cry of Pans over every coffin. / Sing in lines! in strophes! with stringed harmony / In memory of mint along the paths.] (ll. 21–24)

Thus, the modern Russian poets, the Soviet Pans, are as powerless as the forces of nature in face of modernization. They, too, can sing only to the memory of a lost world. And, presumably, they might be able to sustain that memory for a future world.

Contemporary society, as Briusov perceives it, cannot possibly engender lyric expression. In the twentieth century, the voice of the gods from above has been reduced to an ominous groan from the clouds. As the clouds break, the rumble will disappear. At the same time, the voice of a prophet in the desert produces an utterance equally unintelligible to Soviet man and his poet. Thus, Briusov's "Зимой" illustrates the tragic anachronism of the metaphor of the poet as priest or prophet. The modern poet has lost his traditional muses and sources of wisdom, and he no longer has a stable god whom he can serve as interlocutor between the heavens and earth. The contemporary Pans are reduced, then, to singing of a past world, to the "memory of mint."

"Лесная Тьма" ("Forest Gloom"), written five months after "Зимой" ("In Winter"), depicts the direct destruction of the pastoral world by the forces of modern industrialization. The sounds of birds and insects in a forest are drowned by those of the "alien but familiar" motor boats on a nearby river. And, in a seemingly isolated refuge, the sound of a helicopter breaks the countryside's tranquility. The poet remarks that this noise and these intrusions on a harmonious life are "шум, что не ведали дриады" ("noise that the driads did not know") (l. 10). In short, the peace and stability of bucolic Arcadia has been ruptured.

Moreover, the god Pan, roaming through the forest, is disturbed and then frightened by an airplane that appears overhead "хищным шипом василиска" ("with the predatory thorn of a basilisk") (l. 15). The poet Pan is ultimately forced to abandon his pastoral home, as is the entire community of Elysian gods.

Шум листьев в сумрачном хорале
Притих; идут, смелей, грозней,
Электроплуг, электротраллер,
Чудовища грядущих дней.

[The sound of leaves in a gloomy chorus / Is still; prouder, more terrible yet roll / The electric plow, the electric trawler, / Monsters of future days.] (ll. 21–24)

The songs of the gods and those of nature itself have been replaced by the cacophony of a new agricultural collective.

Both "Зимой" and "Лесная Тьма" are simple but forceful expressions of the same conflict that Briusov addresses in his Orphic poetry. Modern society cannot inspire lyric poetry, according to Briusov, because modern innovations and truths attempt to supplant ancient and eternal values and beliefs. In each of these poems, we find that modern life disallows any possibility of complementary fusion between the old and new, forcing instead the destruction of ancient values and aesthetics by the modern. Thus, in Briusov's eyes, modernity is a destructive force in itself, and not the creative force that it might be, were it to provide a complement to ancient aesthetic values rather than their negation.

It is entirely expected, then, that the mythological poetic prototypes within Briusov's work pointedly set themselves apart from their societies in the interest of their art. Indeed, Briusov's 1907 poem, "Поэту" ("To the Poet"), makes this very point in a more general fashion (vol. 1, p. 447). This work counsels the artist to be a "холодный свидетель" ("cold witness") to life (l. 5). He must be militant and dispassionate in his observation and analysis of modern life. Above all, as Victor Erlich observes, he must exhibit absolute devotion to his aesthetic vocation, subordinating his life as a man to his life as an artist, giving exclusive attention to "the stern demands of the Muse."²¹

This fundamental and wrenching dilemma is broached earlier by French symbolists Laforgue, Verlaine, and Mallarmé, and by Briusov's fellow Russian symbolist, Aleksandr Blok. Not only do they all treat this self-reflexive theme, but the Russian poets repeat the poetic personae found in the work of their French predecessors.

Blok frequently employs the *commedia dell'arte* motifs that are found throughout French self-reflexive lyrics. In his work, Harlequin and Pierrot represent the poet, with Colombine presiding as Muse. Moreover, Blok's poetic clowns in "Двойник" ("The Double") strongly resemble those of Laforgue in their multiple, almost schizoid identities. One could also include the masked persona in "Я был весь" ("I was all") and "Свет в окошке шатался" ("Light quivered through the small window") in this comparison. Each poetic clown masks himself and plays a charade with a world he longs to serve, although the world has no interest in him or in his art. More precisely, the poet finds that he must disguise himself before his fellow man because society does not value the poet. In each of these poems, the community ridicules the artistic man and dismisses his work casually and without reflection. Just as Laforgue's poet-Pierrots sleepwalk through a sterile lunar landscape, Blok's poetic clowns wander as aliens in the marketplace ("Двойник" "The Double") and stand just outside the festivities ("Свет в окошке шатался" "Light quivered through the small window").

However, unlike the Laforguean Pierrots, who are bitterly resigned to their plight and have retreated in solipsistic stasis, the poet figures in Blok's poetry continue to struggle. They beg to be heard. Some even appear to preach to their audience. Blok's poetic clowns differ from their French predecessors in that they are still closely allied with their native юродивые ("holy fools") and with the Elizabethan court fool. Blok's poetic clowns still attempt to proclaim a view of the poet as truth-teller ("Двойник"), spinner of fantastic tales ("Я был весь"), and powerful figure ("Свет в окошке"). The vatic and mighty image of the poet is, of course, tarnished for the modern Russian artist. However, the poetic persona continues to struggle for a proud and strong creative identity, which Laforgue's clowns understand as an anachronism.

Valerii Briusov, on the other hand, employs the earlier mythological prototypes, Pan and Orpheus, in his depiction of the poet. Much like Mallarmé's Orphic Igitur, Briusov's Orpheus figures understand that any alliance with modern society precludes artistic activity. Although one Orphic poet in "Ученик Орфея" ("Student of Orpheus") wavers in his singular devotion to his Muse, they consider an affinity to a technological society, its cities, and its rhythms to be incompatible with a poetic vocation. Briusov's Pan also eschews any contact with twentieth-century society, and in this respect the Russian Pan-poets differ radically from those of Mallarmé and Laforgue. Briusov's Pan and Orpheus no longer seek social gratification and no longer seek an audience. For this reason, they are perhaps closer to the French symbolists' Pierrots. Briusov's Pan is as much an alien in an industrial Russia as Laforgue's Pierrots are in a lunar void.

Nonetheless, both the Russian and French symbolist poets reach for the same poetic prototypes in their depiction of the creative self. And regardless of what they seek in their society, these poets—Pan, Orpheus, Pierrot, Harlequin, and *pitre*—uniformly suffer at the hands of a world that either ignores them or ridicules them.

5

An American Mythology of the Poet: Wallace Stevens and Hart Crane

Most critical readers of Wallace Stevens and Hart Crane have observed the marked influence of the French Parnassians and symbolists on these American poets. Critics such as Michel Benamou, Daniel Fuchs, and Robert Storey have examined the profound influence of Laforgue and Verlaine on the poetry of Wallace Stevens; and Warren Ramsey, Monroe Spears, and R. W. B. Lewis have traced in considerable detail the many motifs and attitudes that Crane's poetry shares with that of Corbière, Laforgue, and Rimbaud.[1] Moreover, Stevens and Crane continue the modern lyric tradition of presenting the poet as *pitre*, a tradition they inherit from their French predecessors.

However, the poetic clowns of Wallace Stevens and Hart Crane are not reproductions of the French Pan and Pierrot, the *faune* and the *pitre châtié*, merely displaced to another decade on another continent. Although the American poets applaud by imitation the French representation of the poet as *pitre*, both Crane and Stevens infuse their poetic personae with a distinctly American character. Their poetic clowns are tambourine players, "humpty-dumpty clods," and "conscripts" to the wine bottle; they are "emperors of ice cream," joined by a "weeping burgher" and "castratos of moon mash." Like their French and Russian predecessors, the American poetic clowns are superfluous creatures in their society and testify to the isolation of the poet in twentieth-century America. Both Stevens and Crane have created Pierrots as well. But more important than the exact clownish mask and garb they don are the spirit and character of the poetic personae of Stevens and Crane, and in this aspect as well, their self-reflexive clowns depart from the French poetic *pitres*. Although Stevens and Crane draw on the French poet-*pitre* and poet-Pierrot for their personae, they mock and undercut the symbolist figures. Both reject the wan, impotent poetic persona in favor of a more vital American version.

In "The Comedian as the Letter C," for example, Stevens's Crispin is very much the self-reflexive poet of the French symbolist tradition.[2] He is a *commedia* figure, an aesthete, a "fagot in the lunar fire" (sec. 3, l. 3). However, "The Comedian" is a poem of transformation in that we witness Crispin's rejection of the aesthetic he carried with him from the European continent. In the New World, Crispin understands that as poet he is a clown, but an "aspiring clown" (sec. 4, l. 91). He is a clown who aspires to some measure of reconciliation with his world and its reality.

The poetic masks of Hart Crane, too, approximate the poet-*pitres* of Laforgue and Verlaine. However, Crane's figures are not obsessed with their social isolation and their poetic impotence as were the personae of their European predecessors. Crane's black tambourine player ("The Black Tambourine"), Porphyro ("Porphyro in Akron"), and the abused clown ("Chaplinesque") can also be described as "aspiring clowns."[3] They have not lost their belief in the value and power of the lyric. Although Crane's poetic clowns are social outcasts, and their creative activities are repressed by their world, they retain optimism in the ability of the twentieth century to inspire and then to value lyric poetry.

In their rejection of the poet-*pitre*, Crane and Stevens return to the ancient prototypes of Pan and Orpheus for noble and powerful poetic personae. Stevens's Peter Quince is a Dionysian figure much like the goat-god Pan, and Stevens finds that the creative process of his poet is identical to that of his ancient prototype. Crane's hobo-trekkers are Pan figures as well. Like the ancient god, they tap the native imagination of their land and transform this primal energy into song. In *The Bridge* Crane returns to the Orpheus myth to demonstrate the resilience of poetry in modern society. The Indian king, Maquokeeta, is an Orphic poet whose voice continues to be heard past his sacrificial death. Moreover, the central poetic persona in *The Bridge* is an Orpheus figure who descends into his American past to recover his poetic ideals, and returns to the present time with a firm sense of the power of the lyric. In short, instead of submitting to the world's derision, Crane's and Stevens's poetic personae represent their attempts to "cultivate a more graceful mask against all this."[4]

Wallace Stevens's 1923 collection, *Harmonium*, could alone provide sufficient material for a lengthy study of self-reflexivity. Each of the major lyric compositions in *Harmonium* and many of the shorter ones directly address questions of the nature of poetry and the poet, their status in modern society, and their relationship to reality. However, Stevens's *Harmonium* appears to focus on the role of the poet more than on any other self-reflexive theme. One poem after the other presents the poetic persona in the act of contemplating his creative role. Indeed, Joseph Riddel notes that *Harmonium* is "a pastiche of masks and gestures, of acts which essentially add up to a self (or many faces and gestures of a self) in emergence, and in total to an act of self-discovery."[5] In *Harmonium* alone, Stevens presents Peter Quince, Hoon, Crispin, the man whose pharynx was bad, and the Weeping Burgher, each engaged in anxious introspection and in troubled analysis of the poet's position in the twentieth century. Riddel observes that *Harmonium* "is a poetry of balding amorists (not necessarily Stevens, but the poet as modern self, *l'homme moyen imaginatif*) readjusting himself to a world which is not, as it formerly was, his plum."[6]

Correspondingly, the personae of Stevens within *Harmonium* are, like those of the French symbolists, a readjustment of the traditional poetic persona. Although the poetic persona of Stevens represents a departure from the symbolist poet-*pitre* as well, his poetic prototypes retain their roots in the French poetic identity. The influence of French poetry on Wallace Stevens is pronounced and was recognized very early by such critics as René Taupin, Warren Ramsey, H. R. Hays, and Robert Buttel. Although there exists only sketchy documentation on exactly which French poets Stevens read and when exactly he read them, Wallace Stevens did take several courses in French literature while he was a student at Harvard. There he also read widely from Ernest Dowson and T. S. Eliot, and must have assimilated some notion of French symbolism from these poets who were so intensely influenced by French poetry. In any event, after his introduction to Eliot and Dowson, Stevens began to write short verses à la fête galante, somewhat in the style of Verlaine. And, in 1909 he composed a poem entitled "Pierrot" for the woman who would later become his wife. Beginning in 1908, Stevens's correspondence contained brief statements about his appreciation of Rimbaud and Verlaine. Finally, in a letter to Hi Simons in 1941, Stevens revealed having "read s'thing more or less" of Mallarmé, Laforgue, Verlaine, Valéry, and Baudelaire.[7]

Like many of the poems contained in *Harmonium*, "The Weeping Burgher" exhibits the influence of French poetry on Wallace Stevens. Stevens's weeping burgher appears "as belle design / Of foppish line," and proclaims himself a "ghost" of the fine dandies of the European tradition (p. 61, ll. 12–13, 10). Daniel Fuchs describes the burgher as a poet engaged in a "quest for elegance in an inelegant time and place."[8] Stevens's poet fully realizes that he is an anachronism in the twentieth century. Yet, he longs for the "old speech" of earlier poetry, and for the romance and flourishes of an earlier time (l. 14).

The weeping burgher is an artist who clearly finds no place for himself or his work in twentieth-century America. At the same time, Stevens describes the poet as a burgher in the very title of the poem. To be a burgher is to be a part of a solidly established social class, although Stevens's burgher as poet is depicted as a man apart from his society. Fuchs has observed, then, that "weeping burgher like American dandy seems to be a contradiction in terms, since the burgher . . . is happily absorbed in the world of getting and spending, and has hardly any cause for weeping about his secure social status. Yet, Stevens' persona here is a weeping burgher, an alienated arty burgher who denies his position in favor of a sense of taste which he feels is aristocratic, and he knows, ridiculous for being so."[9] Thus, the burgher's "malice" is that of being foolishly entranced with an aesthetic that is not of his time, and of attempting to "distort the world" to conform to his aesthetic (ll. 1–2).

"Peter Quince at the Clavier" is a more complex study of the poet, in which the artist is presented not as a bizarre or clownish figure, but as a musician (p. 89). The name Peter Quince is that of the theatrical director in *A Midsummer Night's Dream*, in which Quince is a carpenter by trade, a play director for a special occasion, and, according to Bottom, something of a poet. However, in

Stevens's poem, Quince appears to be a descendant of the Dionysian Pan.

In section 1, the artist Peter Quince tells us that the art of music is identical to emotion. More specifically, he reveals that eroticism is music.

> Music is feeling, then, not sound;
> And thus it is that what I feel,
> Here in this room, desiring you.   (sec. 1, ll. 3–6)

In this sense, Quince can be compared to Pan: erotic desire became the sound of Pan's pipes, and, conversely, music evoked his desired nymph. The nymph Syrinx became physically the syrinx, the pan-pipes.

However, within this poem, Stevens also addresses the limits of the poet in his sensual and artistic desire. He does so by exhibiting two extremes of the music created by desire. In section 2, we observe Susanna, the object of Peter Quince's fascination. Susanna is occupied with "concealed imaginings" and ascetic contemplation that yield for her a surfeit of emotion and music (sec. 2, l. 6). "She sighed, / for so much melody" (sec. 2, ll. 7–8). Yet, the "red-eyed elders" yield to their erotic instincts when they find Susanna bathing alone in the garden (sec. 1, l. 12). Their emotion is not sublimated in art, as was that of Peter Quince, Susanna, or Pan, but they allowed their desires to play on "bawdy strings" and to issue "witching chords" (sec. 4, l. 11, sec. 1, l. 14).

Although Quince does not deny his emotional energy that produces music when provoked by his Susanna, Peter Quince, like Pan, transforms his sexual energy into artistic energy. "Thinking of your blue-shadowed silk, / Is music" (sec. 1, ll. 7–8). The contrast between Quince and the elders (or even more pointedly, the elders and Susanna) allows Stevens to exhibit the nature of poetic creation. In his analysis of "Peter Quince at the Clavier," Harold Bloom agrees that "music *is* pathos, Stevens asserts, and is identical with desire or the will-to-possession. But in Stevens, the desire deprecates itself, by an identification with the desire of the elders for Susanna rather than with the more refined and repressed desire of Susanna herself, in Section II of the poem."[10] Stevens believes that art is indeed engendered by the Dionysian spirit that characterizes the activity of the god Pan, but that it is debased by orgiastic excesses of the same emotional energy. In the context of the poem, then, Peter Quince emerges as a true musician or poet in that he, like Pan, participates in a transformation and sublimation of Dionysian instinct into a pure form of art.

Of all the poetic masks of *Harmonium*, Stevens's Crispin most resembles the poetic personae of earlier French symbolist poets with whom Stevens was familiar, yet Crispin also represents the poet's attempt to divorce his persona from the prototypes of Laforgue, Verlaine, and Mallarmé. Moreover, Crispin represents Stevens's view of what the poet in twentieth-century America might be.

Crispin of "The Comedian as the Letter C" owes his name to three very different personages—the third-century Saint Crispin, who was a cobbler although a nobleman; the poet Crispinus, who challenged Horace to see which of them could write faster, his story revived in Ben Jonson's *The Poetaster*; and the *commedia dell'arte* Crispin, known principally in the French theater of the seventeenth and eighteenth centuries.[11] Of these three, the twentieth-century Crispin appears to resemble most the *commedia* valet. Stevens describes his Crispin in this way:

>   . . . Crispin
> The lutanist of fleas, the knave, the thane,
> The ribboned stick, the bellowing breeches, cloak
> Of China, cap of Spain. . . .   (sec. 1, ll. 21–24)

His *commedia* ancestor was a burlesque valet who wore a little hat, black clothing, and boots, and carried a long rapier. Crispin is a knavish figure whose ruses directed at his masters are carried out through flattery and trickery.

Yet, Robert Storey contends that the Crispin of Wallace Stevens is more akin to the *commedia*'s better-known Pierrot. "There is no *commedia* mask, I should point out, that he resembles so closely in temperament at the beginning of his voyage as that of Pierrot."[12] When Storey claims that the twentieth-century Crispin approximates the character of Pierrot, he is speaking not only about the *commedia* Pierrot, but also and perhaps more specifically about the representations of Pierrot in the French poetry of the late nineteenth century. René Taupin has made a similar observation, and writes of Stevens, "Il est parent de Baudelaire; il est aussi parent de Laforgue à qui on l'a comparé pour son ironie nonchalante, le ton 'pierrot' de ses poèmes, même si Pierrot, son maître, est habillé de noir et porte un chapeau de soie."[13]

Consequently, when Crispin sets out on his voyage in "The Comedian as the Letter C," it is not surprising that he departs from the port of Bordeaux, and that he is described much as Laforgue depicted his poet-Pierrots.

> The book of moonlight is not written yet
> Nor half begun, but, when it is, leave room
> For Crispin, fagot in the lunar fire.   (sec. 3, ll. 1–3)

Like his French predecessors, Crispin is a devoté of the sterile moon. He was bred in a high-minded, hypercivilized atmosphere and, as a result, has become "the Socrates / Of snails, musician of pears," "wig / Of things, this nincompated pedagogue" (sec. 1, ll. 2–3, 4–5). Stevens gently mocks his "general lexicographer of mute" and then sets him to sea, bound for the New World (sec. 1, l. 26).

Removed from the rarefied environment of "gelatines and jupes," Crispin questions if he can survive (sec. 1, l. 8). Once a master of "verboseness," the poet is now challenged to master himself and the sea (sec. 1, l. 37). He exchanges his world of the imagination for the New World of reality. Consequently, Crispin becomes an "introspective voyager," and although once he saw himself as a dandy poetic hero, he now knows himself as a "skinny sailor peering in the sea-glass" (sec. 1, ll. 68 and 28).

> Just so an ancient Crispin was dissolved.
> The valet in the tempest annulled.   (sec. 1, ll. 52–53)

At sea, Crispin is faced with a reality that he cannot evade, sublimate, or imagine to be otherwise. Thus, he changes and his aesthetic changes; Crispin becomes a realist.

> . . . The sea
> Severs not only lands but also selves.
> Here was no help before reality.

> Crispin beheld and Crispin was made new.
> The imagination, here, could not evade,
> In poems of plums, the strict austerity
> Of one vast, subjugating, final tone. (sec. 1, ll. 77–83)

Confronting physical reality, Crispin is forced to reexamine the solipsistic world of the imagination that guided his poetry in Europe. *L'azur* and the cult of the moon, the "goblinry" of his past, are impotent forces on the high seas (sec. 3, l. 51). Thus, the poet concedes

> He could not be content with counterfeit,
> With masquerade of thought, with hapless words
> That must belie the racking masquerade,
> With fictive flourishes that preordained
> His passion's permit, hang of coat, degree
> Of buttons, measure of his salt. Such trash
> Might help the blind, not him, serenely sly.
> (sec. 4, ll. 81–87)

And he commands,

> Exit the mental moonlight, exit lex,
> Rex and principium, exit the whole
> Shebang. Exeunt omnes. Here was prose
> More exquisite than any tumbling verse. (sec. 4, ll. 5–8)

Crispin forsakes his "poems of plums" and searches instead for "an aesthetic tough, diverse, untamed, / Incredible to prudes, the mint of dirt" (sec. 1, l. 79; sec. 2, ll. 34–35).

In "The Comedian as the Letter C," Stevens refutes the notion that the poet must reveal other-worldly truth to his reader, and that the poem must afford the world a glimpse of *l'au-delà*. Rather, the poem must offer the reader a clearer vision of his own world and his dealings within that world. Riddel finds that "the poet is not to elevate man but to reinvigorate him, not turn him from the world, but toward it, not offer him future but give him back a present—not 'to console / Nor sanctify, but plainly to propound.'"[14] Michel Benamou concurs, "Stevens veut que le poète nous aide *hic et nunc*, à supporter le fardeau de la civilisation actuelle. Le mythe du héros moderne doit réhabiliter la notion de noblesse humaine."[15] Indeed, in the New World, Crispin learns that man's nobility does not depend upon his ability to transcend his state of being a living, human animal; Crispin learns the nobility of his humanity.

Stevens's poet finds artistic satisfaction in his observation and contemplation of physical reality, the flora and fauna about him. He wanders, subjected to the elements, and ultimately makes his life by working the land. He creates life in the form of four daughters who become "four blithe instruments" for his life's poetry (sec. 6, l. 56). As a student of reality, Crispin devotes himself to the simple and ordinary, the rhythm of his days guided by the crop seasons and the cycle of childbirth.

At the end of "The Comedian," Stevens questions if Crispin's struggles have been "profitless," if submission to physical reality has tamed the poet to the point of his becoming "benign" (sec. 6, ll. 84, 96). But he immediately answers, "So may the relation of each man be clipped" (sec. 6, l. 97). Each poet, each clown, should aspire to what Crispin sought in life. Each should become intimate with his world and with the rituals of human life that render life so valuable. The most that the poetic clown can aspire to is, in Riddel's words, "trying heroically to find his way through the world rather than beyond it."[16]

Like that of Wallace Stevens, Hart Crane's interest in French symbolist poetry was sparked early in his career. In correspondence as early as 1917 he referred to his independent study of the French language, which he hoped would eventually enable him to read French poetry in the original language. Throughout the years from 1915 through 1930, letters to William Wright and Gorham Munson repeatedly refer to Baudelaire, Laforgue, and Rimbaud, as well as to Aragon, Tzara, and Apollinaire. To enrich Crane's reading in the French symbolists, Padraic and Mary Colum suggested in early 1917 that Crane read Arthur Symons's *The Symbolist Movement in Literature*, which Crane promptly did. In his correspondence, Crane continually writes of "running joyfully towards" Baudelaire and Laforgue, of being "deep in Baudelaire's *Fleurs du Mal*," and being "mad about Laforgue."[17] In addition, Crane's respect for these French poets was reinforced by his admiration of Eliot and Pound, who also acknowledge their debt to the French symbolists.

Like the work of his French predecessors, Crane's poetry is riddled with images of the poet in quest of self-understanding and of the artist in the act of self-discovery. Crane's poet is described as "Beauty's fool" ("The Bridge of Estador") (p. 143, l. 25), as a drunken visionary ("Recitative" and "Wine Menagerie") (pp. 23–24), and as a "black man, forlorn in the cellar" ("Black Tambourine") (p. 4, l. 9). He is a Charlie Chaplin figure in "Chaplinesque" (p. 11), a Petrushka in "The Wine Menagerie," and Pierrot in the Laforgue translations, "Locutions des Pierrots" (p. 148). Among the many self-reflexive masks, the ironic, self-deprecating poet predominates. Brom Weber finds that Crane's "romantic and ironic view of himself" was nurtured by his readings in the French poets, who devoted themselves to that approach in their poetry, as well as by his respect for the poetry of those, notably Eliot and Pound, who followed in their paths.[18]

Both Milne Holton and Richard Hutson have observed that much of Crane's early work—like that of the French symbolists he read and admired—is a study of the poetic identity, the creative imagination, and the alienation of the artist in contemporary society.[19] Holton has sketched the development of self-reflexivity in Crane's early poetry and concludes that "if some of the poems of 1919–1920 were obscurely dramatizing Crane's search for sexual identity, other poems confronted other problems in self-definition. And the more fruitful poems now often began to deal tentatively with some of the problems which Hart Crane as a poet confronted."[20] Among those early poems, "My Grandmother's Love Letters" (p. 6) and "The Fernery" (p. 14) introduce the poet's concern for specific artistic skills and the creative process in general, and "Porphyro in Akron" (p. 144) describes the "alienation of the poet-reader from the world around him."[21]

The twentieth-century American city, as Crane describes it in "Porphyro in Akron," is a grim environment for the lyric poet. Porphyro's Akron is "a bunch of smoke-ridden hills / Among rolling Ohio hills," a tainted and polluted area that has infected otherwise clean and virgin land (sec. 1, ll. 11–12). Moreover, the cacophony of industrial Akron neither inspires nor tolerates an artistic sensibility.

> The plough, the sword,
> The trowel,—and the monkey wrench!
> O City, your axles need not the oil of song.
> I will whisper words to myself
> And put them in my pockets. (sec. 1, ll. 17–21)

Much like Briusov's Pan-poet, Crane's Porphyro is an alien within the modern city. He is out of place both on South Main Street and in his mother's parlor. In the modern city, after all, poetry is pronounced a "Bedroom occupation" (sec. 3, l. 21). Indeed, the poet appears "ridiculous" in his attempt to read Keats's "The Eve of St. Agnes" in an Akron hotel room. The stars of Porphyro's unlyrical world are clouded by a dreary, slow rain, and he can barely concentrate on reading for the barroom noises "slung up from the street" (sec. 3, l. 18).

Although Crane's "ridiculous" poet feels himself alienated on South Main in Akron, he also feels an intense affinity to the immigrants in the alleys. The Greeks, Swedes, and Roumanians are as yet unsullied by the crass materialism and revered technological orientation of American society. Equally important, they have retained their memory of purity and their dreams. They recall earlier homes, the fjords and the Aegean. Although the poet appears to have little in common with the shift workers "pressing down" the street to work, Porphyro seems to be drawn to the immigrants' instinctive manner, the quick grins, and casual taunts. He seems to understand their naive, basic desires for a dark horse, sheep, and a pregnant wife. In a sense, Porphyro is a Pan figure who values revelry, raisin-jack, and dance, and who shares the immigrants' dreams of sheep that lamb regularly and a wife who bears likewise. The poet, too, is drawn to an earthy, intuitive way of life; he appreciates their generosity of spirit, their taking time to "pitch quoits with the old men," and their overtipping "because we felt like it" (sec. 1, l. 22; sec. 2, l. 16).

Crane's poetic persona bears the name of Keats's hero in "The Eve of St. Agnes." In this poem, Keats's bold young lover, Porphyro, woke his lady, Madeleine, with an "ancient ditty" on a lute, and with these "chords that tendrest be" he also awakened her love for him.[22] However, Crane's Porphyro is a poor namesake of Keats's hero. Crane's poet only reads of love. Moreover, although he aspires to creative activity, he has not yet realized poetic creation.

In Porphyro's Akron, the modern Pan's world, the suspect act of poetry is whispered softly and concealed "in the pocket" (sec. 1, l. 21). But crucial to Porphyro is the role of lyric impulse, artistic expression that may be extracted from the pocket and proclaimed to a receptive world. Although he reads and dreams of Keats's heroine, Crane's Porphyro is not the lover who won the "full-blown rose Madeleine ("Eve of St. Agnes," sec. 16, l. 1). The only rose in his impoverished world is the solitary bloom on his mother's front-yard bush. Yet, that bloom alone, or rather the memory of that bloom, engages his senses and starts his toes "ridiculously tapping" (sec. 3, l. 15). Ironically, an appreciation of the only beauty that his limited world has to offer makes him appear foolish to that world, and ultimately serves only to alienate him from his society.

Again in 1920 and 1921, Crane addressed the alienation of the poet in modern American society. In "Black Tambourine" the poet is presented as a black man who perhaps at one time was a minstrel singer. R. W. B. Lewis understands this self-reflexive lyric as "a poem about the American Negro in the modern world that becomes a poem also about the American poet in the modern world—and about the destiny of poets generally."[23]

Like Porphyro caught in twentieth-century America while yearning for an earlier time, Crane's black man is trapped in a poetic limbo, "in some mid-kingdom dark" (l. 10). Physically confined to a closed cellar, not dead but excluded from life, the black man as poet is caught between bestiality and humanity. Aesop found joy in writing about small animals, but Crane's black man finds no poetic inspiration in the insects that share his basement. He merely "wanders" in his mid-kingdom. Unable to transform his suffering into lyric verse, he is reduced to stasis.

So, too, the black man recalls his African heritage, but he no longer shares in its music. The poet's artistic expression is confined to the poor tambourine, a minstrel singer's instrument that is as coarse as the shepherd's Pan-pipes. The poet's limbo, then, is twofold. He recalls a vital African heritage and he looks to a poetic prototype in Aesop. Spanning both time and place for his sources of poetic strength, he nonetheless faces an impoverished reality that allows him access to neither. His blackness makes him not tribal shaman, but subhuman, and the rhythms of Aesop are replaced by those of a cheap minstrel tambourine.

As Holton has observed, the final line of "Black Tambourine" lifts the poem from its pessimism. "The poem is replete with images of death—Aesop's grave, the carcass in the final line—and that final image of the "carcass quick with flies," of death paradoxically engendering life, seems to allude to this temporal meaning for "mid-kingdom" and to resolve one of the significant oppositions of the poem itself."[24] The African past, a poetic heritage, both seemingly dead, will engender new life and new song to sing truer and stronger than the slave songs of the moment.

In "Chaplinesque," yet another self-reflexive poem, Crane identifies the modern poet as clown (11). After seeing *The Kid* in October 1921, Crane turned to the modern clown, Charlie Chaplin, for his portrayal of the contemporary poetic prototype. Like Chaplin, Crane's poetic clown is a quintessentially downtrodden, misunderstood, and abused creature. He, too, distinguishes himself by his sensitivity and his humanity. And, in Crane's words, Chaplin represents "the soul imposed upon by modern civilization."[25]

"Chaplinesque" dramatizes the plight of the artist as a homeless vagabond. In this vignette, Charlie Chaplin as poet does his best to provide a home for an abandoned kitten in his threadbare coat and discovers that only he is concerned with this seemingly meaningless love. Moreover, Chaplin's sensitivity has marked him as suspect in the eyes of the police, those who control and protect society from undesirable elements. In a letter to William Wright Crane provides an allegorical key to this poem: "Poetry, the human feelings, 'the kitten,' is so crowded out of the humdrum, rushing, mechanical scramble of today that the man who would preserve them must duck and camouflage for dear life to keep them or keep himself from annihilation."[26] The poet, too, must shift, dodge, and flee in order to protect himself and his work from "the fury of the street," which is "American society's crass indifference to and persecution of excellence."[27]

In addition to his sensitivity and vulnerability, Crane's poetic clown is a visionary and a prophet of sorts. The poet as Chaplin holds priestly powers that effect transfiguration of the common into the sacred. His eyes alone can transform an ash can into a chalice for the Holy Grail. The power of transformation and redemption is the clown's victory—and that of the artist as well. He can laugh in the lonely alleyways, and he can recognize his salvation where other men see only foolishness. He hears the kitten and the *vox clamantis in deserto* of John the Baptist where other men hear nothing.

Crane's clownish poet cuts an awkward and melancholy figure. At the same time, the reader is impressed with his peculiar self-assurance as he faces his responsibility toward the kitten and his poetic vocation. His devotion to the moon that transforms the alleyways is analogous to the poet's commitment to the Muse who inspires poetic creation. And, as disciple of the moon, the poet as Chaplin resembles the poet as Pierrot of Laforgue's "Les Locutions des Pierrots" and "Notre-Dame la Lune." Both poetic clowns are bizarre figures, isolated from any human contact, and fixated on the moon as Muse. In addition, Crane's Chaplin is a prophetic figure much like the Elizabethan fool in motley. Though detached from reality, both have a keen sense of reality. In the midst of the court's merry making and throughout the court's most serious political upheavals, the fool retains a firm hold on truth. So, too, Chaplin maintains his sense of what is important and correct even in the midst of "gaiety and quest" (l. 22). While he walks through the confusion of the street, he nonetheless hears the kitten in the cultural wilderness.

In his analysis of Crane's self-reflexive clown, R. W. B. Lewis, too, observes that Crane's American clown is a synthesis of several clown figures.

> The nineteenth-century French clown, mournful and agile, is reanimated in "Chaplinesque" through the immediate influence of Laforgue and Eliot, but he is reanimated in tonalities that at the same time recover a good deal of the medieval Fool of which the French Pierrot is a scrupulously truncated version. With some assistance from his own archetypal imagination, Crane at once Americanized and transvaluated the

clown of Laforgue by a poetic method at once ironic and ritualistic. The resulting figure does participate in the longstanding modern view of art as derided and humanity as debased, but he also participates in a much more ancient view. In his very shabbiness and clownishness, as he submits to the transfiguring moon, he represents for a second that moment just prior to an immense inversion of values whereby the humble shall be exalted, the foolish become the source of wisdom, and the world shall renew itself by honoring the ridiculous, the disgraced, the outlaw.[28]

The poet as Chaplin is not Crane's only "transvaluated clown." Such is also the status of the black minstrel singer and Porphyro. Thus, to speak more generally about Crane's early personae—both clown figures and clownish figures—each poet exists in spite of the society in which he lives. In addition, Crane portrays contemporary American society as venal and spiritually impoverished. As such, this society cannot nourish its artists; indeed, it debases both the poet and his poetry. Consequently, Crane's early self-reflexive poetry plays out the tragedy of twentieth-century American values. The poet as Chaplin, for example, lives in the back alleys of our cities where his fellow man is suspicious and hostile. Porphyro, too, is made to feel uncomfortable in Akron society; he is ostracised and we find him alone, living in a hotel room above a bar. So too, the black tambourine man is forced to inhabit a cellar crawling with insects. There he is cut off from his cultural heritage and all human exchange.

However, within contemporary society these men alone demonstrate wisdom. Chaplin distinguishes himself by his humanitarianism and holds the power to transform the commonplace and ugly into the holy and extraordinarily beautiful. Porphyro, too, displays traditional values, allies himself with the true and eternal, and, above all, is able to appreciate the one rose that blooms in Akron. As Lewis has indicated, this is the tragedy and irony of the poet's position, that a vision so exalted should maintain a position so diminished in American society.

Society is traditionally understood as the human bond that forms when men come together. The cities of a society should be an expression of the best that men know and can construct. However, the American city is not a true social mecca, according to Crane. Rather, it is a wilderness, a cultural desert where the poet suffers from the "fury of the street" (l. 7). In the imagery of "Chaplinesque," the world offers only wind to fill the "too ample pockets" of the poet's sensibility (l. 4). Porphyro's world, Akron, is likewise described as a "bunch of smoke-ridden hills," which serves only to befoul the pure rural area in which it is located (l. 11). Akron is a "stuffy parlour," a drizzling night, a yard with barren rose bushes, and, most pointedly, a mechanical world whose axles do not "need the oil of song" (sec. 3, l. 7; sec. 1, l. 19).

In addition to his representation of the poet as social outcast, Crane also depicts the poet as the *commedia* Pierrot and turns directly to Laforgue's "Les Locutions des Pierrots" for its image of the poet as the lovelorn, moon-struck clown. In the summer of 1921, Crane began to translate several of Laforgue's sixteen "Locutions." With the assistance of those more familiar with French, Crane produced three poetic translations, which he also entitled "Locutions des Pierrots" (p. 148). R. W. B. Lewis, among others, has studied these poems as translations, but our concern is not for the accuracy of the translation, but for the self-reflexive quality of Crane's "Locutions."[29]

Crane's three compositions depict the poet as Pierrot, the clown and the spurned lover. The poet's "locutions" represent the words of Pierrot addressed to his unwilling lover. However, more than a would-be lover, the object of Pierrot's desire is also his Muse. She is "O prodigal and dilatory lady," Eve, Gioconda, and Dalila (sec. 1, l. 2). Moreover, she represents the moon, a symbol of poetic inspiration that is so evocative for Laforgue. Despite his eloquent claims of "divine infatuation," Pierrot's lady offers only a "stiff denial" to his proposals (sec. 2, ll. 1, 11). To the end, she remains "perversely austere" until Pierrot is reduced to begging,

> Come now—appease me just a little
> With the why-and-wherefore of Your Sex!
>
> (sec. 1, l. 6; sec. 3, ll. 11–12)

More than a scenario of courtship and sexual proposal, Crane's

"Locutions" represents the modern poet's attempt to court the favor of his society and to determine if his society favors him and his work. R. W. B. Lewis argues that "Pierrot's amatory difficulties . . . are also no doubt a bitter-comic representation of Pierrot's relation—that is, the relation of the artist in Laforgue's generation—to the 'perverse austerities' of the modern world, a world he at once courts and denigrates, a world which may claim to love him but has not the wit to understand a word he says."[30] Charming and yearning, bitter and despondent, Pierrot's "Locutions" bespeaks the uncertain and ironic relationship of the modern poet and his world, of Porphyro and his Akron, and of Chaplin and the "fury of the streets."

When he speaks of the poet's role within early self-reflexive lyrics, Hart Crane points to the "inadequacy of the world for the poet," but he also testifies to the poet's ability to withstand the stubborn blindness of his world.[31] In his study of Crane's early work, Sherman Paul finds that "poems such as these tell of the poet's persistence on behalf of an ideal or condition that he knows is already lost in time."[32] In this sense, Crane's self-reflexive work speaks of the optimism which his poet figures retain within an unlyrical world. Figures such as Chaplin, Porphyro, and the black minstrel singer have preserved their memories of the ideal, look to those memories for courage, and attempt to carry their poetic ideals into the future.

As Milne Holton has indicated, *The Bridge* draws on and expands those self-reflexive themes that Crane explored in his earlier, shorter works. In particular, the self-reflexive consideration of the poetic identity is an early thematic strain "which was to become significant in the major work," *The Bridge*.[33] He notes that

> in "Black Tambourine" Crane is now writing more directly about that subject which he had only begun most circuitously to consider in poems like "My Grandmother's Love Letters" and "Porphyro in Akron." Now Crane is addressing himself to the subject of the poet and his imagination in a modern world, and in "Black Tambourine" the outlines of the figures begin to come a bit clearer. Crane's poet [verb omitted] from his world and must move imaginatively backward in historical

time to seek the material for his vision. In one poem the poet tentatively approached his grandmother's old love letters, in another he read Keats in Akron. Now, in a new disguise, he explores the cellar of the racial memory. Soon Crane will search his own schoolboy's knowledge of his nation's history. But the song will be sung and the tambourine will be played out; out of this search Crane's myth will be created.[34]

Crane's myth and his mythology of the poet will be created in their most complete fashion in, of course, *The Bridge*.

Hart Crane's *Bridge* is a complex lyric expression in which the poet addresses a number of self-reflexive issues. The poem is a celebration of the imagination and an analysis of the poetic act; it is a study of the relationship between lyric form and poetic vision, and a discussion of the nature and power of artistic creation in modern society. And, like many of Crane's earlier self-reflexive poems, *The Bridge* speaks directly to the nature of the poet himself and his relationship with twentieth-century American society. Crane's longest and most ambitious self-reflexive work is a testimony to the poet's persistence within an unreceptive society, as Sherman Paul noted.[35] Moreover, it is an account of the poet's effort to recover the artistic ideals that were lost to him.

To reclaim a strong poetic identity, Crane reaches into his lyric past, the historical past, in search of poetic prototypes that would, first, allow him to rid himself of the ironic, self-deprecating persona inherited from the French symbolists, and, second, would aid him in understanding what the poet once was and might again become in twentieth-century America. Lawrence Dembo asserts that "whatever his declared intention, Crane's real purpose in writing *The Bridge* was to create an environment in which the poet was able to transcend the impotent-clown image that was his only face in a nontragic, nonheroic world."[36] Indeed, *The Bridge* is Crane's departure from the ironic mode of his earlier self-reflexive poetry. In *The Bridge*, Crane abandons his examination of the self-deprecating poet and rejects the image of the poet as clown. He does so by calling forth his rich poetic ancestry. Throughout the poem, Crane encounters and examines a wealth of poetic figures drawn mostly from American literature, history, and folklore. These figures provide the modern artist with a renewed sense of his poetic heritage and point to a source of artistry and wisdom to which he is heir.

Thus, *The Bridge* represents a refutation of the image of the poet as an impotent Pan and offers a rebuttal to the symbolist mask of the poet as clown. In direct contrast to this wan, ironic persona, *The Bridge* offers distinctly American poetic prototypes, positive and vigorous figures that will be the primary object of this study. Second, in its rejection of the poet as clown, *The Bridge* also evokes the Orphic ritual of descent. The central movement of *The Bridge* appears to parallel that of the *katábasis* of Orpheus. The composition begins with descent and search and climaxes with an affirmation of poetic power. Finally, the mythic structure of *The Bridge* is not limited to a mere rehearsal of the gross movement of the Orphic *katábasis*. In a more general sense, Hart Crane taps the very nature of ritual and social ceremony in his attempt to understand the poetic self.

The first major poetic prototype encountered in *The Bridge* is the historical figure of Columbus in "Ave Maria" (p. 47). This American hero is not only an explorer and discoverer of the New World, but within *The Bridge* he also serves as "mask of the poet; that is, a poet-figure or 'ancient man,' who in some way re-enacts the narrator's quest and serves as guide."[37] Crane's Columbus is anything but the ironic fool or pale aesthete of the symbolists, a fact established at the outset:

> For I have seen now what no perjured breath
> Of clown nor sage can riddle or gainsay;—
> . . . .
> . . .—I bring you back Cathay!   (ll. 5–6, 8)

Columbus as poet is explorer of a New World in which poetry can thrive; he is explorer of a new sense of the nature of poetry and of a new definition of the poet. The vision and challenge of Columbus is beyond those possible for the self-deprecating fool, or for a sage devoid of the faith that his task requires.

This is not to say that the poet has freed himself of the fears and doubts that resulted in poetic stasis for Crane's earlier poetic figures. Columbus, too, confesses his "trembling heart" (l. 92). Nonetheless, his poetry is born in the chasm between two continents; it is "tested" by the water between the two, and emerges from the test as prophetic as the words of Isaiah (ll. 32–50). R. W. B. Lewis writes that "the heroic mariner's posture is . . . an analogue for that of the poet: standing alone, peering out across vast distances, journeying in imagination between two separated worlds, hoping to join the envisioned splendor of the one to the known actuality of the other, and always fearful of disaster."[38] Like Porphyro, Chaplin, and the black man in the cellar, Columbus stands between reality and that which he dreams might exist. In this position, the poet is vulnerable and lonely, and such is his unalterable fate.

However, Columbus distinguishes himself from the earlier poetic figures in that he steadfastly "utter[s] to loneliness the sail is true" (l. 62). Crane's American poet refuses to indulge himself in vacillation and self-doubt. The ship and the sea will not allow him to do so. Consequently, Columbus is vigilant in his mission; he examines each wave "series on series, infinite" and lives always at the edge of discovery (l. 42). Ultimately, he finds Cathay, the "incognizable Word / Of Eden" (ll. 59–60).

In "The River," Crane's poet continues to journey in the past, allowing himself to leave behind the "din and slogans of the year," which comprise contemporary poetry for American society (l. 63). In this earlier time, the poet encounters a group of "hobo-trekkers," men who appear to be "blind fists of nothing, humpty-dumpty clods" (ll. 57, 63). However, Crane immediately qualifies this description:

> Yet they touch something like a key perhaps.
> From pole to pole across the hills, the states
> —They know a body under the wide rain. (ll. 64–66)

These "clods" are the poetic prototype he is searching for. They are Pan figures, and these awkward, Dionysian characters hold vital knowledge about man, his memory, and his dreams.

As they crisscross the continent, "hopping the slow freight" and "tak[ing] their liquor slow," these men reject the modern obsession for speed (ll. 28, 61). They challenge the idea that rapid communication—represented here by the telephone wires and wireless—means better or more valuable communication. As they "ruminate" through America's cities, these trekkers become intimate with the land and its people (l. 32). They tap its past and its imagination. Serving as American shaman and poet, the hobo-trekker builds a corporate American memory.

John, Jake, or Charley, children "on a loose perch," these men somewhat resemble the earlier clownish poetic personae (l. 53). But they are actually "ancient men" and "ancient clown[s]," resembling more closely Pan, the most ancient of clowns before the gods, who shared with man the gift and power of his song (ll. 55, 102–103). Crane's poet learns to hum from the trekkers; he learns to dream. Caught in this "tideless spell," the poet is able to share in the corporate memory of these tribal shamans and will eventually learn to sing as they do (l. 123). When Crane's poet has "touched hands with some ancient clown" (ll. 102–103), he has found Pan and has begun to discover his poetic ancestry.

In "The Dance," Crane's poetic prototype is not only tribal shaman, but tribal chieftain, Maquokeeta. The poet watches the Indian king in his tribal dance and observes the mythic ritual that brings the morning sun and assures the coming of spring. At last he bears witness to the power of poetry that is chanted and acted out by the highest authorities of a society. No longer a clown or an impotent faun, Crane's Indian poet wields the power of the ancient Greek mythological poets when he chants. Just as the song of Pan made all of nature bow and sway, so the song of Maquokeeta causes the birches to kneel and the oaks to circle. The sky, too, moans when the chieftain dances.

Lewis has noted that "in 'The Dance,' moving onto the smoky ground of a new revelation, Crane indicates what it is those vagrant rustics possess a key *to*, if they did but know. It is a world governed by a mythic apprehension of reality, of nature, of experience—a world in which these things are seen and responded to as elements in a grand and recurring mythic drama. It is the remote and marvel-ridden age of the old rain-gods—those gods who now, in the modern period, lie buried beneath iron (that is, technological) mountains of forgetfulness, of blunted awareness."[39] For the poet

Maquokeeta, the essence of such mystery, experience, and drama is found in the "glacier woman," Pocahontas (l. 2). Virgin bride, a pure woman native to a pure continent, she represents the source of poetic life, of lyric beauty, and of the mythic apprehension Lewis describes. By taking the tribal princess on a bed of leaves, he ensures his immortality through his heirs. Maquokeeta is thus able to perform the sacred dance, to reveal the divine lie, and then to dance to his death.

> Dance, Maquokeeta! snake that lives before,
> That casts his pelt, and lives beyond! Sprout, horn!
> Spark, tooth! Medicine-man, relent, restore—
> Lie to us,—dance us back the tribal morn! (ll. 61–64)

At his death, Maquokeeta also evokes the ancient poet, Orpheus. A sacrificial figure, the Indian king is killed in a Dionysian ritual of frenzied dance. In a continuation of that ritual, his remains are scattered like those of Orpheus. And, like the song of the ancient hero, the poetry of the chieftain, Maquokeeta, will live forever.

As witness to the tribal dance and sacrificial killing of the king, Crane's poet becomes the poetic heir of Maquokeeta. The Indian ritual serves as an initiation rite for the poet in which he is bound "liege / To rainbows currying each pulsant bone" (ll. 66–67). The poet then takes up the dance of Maquokeeta and thus assumes as well the mythic sensibility of the ritual king.

It remains for the poet to retain his primitive vision upon his return and to join it with his modern sensibility. His challenge is to determine what might be the place of the ritual dance and tribal song in the "Years of the Modern!" ("Cape Hatteras," l. 224). In "Cutty Sark" and "Cape Hatteras," the poet confronts such modernity in the inventions of the steam ship, the phonograph, and the airplane, and the poet puzzles:

> Dream cancels dream in this new realm of fact
> From which we wake into the dream of act;
> Seeing himself an atom in a shroud—
> Man hears himself an engine in a cloud!
> ("Cape Hatteras," ll. 43–46)

At this point, Crane's poet encounters yet another poetic ancestor and artistic prototype, Walt Whitman, and asks him,

> Walt, tell me, Walt Whitman, if infinity
> Be still the same as when you walked the beach.
>
> (ll. 48–49)

That is, have the nature of the world and the poetry it requires changed radically from those of the primitive world of Maquokeeta, or can modern poetry retain the essence of the tribal rite that Crane's poet witnessed in the Indian camp? Does the poet still wield the power of Pan over nature, and does he make the sun rise and the spring arrive as did the Indian king through his song? The poet's encounter with Whitman makes him understand that the "new verities, new inklings" of the modern technological world can be incorporated into the poet's primitive vision and can inspire poetry that is "bright with myth" (ll. 71, 66). Heir to Columbus, the ancient clowns, and Maquokeeta, the poet then joins hands with another artistic prototype, Walt Whitman.

> What heritage thou'st signalled to our hands!
> . . . .
>   yes, Walt,
> Afoot again, and onward without halt,—
> Not soon, nor suddenly,—no, never to let go
>   My hand
>   in yours,
>   Walt Whitman—
>   so—
>
> (ll. 225, 232–38)

The poet thus continues his journey to the present time where he retains his early vision of Cathay, the dream of the sacred "multitudinous Verb" ("Atlantis," l. 115). Moreover, he "reclaims" the vision of Whitman, that is, he succeeds in transforming poetic ideals into the Psalm of Cathay, the poetry for which he was searching ("Cape Hatteras," l. 238).

    R. W. B. Lewis claims that Crane's "Proem" serves as "synecdoche of the entire poem," *The Bridge*.[40] This is indeed true for the structure of this composition. The "Proem" is a poem of descent and return, and presents in condensed form the movement of the entire poetic sequence. "Proem" establishes *The Bridge* as a composition structured on a movement analogous to the *katábasis* of Orpheus.

"To Brooklyn Bridge"—or "Proem" (p. 45)—presents the poet's persona as a bizarre figure emerging from "some subway scuttle, cell or loft" (l. 17). With a backdrop of "the sky's acetylene," he races to the top of the bridge and jumps (l. 22). The poet descends to his death and leaves behind him a world that appears to be as sordid and venal as the world of the Maenads was in the eyes of Orpheus. And, like the descent of Orpheus into the underworld, the fall of the Bedlamite poet is meaningful. As the final imperative indicates, his fall will enable him to "descend / And of the curveship lend a myth to God" (ll. 43–44). The poet's descent in "The Tunnel" will give value to his long voyage in the past. It will allow him to reclaim for the present those elements of poetic beauty that he searched for in the past. His descent also challenges him to fuse the Orphic roles, "the prophet's pledge, / Prayer of pariah, and the lover's cry" into a new form of music, a newer form of poetry ("Proem," ll. 31–32).

The descent of "The Tunnel" is again foreshadowed in "Powhatan's Daughter" (p. 53), where Crane's poet voyages in the past to another world, "There, where the first and last gods keep thy tent" ("The Dance," l. 80). In this world found in the past, the poet attempts to recover the "bride immortal" (l. 84). Like his poetic ancestor, Orpheus, the poet travels in search of a nameless woman in whom is vested poetic energy. For Orpheus, this woman is Eurydice, who enables him to sing and for whom he sings. For Crane's poet, she is Powhatan's daughter, Pocahontas, and she serves essentially the same function as Eurydice. In Ovid's account, Orpheus defies time when he descends into hell and sees a wife who existed in the past. But to glimpse his wife was to glimpse supernal beauty. Thus, although Orpheus leaves the underworld without Eurydice, he retains his vision of beauty and recovers his memory of their love. He is then able to sing again and to create art once more. In the glosses to "Van Winkle" we learn that when

Crane's poet discovers Powhatan's daughter, he, too, recovers time and memory (p. 85). With her, he undergoes his artistic initiation and emerges a true poet. The poet's experience with Pocahontas establishes a continuum between himself and Maquokeeta, and he falls heir to the tribal chieftain by virtue of his ritual encounter with this woman. Moreover, through Powhatan's daughter he takes his vows in the mythic poetic priesthood. Lawrence Dembo describes the transformation from man to poet in the Indian ritual: "As the mythic experience begins, the poet leaves the village of the white man and enters the soil in which Pocahontas manifests herself. In the moon he sees her hair ('Your hair's keen crescent running') and follows it until it is replaced by 'one star' that 'bleeds immortally' into the dawn. The star is the same one that he saw in 'The Harbor Dawn' and sees again in 'Atlantis,' the 'one tolling star / That bleeds infinity' and marks the divine 'Ever-presence.' . . . He approaches the purifying fire in which he will find the 'name, unspoke,' 'Creation's blithe and petalled word.'"[41]

After he has undergone his poetic initiation, Crane's poet is challenged to retain his vision of beauty and his artistic legacy as he descends to the underworld. He begins his descent in "The Tunnel." There we find his Hades in the New York subway, an underground system that lies beneath modern urban life. The poet finds twentieth-century America, represented in its underground, to be profane and unlyrical. Dembo asserts that in "The Tunnel," "the poet's main concern is to preserve his faith while living in a world that seems to deny the Ideal."[42]

Like the descent of Orpheus, the *katábasis* of Crane's poet involves a search for a woman. In his underworld, the poet discovers a "Genoese," the "Wop washerwoman" (ll. 102, 105). Although Crane's description of this woman is less than elegant, the image is a complex and positive one. The lady's hair and eyes evoke mother love, the first object of one's affection. As a Genoese, she is also reminiscent of Columbus's quest in "Ave Maria." Finally, this woman represents Pocahontas, the woman by whom the young artist discovered his poetic powers.[43] In a twentieth-century urban setting, the Wop washerwoman is a diminished version of the Indian princess, but she retains her power to inspire the poet. Once he has gazed at her, he sees the "day in birth" from the depths of the subway (l. 109). The poet is then able to begin his return to the upperworld.

For support throughout his voyage and as a reminder of his "Sanskrit charge," the poet looks to the eyes of another urban American poet, Edgar Allan Poe ("Cape Hatteras," l. 144). Crane's poet watches Poe's "eyes like agate lanterns—on and on" and he recalls the "trembling hands" of the earlier artist ("The Tunnel," ll. 74 and 81). Earlier in *The Bridge*, the poet sought the "Hand of Fire" of Columbus and the "hands of some ancient clown" of the hobotrekkers in order to establish his artistic ancestry ("Ave Maria," l. 94; "The River," l. 103). Then, in "Cape Hatteras" he clung to the hand of Walt Whitman. Now in "The Tunnel" the poet retains his contact with the hands of fellow artists until the final lines of the section when he passes from the underground to the upperworld.

At this moment, Crane's poet acts on his "Sanskrit charge," and in "Atlantis" the poet sings (p. 114). Like the music of Orpheus, his song springs from the harp or lyre. It is described as "the flight of strings," which gleam "as though a god were issue of the strings" (ll. 2, 8). They further resemble the ancient instrument of the mythological hero in that they are described as "deathless strings" (l. 56). Moreover, Crane's poet at last takes his place as a true ancestor of the hero Orpheus when he asks, "Atlantis,—hold thy floating singer late" (l. 88). The spirit of the mythological victim of *sparagmós* has been assumed by the modern poet, who, in effect, now takes the place of Orpheus as an artist within his own society. In the final strophe of *The Bridge*, the poet's lyre is firmly identified as "the orphic strings" and they produce—if only in a momentary vision—"the Song," "the Bridge of Fire," "the Psalm of Cathay" (ll. 91, 93, 47).

Finally, when the poem is approached from the more general perspective of mythic structure, *The Bridge* emerges as a testimony to the value of mythology for twentieth-century man. That is, Crane's poet discovers meaning in himself only when he creates what appears to be a mythic social ritual for himself.

The body of *The Bridge* is devoted to the poet's search for past poetic prototypes with whom he might identify and fuse his lot.

He is then confident that his role is truly that of a poet, and that this social role has existed and will continue to exist. This is what Joseph Campbell terms mythic *consciousness*.[44] In order to understand one's self and one's social role, one must view the self in perspective of society, past and present. One does so, according to Campbell, through the vehicle of ritual, which serves

> to translate the individual's life crises and life-deeds into classic, impersonal forms. They disclose him to himself, not as this personality or that, but as the warrior, the bride, the widow, the priest, the chieftain; at the same time rehearsing for the rest of the community the old lesson of the archtypal stages. All participate according to rank and function. The whole society becomes visible to itself as an imperishable living unit. Generations of individuals pass, like anonymous cells from a living body; but the sustaining timeless form remains. By an enlargement of vision to embrace this super-individual, each discovers himself enhanced, enriched, supported, and magnified. His role, however unimpressive, is seen to be intrinsic to the beautiful festival-image of man—the image, potential yet necessarily inhibited, within himself.[45]

To effect such mythic consciousness on the part of the poet in *The Bridge*, Crane uses the construct of ritual to view his poet as part of an ongoing social structure, which, in this poem, is North American civilization in general. Only in this way is he able to secure his identity. The poet's journey into American history and folklore is Crane's analogue for the primitive ritual in which a society recalls its community ancestors and takes one's place among them. Thus, through his mythic voyage, Crane's poet discovers that he assumes the role of the artists who went before him, and through this ritual he is able to call upon his artistic forefathers and witness the continuum of their creative energy through him.

Thus, at the climax of the Indian ritual in "The Dance," Crane asserts the vital importance of such mythic consciousness (p. 73). And we again recall the tribe's continual command to its shaman:

> Dance, Maquokeeta! snake that lives before,
> That casts his pelt, and lives beyond! Sprout, horn!
> Spark, tooth! Medicine-man, relent, restore—
> Lie to us,—dance us back the tribal morn! (ll. 61–64)

This declaration, chanted in the frenzy of the ritual dance, is particularly interesting because it is written in an eternal present that encompasses both past and future. The poet and tribal shaman is compared to a snake, who sheds his skin to allow himself to grow and continue to live, an analogy that can be understood only in mythological terms. The role of the poet is in itself a living entity that is filled, by different individuals at different times in history, yet is always filled by someone. Therefore, when Maquokeeta dances to his death, his tribe understands that another poet will take his place. He will fulfill the same social function; he will be the same snake in a new skin. And, as poet he will dance them to the "tribal morn" (l. 60). The community's act of faith in their social order and in all of nature is expressed in this ritual dance of which the poet is an essential and vital member.

Thus, the structure of Hart Crane's *Bridge* speaks directly to the importance of ancient mythology for the individual and points to the social nature of primitive ritual. Moreover, the movement of *The Bridge* suggests something of the function of mythology in modern poetry in general. In Crane's work, mythic consciousness serves to identify the poet and his special powers. Mythic consciousness not only defines the role of poetry in modern society, but also asserts its importance.

Conclusion

In his discussion of the nature of mythology, Bronislaw Malinowski argues that in primitive society myth is manifest in a special class of sacred stories, apart from the social folk tales and practical historical legend of a given tribe.

> Studied alive, myth . . . is not symbolic, but a direct expression of its subject-matter; it is not an explanation in satisfaction of scientific interest, but a narrative resurrection of a primeval reality, told in satisfaction of deep religious wants, moral cravings, social submissions, assertions, even practical requirements. Myth fulfills in primitive culture an indispensable function: it expresses, enhances, and codifies belief; it safeguards and enforces morality; it vouches for the efficiency of ritual and contains practical rules for the guidance of man. Myth is thus a vital ingredient of human civilization; it is not an idle tale, but a hard-working active force; it is not an intellectual explanation or an artistic imagery, but a pragmatic character of primitive faith and moral wisdom.[1]

Myth, then, serves as a form of sociological charter that binds a group of people together.

Joseph Campbell adds that myth is essential not only for the society as a whole, but also for each individual within society. In *The Hero with a Thousand Faces*, Campbell explains that each man is "only a fraction and distortion of the total image of man."[2] He is limited to experience life in one gender, in one age at each stage of his development, and he functions in society in one occupation at one social level. Although he is aware of other social roles, recalls his childhood, and knows intimately someone of the opposite sex, he is never able at one time to experience the total range of human life. However, through ritual, myth gives man a glimpse of the entire possibility of human existence and affords him an understanding of his place within that body. Myth springs from social ritual—and not the reverse—as Jane Harrison observes in *Themis*.[3] Therefore, through ritual ceremony in primitive society, myth serves to disclose society to the individual and to identify the role of the individual within society.

Consequently, one's view of society and one's view of oneself are two sides of the same coin, and are inseparable constructs. In his observations on the mythic conception of the "I," Ernst Cassirer, too, states that man's mythic consciousness forces him to recognize that his identity and destiny are enmeshed in those of nature and his society. The very idea of the individual is mythically bound to the concept of society; indeed the individual is incomprehensible outside of the larger sphere. "In den ersten Stadien, bis zu denen wir die Entwicklung zurückverfolgen können, finden wir das Selbstgefühl überall noch unmittelbar verschmolzen mit einem bestimmten mythisch-religiösen Gemeinschaftsgefühl. Das Ich fühlt und weiss sich nur, sofern es sich als Gleid einer Gemeinschaft fasst. . . . Nur in ihr und durch sie (eine Gemenschaft, eine Sippe) besitzt es sich selbst; sein eigenes persönliches Dasein und Leben ist in jeder seiner Äusserungen wie mit unsichtbaren magischen Banden an das Leben des umschliessenden Ganzen gebunden."[4] Thus, when the ancient poet looks to his personal god and hero, his mythic prototypes, Pan and Orpheus, he creates a sense of self and sees himself in terms of the totality of life, his society in the past, present, and future.[5] Mythic consciousness, Campbell would insist, is the overwhelming impulse to feel oneself an essential and clearly defined member of a society. That is what compels the poet to look to Pan and Orpheus when he wishes to speak not only of them, but of himself and his self-conception within society.

This is the import of the mythology of Pan and Orpheus for later poets as well. The modern artist finds in these figures a prototype of social identity and an embodiment of man's critical need for lyric expression. Myth is a public profession of man's most intense and most basic impulses. Manifest in his mythology are man's conceptions of morality, death, immortality, and the value of his life's work—issues of true importance to both ancient and modern man. The work of J. G. Frazer teaches, above all, that mythic impulses are universal although diverse in their expression. The power of the poet and the necessity of poetry—universal elements of ancient mythic expression—are ideas that modern poets seek to examine through the mythology of Pan and Orpheus.

Carl Jung tells that the elders of the Elgonyi tribe in Kenya spoke to him of a nocturnal god whom they hear in the wind. A breeze that whistles through the long grass spells something sinister to them. Jung describes this god as an "African Pan."[6] The Greek Pan, after all, is recognized by the noon cry of his pipes, which warns shepherds of impending danger and which causes "panic." Compare this myth of a wind-god with the myth of Orpheus as interpreted by John Fiske in *Myths and Myth-Makers*. Fiske views Orpheus as the power of the wind because he is able to bend trees and raise stones just as the wind might.[7] The music of Orpheus embodies the might of the wind, and Pan, too, wields this power over nature.

The ancient Greeks also believed that the wind held the souls of the dead; this same belief can be found in biblical literature (God breathed a soul into the dust that became man; Christ is the wind in the upper room after his crucifixion) as well as in later commonplaces (the gust of wind and ensuing chill in a room when someone dies). The power of the wind and the breath that rushes into a flute both represent the power of the soul, dead or alive, and this is the element that controls both man and nature. The "something sinister" that grips the Elgonyi tribe is a presentiment of death or a reminder of one who has died. When Orpheus mourns for his wife, he naturally reaches for his lyre because his music, which is the power of the wind, recreates her soul for him and becomes an expression of her. Likewise, when Pan holds his pipes and plays a melody, he expresses his memory of Syrinx and is able to hold onto her through his music. The music creates what was, but what no longer exists; what is not and perhaps never was, but what we desire to be. And so, for example, when Mallarmé's faun wakes from a dream and wishes to recreate the nymph that never existed in reality, he makes music.

When the poet draws on the mythology of Pan and Orpheus in his self-reflexive poetry, his work also asserts the social function of the mythology. That is, such poetry speaks to the social identity of the poet and the role of poetry within a community. Until the late eighteenth century, lyric poets depict Pan as *Allgott* in their self-reflexive work. They do so because they conceive of the poet as an all-powerful creator, a vatic figure within their society. Thus, when the poet wishes to describe his role as artist, he turns to powerful mythological prototypes and asserts the continuity of an artistic heritage that passes from the early poet Pan to himself. The Pan of Jonson, then, is an omnipotent poet, and the goat-god of Ronsard confers eternal life on the subjects of his verse. When Spenser describes the poet as Pan, his mythic model is a private, pastoral poet and a public, prophetic artist as well.

Likewise, early representations of the poet as Orpheus depict the hero as an omnipotent, vatic, godlike creature. Boileau's Orpheus is credited with the civilization of man from a savage state into social and cultural order. When Spenser and Shakespeare describe the powers of Orpheus, we learn that his music is able to enchant flora and fauna such that they sway and bow to the poet.

In the romantic poets, we find a less glorified image of Pan and Orpheus in self-reflexive poetry. Where these figures represent the poet, they are often diminished versions of the earlier mythological personae. The romantic poet gradually abandons the image of Pan as *Allgott* and of Orpheus as a pacific priest. In their stead we find more complex poetic personae whose powers are dark and mysterious, yet whose words are nonetheless brilliant and prophetic. Pushkin depicts his goat-god as a sinister creature able to fuse holy and evil within his verse. Victor Hugo's Pan is initially depicted as a satyr-clown facing an audience that is suspicious of his powers and that challenges the value of his poetry. Although triumphant at the close of the poem, Pan finds that his poetic role is clearly under fire. In the poetry of Robert Browning, the Dionysian goat-god is presented as a rough, lascivious brute. His Pan, as well as those of Shelley and Elizabeth Browning, alienate themselves from their societies by the suffering they inflict on others. All are poets, but none is the revered artist of earlier times. Likewise, the Orphic poet of Hugo demands comparison to his ancient Greek predecessor, but his society belittles such comparison and derides his lyric voice. In these works, the romantic Pan and Orpheus themselves, at times, question their creative roles; yet, at times, fight to retain their vatic identities.

In nineteenth-century French symbolist poetry, the mythic figures are further transformed. The Pan of Mallarmé and Laforgue has become a manic, Dionysian figure, prepared to sacrifice his creative role to satisfy his erotic desire. On the other hand, the Orphic poet of Mallarmé is characterized by his extreme asceticism. Unlike his ancient prototype, the Orphic Igitur devotes himself entirely to his art to the extent that he isolates himself from all social exchange. Indeed, he believes that his isolation from society is a necessary element of true artistic creation. In addition, the French symbolist poets have created poetic masks that are distinct from their mythic personae, yet draw on elements of the ancient Pan and Orpheus. In the work of Mallarmé, we find a poet-*pitre*, a poetic clown whose manic activity is indistinguishable from that of Mallarmé's *faune*. Both seek in sensuality a means of filling the emotional void of their poetic identity. In addition, Laforgue depicts the poet as the *commedia*'s Pierrot. In this guise, the poet is a self-deprecating, naughty clown who, like the Orphic poet of this period, lives in complete isolation from his society. Regardless of the exact mask of the poetic figure, each symbolist persona is an outcast from his society or is, in some measure, an alien among his fellow men.

The same can be said of the personae of the Russian symbolist poets, Aleksandr Blok and Valerii Briusov. The poetic clowns of Blok, like the Pan and *pitre* of Laforgue and Mallarmé, reach out to their fellow man, but are rebuffed at every occasion. Whether *Commedia* figures or poetic *pitres*, they are bizarre men who clearly do not form part of their contemporary societies. Briusov's mythic poets, Pan and Orpheus, suffer the same plight. They find that their role as lyric poets has no place in technological, industrial Russia, and they thus feel that lyricism is incompatible with modernity. Thus, like their French predecessors, the Russian poetic persona is alienated from his society. However, as an expresser of truth, he is nonetheless compelled to speak to his community. Consequently, the French and Russian persona—be he the mythic Pan and Orpheus or the modern clown—must assume a disguise before he can assume a lyric voice and bring his lyric creation to the world. That the disguise is either clownish garb or the tragic mask of a mythological figure testifies to the ironic position of the poet in modern society.

Finally, with the American poets Hart Crane and Wallace Stevens, the poet remains a clown, but seeks to shed his clownish mask. Both Stevens and Crane continue to depict the poet as clown, but their poetic clowns look to a future when they will speak out as dignified men and as true poets. Porphyro and Chaplin retain their vision of the lyric, and Crispin is a clown who aspires to reconciliation with reality and with his fellow man. Likewise, where Crane and Stevens draw upon Pan and Orpheus as mythic prototypes of the artist, these figures seek to revive the poet's lost honor and self-assurance. As Peter Quince, Stevens's Pan rejects the image of the goat-god as a manic, ithyphallic creator, and restores dignity to the Dionysian spirit that engenders lyric poetry. Crane's Orphic poet in *The Bridge*, too, looks toward a renewal of the poetic self and seeks identity in the community of poets that preceded him.

We find in the poetry of Crane and Stevens, then, a rejection of the self-deprecating poetic personae of the earlier nineteenth-century European poets. Correspondingly, their work issues a rejection of the ironic mode of self-reflexive poetry. When they abandon the ironic poetic personae, both Crane and Stevens return to the mythic prototypes; moreover, they infuse these prototypes with the spirit of the ancient mythological figures.

The Pan and Orpheus of Crane and Stevens aspire to an alliance with their fellow man and they long to take part in the rhythm and cycles of contemporary society. Crane's poet in *The Bridge* seeks lyric inspiration in the sounds and inventions of the city, and Stevens's Crispin establishes himself in the New World. The modern poet claims intimate knowledge of his land and its people; he holds their memory and their dreams. Although his is not technological knowledge or commercial insight, he bears poetic truth and for this he is recognized by his fellow man. After he allies himself with his community, the poet finds that he commands the attention of society.

This is not to assert that the modern poet approaches to the status of the mythological poet as hero or god. The modern Pan and Orpheus are not identical to the ancient Pan and Orpheus. The modern poet, however, does share in mythic consciousness that earlier poets had lost. By virtue of such mythic consciousness, he is able to recapture a sense of his poetic identity and to reestablish a place for himself within his society.

The progression of Pan and Orpheus as poets from early lyric verse through twentieth-century poetry appears to correspond to Northrop Frye's theory of fictional modes.[8] Frye's classification of modes begins with the mythic, in which the hero (in our case, the poetic persona) is a god or a godlike being; his fifth and final level concerns the absurd and frustrated hero of the ironic mode. The classification of fictional modes may well describe the depiction of Pan and Orpheus in early poetry as vatic, omnipotent poets, then in romantic and symbolist poetry as diminished and ultimately ironic figures. Northrop Frye further asserts that his modes are cyclical, that the ironic literature tends toward the mythic once again. In a study of the progression of Pan and Orpheus as poetic prototypes, we, too, find that following a period in which these figures are self-deprecating, ironic personae, they begin in twentieth-century American poetry to assume the characteristics and spirit of the mythic heroes once more.

Notes

Chapter 1

1. "'Kann die Harfe durch ihre Propeller schiessen?': Poetologische Lyrik in Amerika," in *Amerikanische Literatur im 20. Jahrhundert*, ed. Alfred Weber and Dietmar Haack (Göttigen: Vandenhoeck und Ruprecht, 1971), 181.
2. Ibid., 184.
3. "Amerikanische Künstlererzählungen und poetologische Gedichte als Dokumente der Poetik," (Lectures presented in Tübingen, West Germany, 1974–75), 32.
4. I use the terms *archetype* and *convention* interchangeably, and employ them not in the sense that Northrop Frye has developed in his theory of myths, but rather in the sense of fluid literary *topoi*, shaped and reshaped by both culture and history. For a detailed discussion of this concept, see E. R. Curtius, *Europäische Literatur und lateinisches Mittelalter*, 3rd. ed. (Bern: A. Francke, 1961), 79; and H. Levin, "Notes on Convention" in *Perspectives of Criticism*, Harvard Studies in Comparative Literature, no. 20 (Cambridge: Harvard University Press, 1950), 55–83.
5. For a thorough treatment of Pan mythology, see Patricia Merivale, *Pan the Goat-God: His Myth in Modern Times*, Harvard Studies in Comparative Literature, no. 30 (Cambridge: Harvard University Press, 1969), 1–16. I draw heavily from the work of Merivale in this outline of Pan mythology.
6. *The Homeric Hymns*, ed. T. W. Allen, W. R. Halliday, and E. E. Sikes (Oxford: Clarendon Press, 1936), 82–83. The translation is from *The Homeric Hymns*, trans. Daryl Hine (New York: Atheneum, 1972), 69–70.
7. *Metamorphoses*, trans. Frank Justus Miller, Loeb Classical Library (New York: G. P. Putnam's Sons, 1921), Book 1, ll. 705–12. All subsequent references to Ovid are from this text.
8. *The Hero with a Thousand Faces* (New York: Pantheon Books, 1949), 82.
9. *Ausführliches Lexikon der Griechischen und Römischen Mythologie*, (Leipzig: B. G. Teubner Verlag, 1897–1909), vol. 3.1, 1407.

10. *Die Mythologie der Griechen: Die Götter- und Menschheitsgeschichten* (Munich: Deutscher Taschenbuch Verlag, 1966), 139.

11. *Orphei Hymni*, ed. Guilelmus Quandt (Berlin: Weidmannsche Buchhandlung, 1955), 12–13. The translation is from *The Mystical Initiations; or, Hymns of Orpheus*, trans. Thomas Taylor (London: By the translator, 1787), 130. All subsequent references to the *Hymns of Orpheus* are from these texts.

12. John Milton, "Elegia Quinta in Adventus Veris," in *The Poetical Works of John Milton*, ed. Helen Darbishire (Oxford: Clarendon Press, 1955), vol. 2, 247, l. 122.

13. Ovid, *Met.*, Book 11.

14. Extensive studies of Orpheus mythology can be found in W. K. C. Guthrie, *Orpheus and the Greek Religion: A Study of the Orphic Movement*, 2nd ed. (London: Methuen, 1952); Jane Ellen Harrison, *Prolegomena to the Study of Greek Religion* 3rd ed. (Cambridge: University Press, 1922), 454–658; and Eva Kushner, *Le Mythe d'Orphée dans la littérature française contemporaine* (Paris: A. G. Nizet, 1961), 11–61. My outline of the Orphic myth draws heavily from these three sources.

15. *Ausführliches Lexikon*, vol. 3.1, 1078.

16. *Satires, Epistles and Ars poetica*, trans. H. Rushton Fairclough, Loeb Classical Library (Cambridge: Harvard University Press, 1942), 1. 391.

17. *Orpheus and the Greek Religion*, 40.

18. *Orphée, civilisateur de l'humanité* (Paris: Zalmoxis, 1939).

19. Guthrie, *Orpheus and the Greek Religion*, 30–31.

20. Eurypides, *Alcestis*, in *Eurypides*, ed. and trans. Arthur S. Way, Loeb Classical Library (New York: G. P. Putnam's Sons, 1922), 357–59; *Isocrates*, ed. and trans. G. Norlin and LaRue VanHook, Loeb Classical Library (Cambridge: Harvard University Press, 1961), vol. 3, 107, l. 8. Detailed discussions of the ancient literary sources for the tale of the victorious Orpheus are found in Maurice Bowra, "Orpheus and Eurydice," *The Classical Quarterly* 2 (1952): 113–26; and Jacques Heurgon, "Orphée et Eurydice avant Virgile," *Mélanges d'archéologie et d'histoire* 49 (1932): 6–60.

21. "The Return of Eurydice," *Classica et Mediaevalia* 23 (1962): 200. For studies of medieval poetry that incorporates the joyful resolution of the Orpheus myth, see Dronke, and J. B. Friedman, *Orpheus in the Middle Ages* (Cambridge: Harvard University Press, 1970), 116, 128, 165–66, 175.

22. *The Dismemberment of Orpheus* (New York: Oxford University Press, 1971), 5.

23. "Erotes," in *Collectanea Alexandrina*, ed. J. U. Powell (Oxford: Oxford University Press, 1925), 106–7. See also Albin Lesky, *Geschichte der Griechischen Literatur* (Bern and Munich: Francke Verlag, 1971), 155.

24. Additional sources for the burial of Orpheus and the ascension of the Orphic lyre include: Phanocles, "Erotes," 107; Philostratus, *The Life of Apollonius of Tyana*, ed. and trans. F. C. Conybeare, Loeb Classical Library

(Cambridge: Harvard University Press, 1960), vol. 4, 375; and Pseudo-Eratosthenes, "Catasterismi" in *Mythographi Graeci*, ed. A. Olivieri (Leipzig: B. G. Teubner, 1897), vol. 3, 28–29.

25. J. B. Frazer, *The Golden Bough, A Study in Magic and Religion*, 3rd ed. (London: McMillan and Co., 1963), vol. 7, 15; and Jane Ellen Harrison, *Themis, A Study of the Social Origins of Greek Religion* (Cambridge: The University Press, 1912; reprint ed., 1927), 523.

26. Frazer, *The Golden Bough*, vol. 7, 13; and Harrison, *Prolegomena*, 489–90.

27. *Philosophie der symbolischen Formen*, vol. 2, *Das mythische Denken* (Darmstadt: Wissenschaftliche Buchgesellschaft, 1964), 236.

28. *Le Mythe d'Orphée*, 47.

29. Guthrie, *Orpheus and the Greek Religion*, 47–48. This theory is supported in the works of André Boulanger, *Orphée, rapports de l'orphisme et du christianisme* (Paris: F. Rieder, 1925), pp. 30ff; Eduard Gerhard, *Über Orpheus und die Orphiker* (Berlin: Königliche Akademie der Wissenschaften, 1961), p. 11; and Kushner, 49.

30. *Orpheus and the Greek Religion*, 48.

31. *Le Mythe d'Orphée*, 55.

32. Ibid., 49.

33. Françoise Joukovsky, *Orphée et ses disciples dans la poésie française et néo-latine du XVIe siècle* (Geneva: Librairie Droz, 1970), 160–61.

34. "Le Regard d'Orphée," in *L'Espace littéraire* (Paris: Gallimard, 1955), 179.

35. Ibid., 181.

36. Ibid.

37. *Des Métaphores obsédentes au mythe personnel: introduction à la psychocritique* (Paris: Librairie José Corti, 1962), 134.

38. *The Dismemberment of Orpheus*, 5–6.

39. "Natura" in *Emblemata*, ed. Claude Minois (Leyden: Ex officina Plantiniana Raphelengii, 1608), 103.

40. Curt Sachs, *The History of Musical Instruments* (New York: W. W. Norton, 1940), 142.

41. Ibid.

42. Ibid., 129.

43. *The Greeks* (Baltimore: Penguin Books, 1957), 198.

44. *Larousse Encyclopaedia of Mythology* (New York: Prometheus Press, 1959), 185.

45. *L'Influence des littératures antiques sur la littérature française moderne: état des travaux* (New Haven: Yale University Press, 1941), 9.

46. Material for the brief outline of the translation, adaptation, and influence of Greek and Latin texts was culled from the following texts: Douglas Bush, *Mythology and the Renaissance Tradition in English Poetry* (New York: W. W. Norton, 1963), 25–35, 230–39; Emile Egger, *L'Hellénisme en*

France (Paris: Didier, 1869); J. B. Friedman, *Orpheus in the Middle Ages*; Joukovsky, *Orphée et ses disciples*, 18–27; Merivale, *Pan the Goat-God*, 1–49; Elizabeth Nitchie, *Vergil and the English Poets* (New York: Columbia University Press, 1919), 16–23, 62–69, 98–99; and Edward K. Rand, *Ovid and His Influence* (New York: Longmans, Green, 1928).

47. *Orpheus in the Middle Ages*, 90.

48. Ibid. See also 114–16.

49. For brief discussions of the nature and influence of the inextant *lai d'Orphée*, see Jean Frappier, *Histoire, mythes et symboles; études de littérature française* (Geneva: Droz, 1976), 22; Joukovsky, *Orphée et ses disciples*, 14; and Marian Edwardes, *A Summary of the Literatures of Modern Europe (England, France, Germany, Italy, Spain) from the Origins to 1400* (New York: E. P. Dutton, 1907; reprint ed. New York: Kraus Reprint Co., 1968), 228.

50. *Mythology and the Renaissance Tradition*, 6.

51. *Pan the Goat-God*, 5.

52. Jean Seznec, *The Survival of the Pagan Gods*, trans. B. F. Sessions (New York: Pantheon, 1953), 166.

53. *Pan the Goat-God*, 49.

54. The brief outline of Russian access to ancient Greek and Roman works is largely drawn from Thais S. Lindstrom, *A Concise History of Russian Literature* (New York: New York University Press, 1966), vol. 1, 32–34.

55. A. N. Afanas'ev, Поэтическія воззрѣнія славянъ на природу (Москва: К. Солдаменковъ, 1865), vol. 1, 695; vol. 2, 326. This source reveals that the Slavic myths contained such figures as льшіе, which were more akin to the satyrs and fauns or the germanic *Waldleute* and *Holzleute*. Slavic льшіе are also reported by J. G. Frazer in *The New Golden Bough*, ed. Theodore H. Gaster (New York: Criterion Books, 1959), 447. There existed a Slavic панъ who claimed kingship and divinity, but no musical power.

56. Lindstrom, *A Concise History*, 34.

57. "Миф об Орфее в творчестве Андрея Белого, Александра Блока и Вячеслава Иванова," New York, 1978 (Mimeographed), 1.

58. *L'Influence des littératures antiques*, 9.

59. *Pagan Myth and Christian Tradition in English Poetry; Jayne Lectures for 1967*, Memoirs of the American Philosophical Society, no. 72 (Philadelphia: American Philosophical Society, 1968), 1.

60. For studies of the adaptation and allegory of pagan myth in Christian literature, see: Bush, *Mythology and the Renaissance Tradition*, 3–83, 251–59; Bush, *Pagan Myth and Christian Tradition*; Frappier, *Histoire*; Lawrence Lerner, *The Uses of Nostalgia, Studies in Pastoral Poetry* (London: Chatto and Windus, 1972), 181–212; and Seznec, *Survival of the Pagan Gods*, 84–121.

61. Merivale offers a discussion of Pan-Christ, pp. 9–32.

62. For a study of the Pan-demon figure, see Merivale, 13–14.

63. J. B. Friedman provides detailed documentation of Orpheus-Christus and the Mosaic Orpheus, *Orpheus in the Middle Ages*, 13–36.

64. Merivale, 20, 22, 33, and 38, discusses the figure of Pan-monarch.

65. Pan as pastoral icon is treated by Renato Poggioli, *The Oaten Flute: Essays on Pastoral Poetry and the Pastoral Ideal* (Cambridge: Harvard University Press, 1975), 24–26; and Merivale, 5.

66. A critical study of these two themes is found in Lerner, *The Uses of Nostalgia*, 130–35; and J. H. Miller, "The Rewording Shell: Image and Emblem in Yeats' Early Poetry" (Paper presented at the Symposium on the Poetological Poem, Wuppertal, West Germany, November 1978).

67. See Kushner, *Le Mythe d'Orphée*, 40; and Friedman, *Orpheus in the Middle Ages*, 146–47.

Chapter 2

1. "Autre epistre dudit Cretin audit Charbonnier" and "Plainte sur le trepas de feu maistre Jehan Braconnier, dit Lourdault, chantre," in *Oeuvres poétiques* (Paris: Firmin-Didot, 1932), 214, l. 123, and 287, l. 179.

2. See especially J. A. de Baïf's "Hymne de Pan" in *Evres en rime de Ian Antoine de Baïf*, vol. 10 of *La Pléiade Françoise*, ed. Charles Joseph Marty-Laveaux (Paris: A. Lemerre, 1881–90; rpt. Geneva: Slatkine, 1965), 304.

3. *Oeuvres complètes*, Bibliotheque de la Pléiade (Paris: Editions Gallimard, 1958), vol. 1, 444, ll. 15–21.

4. *Ben Jonson*, ed. Herford and Simpson (Oxford: Clarendon Press, 1941), vol. 7, ll. 171, 176, 180, 184. All subsequent references to *Pans Anniversarie* are from this text.

5. "June," in *Spenser's Minor Poems*, vol. 1 of *The Poetical Works of Edmond Spenser*, ed. Ernest de Sélincourt (Oxford: Clarendon Press, 1910), ll. 70–72.

6. "Authorship, Anonymity, and *The Shepheardes Calender*," *Modern Language Quarterly* 40 (September 1979): 234.

7. "The New Poet Presents Himself; Spenser and the Idea of a Literary Career," *PMLA* 93 (October 1978): 899.

8. For an account of Pan's activity in the Battle of Marathon, see Roscher, *Ausführliches Lexikon der Griechischen und Römischen Mythologie* (Leipzig: B. G. Teubner Verlag, 1897–1909), vol. 3.1, 1347–1482.

9. "Authorship, Anonymity," 228.

10. *Orphée et ses disciples dans la poésie française et néo-latine du XVIe siècle* (Geneva: Librairie Droz, 1970), 36.

11. *Testament*, in *Oeuvres*, ed. André Lanly (Paris: Editions Champion, 1974), vol. 1, 114, ll. 633–36. See also Crétin's "Deploration Dudit Crétin sur le trepas de feu Okergan, Tresorier de Sainct Martin de Tours."

12. *Oeuvres*, ed. Ernest Hoepffner (Paris: Firmin-Didot, 1908–21), vol. 3, 1–142. Lines 2277–2644 directly concern the mythology of Orpheus.

13. *Oeuvres*, vol. 1, ll. 144–46.

14. *Oeuvres complètes*, vol. 12, ll. 269–80.

15. *Orphée et ses disciples*, 62.

16. "L'Art poétique," in *Oeuvres complètes de Boileau* (Paris: Société Les Belles Lettres, 1967), vol. 2, chant 4, ll. 133–52.

17. For detailed discussions of classical motifs and medieval Christian allegory in *Sir Orfeo*, see M. D. Bristol, "The Structure of the Middle English *Sir Orfeo*," *Papers in Language and Literature* 6 (Fall 1970): 339–47; Constance Davies, "Classical Threads in 'Orfeo,'" *The Modern Language Review* 56 (April 1961): 161–66; and J. B. Friedman, "Eurydice, Heurodis, and the Noon-Day Demon," *Speculum* 41 (January 1966): 22–29.

18. Kenneth R. R. Gros Louis, "The Significance of Sir Orfeo's Self-Exile," *The Review of English Studies* 18 (August 1967): 247.

19. "An Interpretation of *Sir Orfeo*," *Leeds Studies in English* 6 (1972): 2.

20. *Sir Orfeo*, ed. A. J. Bliss (London: Oxford University Press, 1954), ll. 593–95.

21. *The Complete Works*, ed. G. B. Harrison (New York: Harcourt, Brace and World, 1968), act 3, sc. 1, ll. 3–5.

22. *Sidney's Apologie for Poetrie*, ed. J. Churton Collins (Oxford: The Clarendon Press, 1907), 11.

23. "L'Art poétique," chant 1, l. 3.

24. *Anatomy of Criticism: Four Essays* (Princeton: Princeton University Press, 1971), 55.

25. *Orphée et ses disciples*, 8.

26. *Mythology and the Renaissance Tradition in English Poetry* (New York: W. W. Norton, 1963), 296. Henri Peyre also notes "combien lâches sont les rapports entre la littérature française du XVIIe siècle et celle de l'antiquité," in *Le Classicisme français* (New York: Editions de la Maison Française, 1942), 32.

27. See "Ода на день врачногосочетания их императорских высочеств государя великого князя Петра Федорьвича . . ." (104, ll. 121–26) and "Ода на прибытие ее величества великая государыне императрицы Елизаветы Петровны по коронации" (88, ll. 17–20), in *Избранные произведения* (Москва-Ленинград: Библиотека Поета, 1965).

28. *The Poems and Letters of Andrew Marvell*, ed. H. M. Margoliouth, vol. 1 (Oxford: The Clarendon Press, 1927), 18.

29. "Theorie im Gedicht und Theorie als Gedicht," in *Literaturwissenschaft zwischen Extremen* (Berlin: Walter de Gruyter, 1977), 151–56.

30. In *Discriminations: Further Concepts of Criticism* (New Haven: Yale University Press, 1970), 261.

31. "Authorship, Anonymity," 219.

32. *Icarus: The Image of the Artist in French Romanticism* (Cambridge: Harvard University Press, 1961), 40.

33. Ibid., 40–45.

34. Ibid., 49.

35. *The Mirror and the Lamp: Romantic Theory and the Critical Tradition* (London and New York: Oxford University Press, 1953; reprint ed., 1974).

See especially "Science and Poetry in Romantic Criticism," 298–335.

36. *The Hero in French Romantic Literature* (Athens, Ga.: University of Georgia Press, 1959), 76–77.

37. Guillaume Apollinaire makes this very point in his 1912 poem, "Zone": "Tu lis les prospectus les catalogues les affiches qui chantent tout haut / Voilà la poésie ce matin et pour la prose il y a les journaux," in *Oeuvres poétiques*, Bibliothèque de la Pléiade (Paris: Editions Gallimard, 1956), 39, ll. 12–13.

38. *Dionysus and the City: Modernism in Twentieth Century Poetry* (New York: Oxford University Press, 1970), 60.

39. "Poetic Knowledge in Mallarmé's 'Prose pour des Esseintes,'" (Paper presented at the Symposium on the Poetological Poem, Wuppertal, West Germany, November 1978).

40. *Die Struktur der modernen Lyrik* (Hamburg: Rowohlt, 1956; reprint ed., 1977), 139.

41. *Romantic Image* (London: Routledge and Kegan Paul, 1957), 142.

42. Ibid., 143.

43. "Hymn of Pan," in *Endymion*, in *The Poetical Works of John Keats*, ed. H. W. Garrod (London: Oxford University Press, 1956), 61, ll. 246, 262, 278.

44. "Песнь Четвертая," Руслан и Людмила ("Fourth Song," *Ruslan and Liudmila*), in Полное собрание сочинений, (Москва: Издательство Академии Наук СССР, 1956–58), том 4, 50–51. All further references to the poetry of Pushkin are from this text.

45. *Oeuvres poétiques*, ed. Pierre Albouy, Bibliothèque de la Pléiade (Paris: Editions Gallimard, 1964), vol. 1, 803–4, ll. 1–3, 6–7. All subsequent references to "Pan" and "Le Poëte" are from this text. See also Hugo's "Les Mages" in which the mythic Pan figures, although not as a poetic persona. Much as "Pan," "Les Mages" is a confrontational work addressed to the poet's audience, and which begins: "Pourquoi donc faites-vous des prêtres / Quand vous en avez parmi vous?" (vol. 2, 780, ll. 1–2). His poet-priests are then described as "ceux que Pan formidable enivre" (l. 27).

46. *La Légende des siècles*, ed. Jacques Truchet, Bibliothèque de la Pléiade (Paris: Editions Gallimard, 1950), 417, ll. 7, 19.

47. Albert Py, *Les Mythes grecs dans la poésie de Victor Hugo* (Geneva: Librairie Droz, 1963), 186.

48. *The Complete Works of Percy Bysshe Shelley*, ed. R. Ingpen and W. E. Peck (New York: Gordian Press, 1965), vol. 4, 69, l. 58. All further references to the poetry of Shelley are from this text.

49. This point has been made by Milton Wilson, *Shelley's Later Poetry, A Study of the Prophetic Imagination* (New York: Columbia University Press, 1959), 34; and by Earl Wasserman, *Shelley, a Critical Reading* (Baltimore: Johns Hopkins University Press, 1971), 52.

50. *Poetical Works* (London: Oxford University Press, 1905; reprint ed.,

1967), 621, ll. 66, 83. All further references to the poetry of Browning are from this text.

51. *Complete Works of Elizabeth Barrett Browning*, ed. C. Porter and H. A. Clarke (New York: Thomas G. Crowell, 1900), vol. 6, 44.

Chapter 3

1. "The Artist as Hero: A Disconsolate Chimera," in *The Lion and the Honeycomb: Essays in Solicitude and Critique* (New York: Harcourt, Brace, 1955), 44.
2. *The Hero in French Decadent Literature* (Athens, Ga.: University of Georgia Press, 1961), 105.
3. *La Préface de "Mademoiselle de Maupin,"* ed. Georges Matoré (Paris: Librairie Droz, 1946) and "Hérésies artistiques," in *Oeuvres complètes*, ed. H. Mondor and G. Jean-Aubry, Bibliothèque de la Pléiade (Paris: Editions Gallimard, 1945), 257–60.
4. "Existence du Symbolisme," in *Oeuvres de Paul Valéry*, vol. 1, ed. Jean Hytier, Editions de la Pléiade (Paris: Gallimard, 1968), 691.
5. *La Préface de "Mademoiselle de Maupin,"* 31.
6. I draw from the following sources in my outline of the Pierrot figure: Kay Dick, *Pierrot* (London: Hutchinson, 1960); Maurice Sand, *The History of the Harlequinade*, vol. 1 (Philadelphia, 1915; reprint ed., New York and London: Benjamin Bloom, 1968), 192–208; and Robert F. Storey, *Pierrot, A Critical History of a Mask* (Princeton: Princeton University Press, 1978).
7. *Pierrot*, 30.
8. G. Sand, "Preface," in *Masques et Bouffons* by Maurice Sand (Paris: Michel Lévy, 1860).
9. "Etude du personnage de Pierrot" (Ph.D. diss., Stanford University, 1976).
10. *The Clown's Grail* (London: Dennis Dobson, 1948), 94.
11. *Portrait de l'artiste en saltimbanque* (Geneva: Editions d'Art Albert Skira, 1970), 9.
12. Ibid., 9, 10.
13. For a detailed comparative study of European clowns and their reception throughout history, see Enid Welsford, *The Fool: His Social and Literary History* (London: Faber and Faber, 1935).
14. *The Poetry of Hart Crane: A Critical Study* (Princeton: Princeton University Press, 1967), 58.
15. *Anatomy of Criticism: Four Essays* (Princeton: Princeton University Press, 1971), 41–45.
16. *Emaux et Camées* (Paris: Bibliothèque Charpentier, 1918), ll. 61–68. All further references to the poetry of Gautier will be from this text.

17. *Jules Laforgue and the Ironic Inheritance* (New York: Oxford University Press, 1953), 143.
18. "Pierrots," in *Oeuvres complètes de Jules Laforgue* (Paris: Mercure de France, 1951), ll. 3-8, 13-16. All further references to the poetry of Laforgue will be from this text.
19. "Pierrot et Fin de Siècle," in *Romantic Mythologies*, ed. Ian Fletcher (London: Routledge and Kegan Paul, 1967), 218.
20. *Moralités légendaires* (Paris: Mercure de France, 1964), 158. All further references to "Pan et la Syrinx" will be from this text.
21. This declaration will be echoed in the opening lines of Mallarmé's "L'Après-midi d'un faune"—"Ces nymphes, je les veux perpétuer." Mallarmé elaborates on the theme of the artist caught between the pain and pleasure of reverie in solitude, a topic that will be treated later in this chapter.
22. *The Hero with a Thousand Faces*, Bollingen Series, no. 17 (New York: Pantheon Books, 1949), 388.
23. *Oeuvres poétiques complètes*. Bibliothèque de la Pléiade (Paris: Editions Gallimard, 1948), 200. All further references to the poetry of Verlaine will be from this text.
24. The third line of "Pierrot" also echoes the Laforgue sequences in its reworking of the traditional tune, "Au Clair de la lune." The folk lyrics, "Ma chandelle est morte. Je n'ai plus de feu." are altered by Laforgue in "Complainte de Lord Pierrot" to read "Ma cervelle est morte. Que le Christ l'emporte!" Now, in Verlaine, the lines are synthesized and become "Sa gaîté, comme sa chandelle, hélas! est morte."
25. Robert F. Storey, "Verlaine's Pierrots," *Romance Notes* 20 (1980): 228.
26. *Portrait de l'artiste en saltimbanque* (Geneva: Editions d'Art Albert Skira, 1970), p. 8.
27. "The Poet as Clown: Variations on a Theme in Nineteenth-Century French Poetry," *Orbis Literarum* 33 (1978): 246.
28. *Mallarmé* (Chicago: University of Chicago Press, 1970), 91.
29. *Oeuvres complètes*, 1416. The later version is found on p. 31. All further references to "Le Pitre châtié" and to "L'Après-midi d'un faune" are from this text.
30. *Mallarmé e l'estetica* (Milan: U. Mursia, 1969), 56.
31. "Dilemma and Dramatic Structure in Mallarmé's Parnasse Poems," *The French Review* 46 (Spring 1973): 73.
32. *Mallarmé e l'estetica*, 57.
33. "Mallarmé's Faun: Hero, or Anti-Hero?," *The Romanic Review* 44 (March 1973): 114.
34. Austin, "'L'Après-midi d'un faune,' essai d'explication," *Synthèses* (December–January 1968): 25; and Cohn, *Toward the Poems of Mallarmé* (Berkeley and Los Angeles: University of California Press, 1965), 13, 14.
35. "'L'Après-midi d'un faune,' essai d'explication," 24-35.

36. *Mallarmé*, 166.
37. "Mallarmé's Faun: Hero or Anti-Hero?," 112.
38. Ibid., 117.
39. Ibid., 124.
40. See especially Théodore de Banville's "Adieu, Paniers" in "Odes funambulesques," *Poésies complètes* (Paris: Charpentier, 1883), vol. 1, 29, which begins:

> Lyre d'argent, gagne-pain trop précaire,
> Dont les chansons n'ont qu'un maigre salaire,
> Je vous délaisse et je vous dis adieu.
> Mieux vaut cent fois jeter nos vers au feu
> Et fuir bien loin ce métier de galère.

41. For an analysis of the Orphic myth in the prose of Nerval, see Walter Strauss, *Descent and Return; the Orphic Theme in Modern Literature* (Cambridge: Harvard University Press, 1971), 50–80.
42. "The Poet and his Moira: 'El Desdichado,'" *PMLA* 75 (September 1960): 402–9.
43. "Images, Structure et Thèmes dans 'El Desdichado,'" *Modern Language Review* 58 (1958): 509.
44. *Oeuvres*, Bibliothèque de la Pléiade (Paris: Editions Gallimard, 1952), vol. 1, 2. All further references to the poetry of Nerval are from this text.
45. For detailed discussions of the classical and medieval allusions in "El Desdichado," see Gérard and Kneller.
46. In this I disagree with the autobiographical criticism of John Senior, *The Way Down and Out: The Occult in Symbolist Literature* (Ithaca: Cornell University Press, 1959), 74–88. His explication of "El Desdichado" is founded on the premise that "there is no separation possible between Gérard de Nerval and his work" (74).
47. *Igitur* (Paris: Librairie Gallimard, 1965), 53. All further references to *Igitur* are from this text.
48. 18 February 1869, *Correspondance 1862–1871*, ed. Henri Mondor (Paris: Gallimard, 1959), 301.
49. *Vers une explication rationnelle du "Coup de dés"* (Paris: Librairie José Corti, 1953), 54.
50. 14 May 1867, *Correspondance 1862–1871*, 242. For a comparison of the biographical Mallarmé, as seen through his correspondence, with the work of the poet, see Guy Michaud, *Mallarmé: l'homme et l'oeuvre* (Paris: Hatier, 1953). Fowlie finds that "the prose of *Igitur* may be considered a close note-taking on Mallarmé's dangerous psychic crisis between 1865 and 1870, which was in many ways the dream of self-annihilation" (*Mallarmé*, 118).
51. *Pure Poetry: Studies in French Poetic Theory and Practice 1746–1945* (Oxford: Clarendon Press, 1971), 142–143.
52. Ibid., 143.

53. In this context, it is interesting to note Mallarmé's 18 February 1869 letter to Cazalis in which the poet writes: ". . . mon cerveau, envahi par le Rêve, se refusant à ses fonctions extérieurs qui ne le sollicitaient plus, allait périr dans son insomnie permanente; j'ai imploré la grand Nuit, qui m'a exaucé et a étendu ses ténèbres. La première phase de ma vie a été finie. La conscience, excédée d'ombres, se réveille, lentement, formant un homme nouveau, et doit retrouver mon Rêve après la création de ce dernier. Cela durera quelques années pendant lesquelles *j'ai à revivre la vie de l'humanité depuis mon enfance et prenant conscience d'elle-même*" (*Correspondance 1862–1871*, 301) [emphasis mine].
54. *Pure Poetry*, 141.
55. *Descent and Return*, 120.
56. Ibid., 138.
57. *Le Soleil des morts* (Paris: Ollendorff, 1924), 24.

Chapter 4

1. *The Influence of French Symbolism on Russian Poetry* (The Hague: Mouton, 1958). Donchin's thesis is also supported by C. M. Bowra, *The Heritage of Symbolism* (London: Macmillan, 1943; reprint ed. New York: Saint Martin's Press, 1962); O. A. Maslenikov, *The Frenzied Poets: Andrei Biely and the Russian Symbolists* (Berkeley and Los Angeles: University of California Press, 1952); and R. Poggioli, *The Russian Poets, 1890–1930* (Cambridge: Harvard University Press, 1960).
2. "Genius and Madness: The Return of the Romantic Concept of the Poet in Russia at the End of the Nineteenth Century," in *American Contributions to the Seventh International Congress of Slavists*, ed. Victor Terras (The Hague: Mouton, 1963), 253.
3. "Images of the Poet and of Poetry in Slavic Romanticism and Neo-Romanticism," in *American Contributions to the Fifth International Congress of Slavists* (The Hague: Mouton, 1963), vol. 2, 79.
4. "Masks and Doubles in Blok's Early Poetry," *Russian Language Journal* 30 (Winter 1976): 60.
5. "The Archetype of the Fool in Russian Literature," *Canadian Slavonic Papers* 15 (Autumn 1973), 245–73. See also Thompson, "Russian Holy Fools and Shamanism," *American Contributions to the Eighth International Congress of Slavists*, ed. Victor Terras (Columbus, Ohio: Slavica Publishers, 1978), vol. 2, 691–706.
6. "The Archetype of the Fool in Russian Literature," 248.
7. I draw heavily from Thompson in the articles cited above for the outline of the Russian holy fool.
8. "Il Follo Sacro e le sue trasformazioni nella letteratura russa," *Strumenti Critici* 9 (June 1975): 171–72.
9. *The Court Masque: A Study in the Relationship between Poetry and the*

Revels (Cambridge: Cambridge University Press, 1927), 381. See also Welsford, *The Fool: His Social and Literary History* (London: Faber and Faber, 1935), 243–70. For a discussion of the contact between the Elizabethan court fool and the Italian *commedia*'s *zanni*, see Olive M. Busby, *Studies in the Development of the Fool in the Elizabethan Drama* (London: Oxford University Press, 1923).

10. *Стихотворения в двух томах* (*Poetry in Two Volumes*) (Ленинград: Художественная Литература, 1972), vol. 1, 203. All further references to the poetry of Blok are from this text.

11. The sketch of the *commedia* Harlequin is drawn from Giacomo Oreglia, *The Commedia dell'arte* (London: Methuen, 1968), 56–70; and Maurice Sand, *The History of the Harlequinade* (Philadelphia: J. B. Lippincott, 1915; reprint ed., New York: B. Blom, 1968), vol. 1, pp. 57–65. This text is a translation of Sand, *Masques et bouffons* (Paris: Michel Lévy, 1860).

12. *Jules Laforgue and the Ironic Inheritance* (New York: Oxford University Press, 1953), 189.

13. *Собрание сочинений в восьми томах* (*Collected Works in Eight Volumes*) (Москва-Ленинград: Художественная Литература, 1960–1963), vol 8, p 46

14. Compare the bestial metaphor with that of "Двойник": "О, люди! О, звери!" ("Oh, people! Oh, beasts!").

15. An interesting parallel to Blok's poem can be found in Boris Pasternak's "Гамлет" ("Hamlet"), in which the poet is an unwilling actor, forced to play a false role before an audience of "a thousand binoculars on an axis": "На меня наставлен сумрак ночи / Тысячью биноклей на оси."

16. "Masks and Doubles in Blok's Early Poetry," 73.

17. *En attendant Godot* (Paris: Editions du Minuit, 1952), 105.

18. "The Great Escape: Principal Themes in Valerij Brjusov's Poetry," *Slavic and East European Journal* 12 (Winter 1968): 407–23.

19. *Metamorphoses*, trans. Frank Justus Miller, Loeb Classical Library (New York: G. P. Putnam's Sons, 1921), book 10, ll. 56–57.

20. *Собрание сочинений* (*Collected Works*) (Москва: Художественная Литература, 1973), vol. 1, 385, ll. 13–14. All further references to the poetry of Briusov are from this text.

21. *The Double Image: Concepts of the Poet in Slavic Literature* (Baltimore: Johns Hopkins University Press, 1964), 77.

Chapter 5

1. Benamou, *Wallace Stevens and the Symbolist Imagination* (Princeton: Princeton University Press, 1972); Fuchs, *The Comic Spirit of Wallace Stevens* (Durham, NC: Duke University Press, 1963), 3–30; Storey, *Pierrot: A Critical History of a Mask* (Princeton: Princeton University Press, 1978), 168–81;

Ramsey, *Jules Laforgue and the Ironic Inheritance* (New York: Oxford University Press, 1953), 213–22; Spears, *Hart Crane*, University of Minnesota Pamphlets on American Writers, no. 47 (Minneapolis: University of Minnesota Press, 1965); Lewis, *The Poetry of Hart Crane: A Critical Study* (Princeton: Princeton University Press, 1967), 61–65.

See also Robert Buttel, "Dandy, Eccentric, Clown," in *Wallace Stevens: The Making of "Harmonium"* (Princeton: Princeton University Press, 1967), 169–202; H. R. Hays, "Laforgue and Stevens," *Romanic Review* 25 (1934): 242–48; Warren Ramsey, "Wallace Stevens and Some French Poets," *Trinity Review* 8 (May 1954): 36–40; René Taupin, *L'Influence du symbolisme français sur la poésie américaine* (de 1910 à 1920) (Paris: H. Champion, 1929); and Linda Ross Wheat, "A Comparative Study of Jules Laforgue and Hart Crane," (Ph.D. diss., Vanderbilt University, 1970).

2. *The Collected Poems of Wallace Stevens* (New York: Alfred Knopf, 1972), 27. All following references to the poetry of Wallace Stevens are from this text.

3. *Complete Poems*, ed. Waldo Frank (Garden City, N.Y.: Doubleday, 1966), 4, 11, 144. All further references to the poetry of Hart Crane are from this text.

4. To Gorham Munson, 21 November 1921, *The Letters of Hart Crane*, ed. Brom Weber (New York: Hermitage House, 1952; rpt., Berkeley and Los Angeles: University of California Press, 1965), 71.

5. *The Clairvoyant Eye, The Poetry and Poetics of Wallace Stevens* (Baton Rouge: Louisiana State University Press, 1965), 272.

6. Ibid., 44.

7. To Hi Simons, 8 July 1941, *Letters of Wallace Stevens*, ed. Holly Stevens (New York: Alfred Knopf, 1966), 391. See also To Leonard C. van Geyzel, 24 May 1940, *Letters*, 355; and To Elsie Moll, 7 December 1908, *Letters*, 110.

8. *The Comic Spirit of Wallace Stevens*, 9.

9. Ibid., 7.

10. *Wallace Stevens: The Poems of Our Climate* (Ithaca: Cornell University Press, 1976), 36.

11. Discussions of the origin of the figure of Crispin are found in Riddel, *The Clairvoyant Eye*, 95; Robert F. Storey, *Pierrot*, 81; and A. Walton Litz, *Introspective Voyager: The Poetic Development of Wallace Stevens* (New York: Oxford University Press, 1972), 122–24.

12. *Pierrot*, 181, n. 41.

13. *L'Influence du symbolisme français sur la poésie américaine*, 275.

14. *The Clairvoyant Eye*, 174.

15. "Le Thème du héros dans la poésie de Wallace Stevens," *Etudes Anglaises* 12 (July–September 1959): 230.

16. *The Clairvoyant Eye*, 57.

17. To Mother, 31 October 1917, *Letters*, 10; To William Wright, 5 Feb-

ruary 1920, *Letters*, 33; To Gorham Munson, 20 October 1920, *Letters*, 45; To Gorham Munson, 19 April 1922, *Letters*, 84; To Charmion Wiegand, 6 May 1922, *Letters*, 85–86; and To Allen Tate, 16 May 1922, *Letters*, 88. See also John Unterecker, *Voyager, A Life of Hart Crane* (New York: Farrar, Straus and Giroux, 1969), 59.

18. *Hart Crane: A Biographical and Critical Study* (New York: Bodley Press, 1948), 107. See also 144–150.

19. Holton, "'A Baudelairesque Thing': The Directions of Hart Crane's 'Black Tambourine,'" *Criticism* 9 (Summer 1967): 218–19; Hutson, "Exile Guise: Irony and Hart Crane," *Mosaic* 2 (Summer 1969): 71–74.

20. "'A Baudelairesque Thing,'" 218–19.

21. Ibid., 219.

22. *The Poetical Works of John Keats*, ed. H. W. Garrod (London: Oxford University Press, 1956), 204, sec. 33, ll. 2–3.

23. *The Poetry of Hart Crane*, 26.

24. "'A Baudelairesque Thing,'" 227.

25. To Charmion Wiegand, 6 May 1922, *Letters*, 85.

26. To William Wright, 17 October 1921, *Letters*, 68.

27. Herbert Leibowitz, *Hart Crane: An Introduction to the Poetry* (New York: Columbia University Press, 1968), 39.

28. *The Poetry of Hart Crane*, 78–79.

29. Ibid., 58, 61–65.

30. Ibid., 59.

31. Hutson, "Exile Guise," 71.

32. *Hart's Bridge* (Urbana: University of Illinois Press, 1972), 8.

33. "'A Baudelairesque Thing,'" 216.

34. Ibid., 227–228.

35. *Hart's Bridge*, p. 8.

36. *Hart Crane's Sanskrit Charge: A Study of "The Bridge"* (Ithaca: Cornell University Press, 1960), 19.

37. Ibid., 30.

38. *The Poetry of Hart Crane*, 256.

39. Ibid., 284.

40. Ibid., 250.

41. *Hart Crane's Sanskrit Charge*, 75–76.

42. Ibid., 85.

43. The triple significance of the "Genoese" has been noted by Dembo, ibid., 123.

44. *The Hero with a Thousand Faces*, Bollingen Series, no. 17 (New York: Pantheon Books, 1949), 388–91.

45. Ibid., 383.

Chapter 6

1. *Myth in Primitive Psychology* (New York: W. W. Norton, 1926), 19.
2. *The Hero with a Thousand Faces*, Bollingen Series, no. 17 (New York: Pantheon Books, 1949), 382.
3. *Themis, A Study of the Social Origins of Greek Religion* (Cambridge: The University Press, 1912; reprint edition, 1927), 257.
4. *Philosophie der symbolischen Formen*, vol. 2, *Das mythische Denken* (Darmstadt: Wissenschaftliche Buchgesellschaft, 1964), 209–10.
5. For a discussion of the concept of the personal god and one's mythic self-conception, see ibid., 238–61.
6. *The Archetypes and the Collective Unconscious*, vol. 9.1 of *The Collected Works of C. G. Jung*, trans. R. T. C. Hull, Bollingen Series, no. 20 (New York: Pantheon Books, 1959), 17.
7. *Myths and Myth-Makers* (Boston: Houghton Mifflin, 1872), p. 32.
8. *Anatomy of Criticism: Four Essays* (Princeton: Princeton University Press, 1971), 33–52.

Bibliography

PRIMARY SOURCES

Greek and Latin

Alciati, Andrea. *Emblemata.* Edited by Claude Minois. Leyden: Ex officina Plantiniana Raphelengii, 1608.
Euripides. *Euripides.* Edited and translated by Arthur S. Way. Vol. 4, *Alcestis.* Loeb Classical Library. New York: G. P. Putnam's Sons, 1922.
Homer. *Chapman's Homer.* Edited by Allardyce Nicoll. Translated by George Chapman. Bollingen Series, vol. 41. New York: Pantheon Books, 1956.
———. *The Homeric Hymns.* Edited by T. W. Allen, W. R. Halliday, and E. E. Sikes. Oxford: Clarendon Press, 1936.
———. *The Homeric Hymns.* Translated by Daryl Hine. New York: Atheneum, 1972.
Horace. *Satires, Epistles and Ars poetica.* Translated by H. Rushton Fairclough. Loeb Classical Library. Cambridge: Harvard University Press, 1942.
Isocrates. *Isocrates.* 3 vols. Edited and translated by G. Norlin and LaRue VanHook. Loeb Classical Library. Cambridge: Harvard University Press, 1961.
Orpheus. *The Mystical Initiations; or, Hymns of Orpheus.* Translated by Thomas Taylor. London: By the translator, 1787.
———. *Orphei hymni.* Edited by Guilelmus Quandt. Berlin: Weidmannsche Buchhandlung, 1955.
Ovid. *Metamorphoses.* 2 vols. Translated by Frank Justus Miller. Loeb Classical Library. New York: G. P. Putnam's Sons, 1921.
———. *Shakespeare's Ovid: The Metamorphoses.* Edited by W. H. D. Rouse. Translated by Arthur Golding. London: Willyan Series, 1567; reprint ed., Carbondale, Illinois: Southern Illinois University Press, 1961.
Phanocles. "Erotes." In *Collectanea Alexandrina,* edited by J. U. Powell. Oxford: Oxford University Press, 1925.

Philostratus. *The Life of Apollonius of Tyana*. 2 vols. Edited and translated by F. C. Conybeare. Loeb Classical Library. Cambridge: Harvard University Press, 1960.
Pseudo-Eratosthenes. "Catasterismi." Vol. 3 of *Mythographi Graeci*. 5 vols. Edited by Alessandro Olivieri. Leipzig: B. G. Teubner, 1897.
Virgil. *Georgics*. Translated by H. Rushton Fairclough. Loeb Classical Library. Cambridge: Harvard University Press, 1950.

French

Apollinaire, Guillaume. *Oeuvres poétiques*. Bibliothèque de la Pléiade. Paris: Editions Gallimard, 1956.
Baïf, Jean Antoine de. *La Pléiade Françoise*, edited by Charles Joseph Marty-Laveaux. *Evres en rime de Ian Antoine de Baif*. Vol. 10. Paris: A. Lemerre, 1881–90; reprint ed. Geneva: Slatkine, 1965.
Banville, Théodore de. *Poésies complètes*. 3 vols. Paris: Charpentier, 1883.
Beckett, Samuel. *En attendant Godot*. Paris: Editions de Minuit, 1952.
Boileau-Despréaux, Nicolas. *Oeuvres complètes de Boileau*. 7 vol. Paris: Société Les Belles Lettres, 1967.
Crétin, Guillaume. *Oeuvres poétiques*. Paris: Firmin-Didot, 1932.
duBellay, Joachim. *Oeuvres poétiques*. Paris: Librairie Hachette, 1919.
Gautier, Théophile. *Emaux et Camées*. Paris: Bibliothèque Charpentier, 1918.
———. *La Préface de "Mademoiselle de Maupin."* Edited by Georges Matoré. Paris: Librairie Droz, 1946.
Hugo, Victor. *La Légende des siècles*. Edited by Jacques Truchet. Bibliothèque de la Pléiade. Paris: Editions Gallimard, 1950.
———. *Oeuvres poétiques*. 2 vols. Edited by Pierre Albouy. Bibliothèque de la Pléiade. Paris: Editions Gallimard, 1964.
Huysmans, Joris-Karl. *A Rebours*. Paris: Fasquelle Editeurs, 1970.
Laforgue, Jules. *Moralités légendaires*. Paris: Mercure de France, 1964.
———. *Oeuvres complètes de Jules Laforgue*. Paris: Mercure de France, 1951.
Machaut, Guillaume de. *Oeuvres*. 3 vols. Edited by Ernest Hoepffner. Paris: Firmin-Didot, 1918–21.
Mallarmé, Stéphane. *Correspondance 1862–1871*. Edited by Henri Mondor. Paris: Gallimard, 1959.
———. *Igitur*. Paris: Librairie Gallimard, 1965.
———. *Oeuvres complètes*. Edited by Henri Mondor and G. Jean-Aubry. Bibliothèque de la Pléiade. Paris: Editions Gallimard, 1945.
Mauclair, Camille. *Le Soleil des Morts*. Paris: Ollendorff, 1924.
Nerval, Gérard de. *Oeuvres*. 2 vols. Bibliothèque de la Pléiade. Paris: Editions Gallimard, 1952.
Ronsard, Pierre de. *Oeuvres complètes*. 2 vols. Bibliothèque de la Pléiade. Paris: Editions Gallimard, 1958.

Valéry, Paul. *Oeuvres de Paul Valéry.* Edited by Jean Hytier. Bibliothèque de la Pléiade. Paris: Editions Gallimard, 1968.

Verlaine, Paul. *Oeuvres poétiques complètes.* Bibliothèque de la Pléiade. Paris: Editions Gallimard, 1948.

Villon, François. *Oeuvres.* Edited by André Lanly. Paris: Editions Champion, 1974.

Russian

Блок, Александр. *Собрание сочинений в восьми томах.* Москва-Ленинград: Художественная Литература, 1960–1963.

———. *Стихотворения в двух томах.* Ленинград: Художественная Литература, 1972.

Брюсов, Валерий. *Собрание сочинений.* 7 тома. Москва: Художественная Литература, 1973.

Лермонтов, М. Ю. *Избранные произведения.* 2 тома. Москва-Ленинград: Библиотека Поэта, 1964.

Ломоносов, М. В. *Избранные произведения.* Москва-Ленинград: Библиотека Поэта, 1965.

Пушкин, А. С. *Полное собрание сочинений.* 10 тома. москва: Издательство Академии Наук СССР, 1956–58.

British and American

Browning, Elizabeth Barrett. *Complete Works of Elizabeth Barrett Browning.* 6 vols. Edited by Charlotte Porter and Helen A. Clarke. New York: Thomas G. Crowell, 1900.

Browning, Robert. *Poetical Works.* London: Oxford University Press, 1905; reprint ed., 1967.

Crane, Hart. *Complete Poems.* Edited by Waldo Frank. Garden City, New York: Doubleday, 1966.

———. *The Letters of Hart Crane.* Edited by Brom Weber. New York: Hermitage House, 1952; reprint ed., Berkeley and Los Angeles: University of California Press, 1965.

Jonson, Ben. *Ben Jonson.* 11 vols. Edited by Herford and Simpson. Oxford: The Clarendon Press, 1941.

Keats, John. *The Poetical Works of John Keats.* Edited by H. W. Garrod. London: Oxford University Press, 1956.

Marvell, Andrew. *The Poems and Letters of Andrew Marvell.* 2 vols. Edited by H. M. Margoliouth. Oxford: The Clarendon Press, 1927.

Milton, John. *The Poetical Works of John Milton.* Edited by Helen Darbishire. Oxford: The Clarendon Press, 1955.

Shakespeare, William. *The Complete Works.* Edited by G. B. Harrison. New York: Harcourt, Brace and World, 1968.

Shelley, Percy Bysshe. *The Complete Works of Percy Bysshe Shelley*. 10 vols. Edited by Robert Ingpen and Walter E. Peck. New York: Gordian Press, 1965.
Sidney, Philip. *Apologie for Poetrie*. Edited by J. Churton Collins. Oxford: The Clarendon Press, 1907.
Sir Orfeo. Edited by A. J. Bliss. London: Oxford University Press, 1954.
Spenser, Edmond. *The Poetical Works of Edmond Spenser*. Vol. 1, *Spenser's Minor Poems*. Edited by Ernest de Sélincourt. Oxford: The Clarendon Press, 1910.
Stevens, Wallace. *The Collected Poems of Wallace Stevens*. New York: Alfred A. Knopf, 1972.
———. *Letters of Wallace Stevens*. Edited by Holly Stevens. New York: Alfred A. Knopf, 1972.

SECONDARY SOURCES

Abrams, M. H. *The Mirror and the Lamp: Romantic Theory and the Critical Tradition*. London: Oxford University Press, 1953; reprint ed., 1974.
Afanas'ev, A. N. Поэтическія воззрѣнія славянъ на природу. 3 тома. Москва: К. Солдаменков, 1865.
Austin, R. J. "'L'Après-midi d'un faune,' essai d'explication." *Synthèses* (December–January 1968): 24–35.
Benamou, Michel. "Le Thème du héros dans la poésie de Wallace Stevens." *Etudes Anglaises* 12 (July–September 1959): 222–30.
———. *Wallace Stevens and the Symbolist Imagination*. Princeton: Princeton University Press, 1972.
Blackmur, R. P. *The Lion and the Honeycomb: Essays in Solicitude and Critique*. New York: Harcourt, Brace, 1955.
Blanchot, Maurice. *L'Espace littéraire*. Paris: Gallimard, 1955.
Bloom, Harold. *Wallace Stevens, The Poems of Our Climate*. Ithaca: Cornell University Press, 1976.
Boulanger, André. *Orphée; rapports de l'orphisme et du christianisme*. Paris: F. Rieder, 1925.
Bowra, C. M. *The Heritage of Symbolism*. London: Macmillan, 1943; reprint edition, New York: Saint Martin's Press, 1962.
Bowra, Maurice. "Orpheus and Eurydice." *The Classical Quarterly* 2 (1952): 113–26.
Bristol, Michael D. "The Structure of the Middle English *Sir Orfeo*." *Papers in Language and Literature* 6 (Fall 1970): 339–47.
Busby, Olive M. *Studies in the Development of the Fool in the Elizabethan Drama*. London: Oxford University Press, 1923.
Bush, Douglas. *Mythology and the Renaissance Tradition in English Poetry*. New York: W. W. Norton, 1963.

———. *Pagan Myth and Christian Tradition in English Poetry; Jayne Lectures for 1967.* Memoirs of the American Philosophical Society, no. 72. Philadelphia: American Philosophical Society, 1968.
Buttel, Robert. *Wallace Stevens, The Making of "Harmonium."* Princeton: Princeton University Press, 1967.
Campbell, Joseph. *The Hero with a Thousand Faces.* Bollingen Series, no. 17. New York: Pantheon Books, 1949.
Cassirer, Ernst. *Philosophie der symbolischen Formen.* Vol. 2, *Das mythische Denken.* Darmstadt: Wissenschaftliche Buchgesellschaft, 1964.
Cohn, Robert Greer. *Toward the Poems of Mallarmé.* Berkeley and Los Angeles: University of California Press, 1965.
Coman, Jean. *Orphée, civilisateur de l'humanité.* Paris: Zalmoxis, 1939.
Curtius, Ernst Robert. *Europäische Literatur und lateinisches Mittelalter.* 3rd ed. Bern and Munich: Francke Verlag, 1961.
Davies, Constance. "Classical Threads in *Orfeo.*" *Modern Language Review* 56 (April 1961): 161–66.
Davies, Gardner. *Vers une explication rationelle du "Coup de dés."* Paris: Librairie José Corti, 1953.
Dembo, Lawrence S. *Hart Crane's Sanskrit Charge: A Study of "The Bridge."* Ithaca: Cornell University Press, 1960.
Dick, Kay. *Pierrot.* London: Hutchinson, 1960.
Donchin, Georgette. *The Influence of French Symbolism on Russian Poetry.* The Hague: Mouton, 1958.
Dronke, Peter. "The Return of Eurydice." *Classica et Mediaevalia* 23 (1962): 198–215.
Edwardes, Marian. *A Summary of the Literatures of Modern Europe (England, France, Germany, Italy, Spain) from the Origins to 1400.* New York: E. P. Dutton, 1907; reprint edition, New York: Kraus Reprint Co., 1968.
Egger, Emile. *L'Hellénisme en France.* Paris: Didier, 1869.
Erlich, Victor. *The Double Image; Concepts of the Poet in Slavic Literature.* Baltimore: Johns Hopkins University Press, 1964.
———. "Images of the Poet and of Poetry in Slavic Romanticism and Neo-Romanticism." In *American Contributions to the Fifth International Congress of Slavists,* vol. 2, 79–113. The Hague: Mouton, 1963.
Fiske, John. *Myths and Myth-makers.* Boston: Houghton Mifflin, 1872.
Fowlie, Wallace. *The Clown's Grail.* London: Dennis Dobson, 1948.
———. *Mallarmé.* Chicago: University of Chicago Press, 1970.
Frank, Armin Paul. *Literatur zwischen Extremen.* Berlin: Walter de Gruyter, 1977.
Frappier, Jean. *Histoire, mythes et symboles; études de littérature française.* Geneva: Librairie Droz, 1976.
Frazer, Sir James G. *The Golden Bough: A Study in Magic and Religion.* 12 vols. 3rd ed. London: Macmillan, 1963.
———. *The New Golden Bough.* Edited by Theodor H. Gaster. New York: Criterion Books, 1959.

Friedman, John Block. "Eurydice, Heurodis, and the Noon-Day Demon." *Speculum* 41 (January 1966): 22–29.

———. *Orpheus in the Middle Ages*. Cambridge: Harvard University Press, 1970.

Friedrich, Hugo. *Die Struktur der modernen Lyrik*. Hamburg: Rowohlt, 1956; reprint ed., 1977.

Frye, Northrop. *Anatomy of Criticism: Four Essays*. Princeton: Princeton University Press, 1971.

Fuchs, Daniel. *The Comic Spirit of Wallace Stevens*. Durham, N.C.: Duke University Press, 1963.

Gérard, Albert S. "Images, Structure et Thèmes dans 'El Desdichado.'" *Modern Language Review* 58 (1963): 507–15.

Gerhard, Eduard. *Über Orpheus und die Orphiker*. Berlin: Königliche Akademie der Wissenschaften, 1861.

Greg, Walter W. *Pastoral Poetry and Pastoral Drama*. London: A. H. Bullen, 1906.

Gros Louis, Kenneth R. R. "The Significance of Sir Orfeo's Self-Exile." *The Review of English Studies* 18 (August 1967): 245–52.

Grossman, Joan Delaney. "Genius and Madness: The Return of the Romantic Concept of the Poet in Russia at the End of the Nineteenth Century." In *American Contributions to the Seventh International Congress of Slavists, Warsaw, August 1973*, edited by Victor Terras, 247–60. The Hague: Mouton, 1973.

Guirand, Felix, ed. *Larousse Encyclopedia of Mythology*. Translated by Richard Aldington and Delano Ames. New York: Prometheus Press, 1959.

Guthrie, W. K. C. *Orpheus and the Greek Religion: A Study of the Orphic Movement*. 2nd ed. London: Methuen, 1952.

Harrison, Jane Ellen. *Prolegomena to the Study of Greek Religion*. 3rd ed. Cambridge: The University Press, 1922.

———. *Themis, A Study of the Social Origins of Greek Religion*. Cambridge: The University Press, 1912; reprint ed., 1927.

Hassan, Ihab. *The Dismemberment of Orpheus: Toward a Postmodern Literature*. New York: Oxford University Press, 1971.

Hays, H. R. "Laforgue and Stevens." *Romanic Review* 25 (1934): 242–48.

Helgerson, Richard. "The New Poet Presents Himself; Spenser and the Idea of a Literary Career." *PMLA* 93 (October 1978): 893–911.

Heurgon, Jacques. "Orphée et Eurydice avant Virgile." *Mélanges d'archéologie et d'histoire* 49 (1932): 6–60.

Holton, Milne. "'A Baudelairesque Thing': The Directions of Hart Crane's 'Black Tambourine.'" *Criticism* 9 (Summer 1967): 215–28.

Huerre, Pauline Baggio. "Etude du Personnage de Pierrot." Ph.D. diss., Stanford University, 1976.

Hutson, Richard. "Exile Guise: Irony and Hart Crane." *Mosaic* 2 (Summer 1969): 71–86.

Jeffrey, David Lyle. "The Exalted King: Sir Orfeo's Harp and the Second Death of Eurydice." *Mosaic* 9 (Winter 1976): 45–60.

Joukovsky, Françoise. *Orphée et ses disciples dans la poésie française et néolatine du XVIᵉ siècle*. Geneva: Librairie Droz, 1970.

Jung, C. G. *The Collected Works of C. G. Jung*. Vol. 9.1, *The Archetypes and the Collective Unconscious*. Translated by R. F. C. Hull. Bollingen Series, no. 20. New York: Pantheon Books, 1959.

Kerényi, Karl. *Die Mythologie der Griechen: Der Götter- und Menschheitsgeschichten*. Munich: Deutscher Taschenbuch Verlag, 1966.

Kermode, Frank. *Romantic Image*. London: Routledge and Kegan Paul, 1957.

Kern, Otto, ed. *Orphicorum fragmenta*. Berlin: Wiedmann, 1922.

King, Russell S. "The Poet as Clown: Variations on a Theme in Nineteenth-Century French Poetry." *Orbis Literarum* 33 (1978): 238–52.

Kitto, H. D. F. *The Greeks*. Baltimore: Penguin Books, 1957.

Kneller, John W. "The Poet and his Moira: 'El Desdichado.'" *PMLA* 75 (September 1960): 402–9.

Kushner, Eva. *Le Mythe d'Orphée dans la littérature française contemporaine*. Paris: A. G. Nizet, 1961.

Lehmann, A. G. "Pierrot and Fin de Siècle." In *Romantic Mythologies*, edited by Ian Fletcher, 209–24. London: Routledge and Kegan Paul, 1967.

Leibowitz, Herbert A. *Hart Crane, An Introduction to the Poetry*. New York: Columbia University Press, 1968.

Lerner, Lawrence. *The Uses of Nostalgia, Studies in Pastoral Poetry*. London: Chatto and Windus, 1972.

Lesky, Albin. *Geschichte der Griechischen Literatur*. Bern and Munich: Francke Verlag, 1971.

Levin, Harry. *Perspectives of Criticism*. Harvard Studies in Comparative Literature, no. 20. Cambridge: Harvard University Press, 1950.

Lewis, R. W. B. *The Poetry of Hart Crane: A Critical Study*. Princeton: Princeton University Press, 1967.

Lindstrom, Thaïs S. *A Concise History of Russian Literature*. 2 vols. New York: New York University Press, 1966.

Litz, A. Walton. *Introspective Voyager: The Poetic Development of Wallace Stevens*. New York: Oxford University Press, 1972.

Lucas, Peter J. "An Interpretation of *Sir Orfeo*." *Leeds Studies in English* 6 (1972): 1–9.

Malinowski, Bronislaw. *Myth in Primitive Psychology*. New York: W. W. Norton, 1926.

Maslenikov, O. A. *The Frenzied Poets: Andrei Biely and the Russian Symbolists*. Berkeley and Los Angeles: University of California Press, 1952.

Mauron, Charles. *Des Métaphores obsédentes au mythe personnel: introduction à la psychocritique*. Paris: Librairie José Corti, 1962.

Merivale, Patricia. *Pan the Goat-God: His Myth in Modern Times*. Harvard

Studies in Comparative Literature, no. 30. Cambridge: Harvard University Press, 1969.
Michaud, Guy. *Mallarmé: l'homme et l'oeuvre*. Paris: Hatier, 1953.
Miller, David L. "Authorship, Anonymity, and *The Shepheardes Calender*." *Modern Language Quarterly* 40 (September 1979): 219–36.
Miller, J. Hillis. "The Rewording Shell: Image and Emblem in Yeats' Early Poetry." Paper presented at the Symposium on the Poetological Poem, Wuppertal, West Germany, November 1978.
Mossop, D. J. *Pure Poetry: Studies in French Poetic Theory and Practice 1746–1945*. Oxford: Clarendon Press, 1971.
Nitchie, Elizabeth. *Vergil and the English Poets*. New York: Columbia University Press, 1919.
Oreglia, Giacomo. *The Commedia dell'Arte*. London: Methuen, 1968.
Paul, Sherman. *Hart's Bridge*. Urbana, Ill.: University of Illinois Press, 1972.
Peyre, Henri. *L'Influence des littératures antiques sur la littérature française moderne: état des travaux*. New Haven: Yale University Press, 1941.
———. *Le Classicisme français*. New York: Editions de la Maison Française, 1942.
Piselli, Francesco. *Mallarmé e l'estetica*. Milan: U. Mursia, 1969.
Poggioli, Renato. *The Oaten Flute, Essays on Pastoral Poetry and the Pastoral Ideal*. Cambridge: Harvard University Press, 1975.
———. *The Russian Poets 1890–1930*. Cambridge: Harvard University Press, 1960.
Preller, Ludwig. *Griechische Mythologie und landschaftliche Sagen*. Berlin: Wiedmann, 1966.
———. *Griechische Mythologie: Theogonie und Götter*. Berlin: Wiedmann, 1964.
Py, Albert. *Les Mythes grecs dans la poésie de Victor Hugo*. Geneva: Librairie Droz, 1963.
Ramsey, Warren. *Jules Laforgue and the Ironic Inheritance*. New York: Oxford University Press, 1953.
———. "Wallace Stevens and Some French Poets." *Trinity Review* 8 (May 1954): 36–40.
Rand, Edward K. *Ovid and His Influence*. New York: Longmans, Green, 1928.
Reichel, Edward. "Poetic Knowledge in Mallarmé's 'Prose pour des Esseintes.'" Paper presented at the Symposium on the Poetological Poem, Wuppertal, West Germany, November 1978.
Riddel, Joseph N. *The Clairvoyant Eye, The Poetry and Poetics of Wallace Stevens*. Baton Rouge: Louisiana State University Press, 1965.
Ridge, George Ross. *The Hero in French Decadent Literature*. Athens, Georgia: University of Georgia Press, 1961.
———. *The Hero in French Romantic Literature*. Athens, Georgia: University of Georgia Press, 1959.

Roscher, W. H. *Ausführliches Lexikon der Griechischen und Römischen Mythologie.* 4 vols. Leipzig: B. G. Teubner Verlag, 1897–1909.
Sachs, Curt. *The History of Musical Instruments.* New York: W. W. Norton, 1940.
Sand, George. "Preface" to *Masques et Bouffons* by Maurice Sand. Paris: Michel Lévy, 1860.
Sand, Maurice. *The History of the Harlequinade.* 2 vols. Philadelphia, 1915; reprint ed., New York and London: Benjamin Blom, 1968.
Senior, John. *The Way Down and Out: The Occult in Symbolist Literature.* Ithaca: Cornell University Press, 1959.
Seznec, Jean. *The Survival of the Pagan Gods.* Translated by B. F. Sessions. New York: Pantheon Books, 1953.
Shroder, Maurice Z. *Icarus: The Image of the Artist in French Romanticism.* Cambridge: Harvard University Press, 1961.
Smith, Harold J. "Dilemma and Dramatic Structure in Mallarmé's Parnasse Poems." *The French Review* 46 (Spring 1973): 66–76.
———. "Mallarmé's Faun: Hero or Anti-Hero?" *The Romanic Review* 44 (March 1973): 111–24.
Spears, Monroe K. *Dionysus and the City: Modernism in Twentieth Century Poetry.* New York: Oxford University Press, 1970.
———. *Hart Crane.* University of Minnesota Pamphlets on American Writers, no. 47. Minneapolis: University of Minnesota Press, 1965.
Starobinski, Jean. *L'Œil vivant.* Paris: Gallimard, 1961.
———. *Portrait de l'artiste en saltimbanque.* Geneva: Editions d'Art Albert Skira, 1970.
Storey, Robert F. *Pierrot: A Critical History of a Mask.* Princeton: Princeton University Press, 1978.
———. "Verlaine's Pierrots." *Romance Notes* 20 (1980): 223–30.
Strauss, Walter A. *Descent and Return: The Orphic Theme in Modern Literature.* Cambridge: Harvard University Press, 1971.
Struk, Danylo. "The Great Escape: Principal Themes in Valerij Brjusov's Poetry." *Slavic and East European Journal* 12 (Winter 1968): 407–23.
Taupin, René. *L'Influence du symbolisme français sur la poésie américaine (de 1910 à 1920).* Paris: H. Champion, 1929.
Thompson, Ewa M. "The Archetype of the Fool in Russian Literature." *Canadian Slavonic Papers* 15 (Autumn 1973): 245–73.
———. "Il Folle sacro e le sue trasformazioni nella letteratura russa." *Strumenti Critici* 9 (June 1975): 157–71.
———. "Russian Holy Fools and Shamanism." In *American Contributions to the Eighth International Congress of Slavists,* edited by Victor Terras, 691–706. Columbus, Ohio: Slavica, 1978.
Thomson, J. A. K. *The Classical Background of English Literature.* New York: Macmillan, 1948.
Unterecker, John. *Voyager, A Life of Hart Crane.* New York: Farrar, Straus and Giroux, 1969.

Vogel, Lucy. "Masks and Doubles in Blok's Early Poetry." *Russian Language Journal* 30 (Winter 1976): 60–76.
Wasserman, Earl. *Shelley, a Critical Reading*. Baltimore: Johns Hopkins University Press, 1971.
Weber, Alfred. "Amerikanische Künstlererzählungen und poetologische Gedichte als Dokumente der Poetik." Lectures presented in Tübingen, West Germany, 1974–75. (Typewritten.)
———. "'Kann die Harfe durch ihre Propeller schiessen?': Poetologische Lyrik in Amerika." In *Amerikanische Literatur im 20. Jahrhundert*, edited by Alfred Weber and Dietmar Haack, 175–88. Göttigen: Vandenhoeck und Ruprecht, 1971.
Weber, Brom. *Hart Crane, a Biographical and Critical Study*. New York: Bodley Press, 1948.
Wellek, René. *Discriminations; Further Concepts of Criticism*. New Haven: Yale University Press, 1970.
Welsford, Enid. *The Court Masque: A Study in the Relationship between Poetry and the Revels*. Cambridge: Cambridge University Press, 1927.
———. *The Fool: His Social and Literary History*. London: Faber and Faber, 1935.
Wheat, Linda Ross. "A Comparative Study of Jules Laforgue and Hart Crane." Ph.D. diss., Vanderbilt University, 1970.
Wilson, Milton. *Shelley's Later Poetry, A Study of the Prophetic Imagination*. New York: Columbia University Press, 1959.
Yur'eva, Zoia. "Миф об Орфее в творчестве Андрея Белого, Александра Блока и Вячеслава Иванова." New York, 1978. (Mimeographed.)

Index

Abrams, M. H., 38
Afanasiev, A. N., 158 (n.55)
Alciati: *Emblemata*, 20
Apollinaire, Guillaume, 161 (n.37)
Apollo, 10–12, 15, 21–22, 44
Aristaeus, 13, 22
Arnold, Matthew: "Lines Written in Kensington Garden," 28
Arnulf of Orléans: *Allegoriae super Ovidii Metamorphosin*, 24
Arseniev, K. K., 89
l'Art pour l'Art, 38, 48
"Au Clair de la lune," 51, 163 (n.24)
Austin, R. J., 73, 74

Baudelaire, Charles, 67, 90
Beckett, Samuel: *En attendant Godot*, 104
Benamou, Michel, 119, 126–27
Blackmur, R. P., 48–49
Blanchot, Maurice, 18–19
Blok, Aleksandr, 90–91; and French Symbolism, 89–91, 95, 104, 117–18; "Двойник," 95–99, 103, 117, 166 (n.14); "Я был весь в пестрых лоскутьях," 99–100, 117; "Свет в окошке шатался," 100–102, 117; "В час, когда пьянеют нарциссы," 102; "Балаган," 102–3

Bloom, Harold, 123
Boethius: *Consolation of Philosophy*, 24
Boileau, Nicolas: "L'Art poétique," 34–36
Boulanger, André, 16, 157 (n.29)
Bowra, C. M., 165 (n.1)
Bowra, Maurice, 156 (n.20)
Bristol, Michael D., 160 (n.17)
Briusov, Valerii: and French Symbolism, 89–91, 104–5, 117–18; *Француские лирики в XIXв*, 90; "Орфей и Эвридика" 105–6, 108; "Орфей," 106–9, 111, 112; "Ученик Орфея," 109–13, 118; "Вечерний Пан," 113–14; "Снова сумрак," 113; "Эимой," 114–16; "Лесная Тьма," 114–16, 129; "Поэту," 116–17
Browning, Elizabeth: "A Musical Instrument," 45–47
Browning, Robert: "Pan and Luna," 44–45, 47
Busby, Olive M., 166 (n.9)
Bush, Douglas, 24, 26, 36–37, 157 (n.46), 158 (n.60)
Buttel, Robert, 121, 167 (n.1)

Calliope, 11
Campbell, Joseph, 62, 145, 147, 148

Cassirer, Ernst, 15, 148, 169 (n.5)
Chénier, André: "Les Nymphes et les satyres," 37
Cohn, Robert G., 73
Coman, Jean, 12, 16
Corbière, Tristan, 119
Crane, Hart: and French Symbolism, 119–20, 127–28; "The Black Tambourine," 120, 128, 130–31, 135, 138; *The Bridge*, 120–21, 135–46; "Chaplinesque," 120, 128, 131–34, 135, 138; "Porphyro in Akron," 120, 128–30, 134, 135, 138; "The Bridge of Estador," 128; "The Fernery," 128; "Locutions des Pierrots," 128, 134–35; "Recitative," 128; "Wine Menagerie," 128; "My Grandmother's Love Letters," 128, 135
Crétin, Guillaume, 30, 32, 159 (n.11)
Curtius, Ernst R., 9, 155 (n.4)

Davies, Constance, 160 (n.17)
Davies, Gardner, 82
deBaif, J.-A., 30, 159 (n.2)
de Banville, Théodore, 164 (n.40)
deMachaut, Guillaume: "Le Confort d'Ami," 32; "Prologue," 32–33
Dembo, Lawrence S., 136, 143, 168 (n.43)
Dick, Kay, 52, 162 (n.6)
Dionysus, 14–17
Donchin, Georgette, 89
Dowson, Ernest, 121
Dronke, Peter, 13
Dryope, 6, 11

Edwardes, Marian, 158 (n.49)
Egger, Emile, 157 (n.46)
Eliot, T. S., 121

Erlich, Victor, 90, 116–17
Euripides: *Alcestis*, 13
Eurydice, 12–14, 18–19, 22, 24, 32, 35, 42, 149; in the poetry of Briusov, 105–6; in the poetry of Crane, 142

Faun. *See* Pan
Fiske, John, 149
Flaubert, Gustave, 53
Fool, Elizabethan, 5, 94; and Blok, 95, 117; and Crane, 132. *See also* Harlequin; *Iurodivyi*; Pierrot; *Pitre*
Fowlie, Wallace, 53, 68, 74
Frank, Armin Paul, 37
Frappier, Jean, 158 (nn.49, 60)
Frazer, Sir James G., 149, 158 (n.55)
Friedman, John Block, 24, 156 (n.21), 158 (nn.46, 63), 159 (n.67), 160 (n.14)
Friedrich, Hugo, 39
Frost, Robert: "Pan With Us," 28
Frye, Northrop, 36, 54–55, 153
Fuchs, Daniel, 119, 122

Gautier, Théophile, 67; *La Préface de Mademoiselle de Maupin*, 49; "Bûchers et Tombeaux," 55–57; "L'Art," 56
Gérard, Albert S., 78, 157 (n.29), 164 (n.45)
Gerhard, Eduard, 157 (n.29)
Gros Louis, Kenneth, 35
Grossman, Joan D., 90
Guirand, Felix, 22
Guthrie, W. K. C., 12, 16, 156 (n.14)

Harlequin, 5, 96; in the poetry of Blok, 90–91, 94–103, 117
Harrison, Jane Ellen, 148, 156 (n.14)
Hassan, Ihab, 14, 19–20

Hays, H. R., 121, 167 (n.1)
Helgerson, Richard, 31
Hermes, 6–7, 21–22
Herodotus, 7
Heurgon, Jacques, 156 (n.20)
Heurre, Pauline, 52
Holton, W. Milne, 128, 131, 135–36
"Homeric Hymn to Pan," 7, 9
Horace: *Ars poetica*, 3, 11–12
Hugo, Victor: "Pan," 40–41, 47; "Le Satyre," 40–41, 47; "Le Poëte dans les Révolutions," 41–42, 47
Hutson, Richard, 128, 135
Huysmans, Joris-Karl: *A Rebours*, 49, 67

Isocrates, 13
Iurodivyi, 91–94; resemblance to Elizabethan fool, 94; in the poetry of Blok, 95–117

Jarry, Alfred, 53
Jonson, Ben: *Pans Anniversarie*, 30–31
Joukovsky, Françoise, 17–18, 32–33, 36, 158 (nn.46, 49)
Joyce, James, 53
Jung, C. G., 149

Keats, John: *Endymion*, 39–40; "The Eve of St. Agnes," 129–30
Kerényi, Karl, 9
Kermode, Frank, 39
King, Russell S., 68
Kitto, H. D. F., 21–22
Kneller, John, 77–78, 164 (n.45)
Kushner, Eva, 15–18, 156 (n.14), 157 (n.29), 159 (n.67)

Laforgue, Jules, 49, 53, 55; "Les Locutions des Pierrots," 57–61, 87–88, 132, 134; "Complainte de Lord Pierrot," 57, 59–60; *Moralités légendaires*, 57, 60–63, 73, 79
Lai d'Orphée, 24
Lehmann, A. G., 60
Leibowitz, Herbert, 131
Lerner, Lawrence, 158 (n.60), 159 (n.66)
Lesky, Albin, 156 (n.23)
Levin, Harry, 155 (n.4)
Lewis, R. W. B., 54, 119, 130, 132–34, 138, 139, 141–42
Lindstrom, Thaïs, 26, 158 (n.54)
Litz, A. Walton, 167 (n.11)
Lomonosov, M. V., 37
Lucas, Peter, 35
Lyre, of Orpheus, 11, 20–21, 45
Lyrik, poetologische. *See* Poetry, self-reflexive

Maenads, 13–14; in poetry of Briusov, 106–9, 111–13; in poetry of Crane, 142
Malinowski, Bronislaw, 147
Mallarmé, Stephané: "L'Art pour Tous," 49; "Le Pitre châtié," 49, 50, 68–71, 74–75, 80, 82; "L'Après-midi d'un faune," 49, 68, 71–79, 80, 82, 87–88, 163 (n.21); *Igitur*, 50, 68, 77, 80–87; "Le Sonneur," 67, 68; "Le Guignon," 67, 68; "Une dentelle s'abolit," 67, 80; "Las de l'amer repos," 67, 80; "Salut," 67, 80; "Mes bouquins refermés," 72, 84
Marot, Clément, 25, 28
Marvell, Andrew, 37
Masks, poetic, 4–6, 54–55, 91, 136–37
Maslenikow, O. A., 165 (n.1)
Mauclair, Camille: *Le Soleil des morts*, 86–87
Mauron, Charles, 19
Maurus, Rabanus: *De rerum naturis*, 25

Merezhkovskii, D., 89
Merivale, Patricia, 24–25, 155 (n.5), 158 (nn.46, 61, 62), 159 (nn.64, 65)
Meta-poetry. *See* Poetry, self-reflexive
Michaud, Guy, 164 (n.50)
Midas, 10, 30
Miller, David, 31–32, 37
Miller, J. Hillis, 159 (n.66)
Milton, John: "Elegia Quinta in Adventus Veris," 10; "On the Morning of Christ's Nativity," 11, 27; *Paradise Regained*, 27
More, Henry: *Praeexistency of the Soul*, 27
Mossop, D. J., 83, 85
Musset, Alfred de, 53
Myth: in modern literature, 136–37, 144–46, 148–53; in society, 145–50

Nerval, Gerard de: "El Desdichado," 50, 55, 77–80, 87–88
Nitchie, Elizabeth, 158 (n.46)

Oeagrus, 11
Onomakritos, 9
Oreglia, Giacomo, 166 (n.11)
Orpheus: in ancient mythology, 11–23, 148–50; as Apollonian priest, 11–12, 15–18, 20, 22–33; and the *katábasis*, 12–15, 17–19, 22, 80–81, 105–9, 112, 137, 142–44; and the *sparagmós*, 13–15, 17–20, 108–9, 111, 140, 144; in medieval literature, 13, 23–25, 27; as Dionysian figure, 14–18, 22–23; introduction into Russian literature, 25–26; as prefiguration of Christ, 27; in the poetry of Mallarmé, 68, 80–87; in the poetry of Nerval, 77–81; in the poetry of Briusov, 91, 104–13, 118; in the poetry of Crane, 120, 137, 140, 142–44
"Orphic Hymn to Pan," 9–10, 25
Ovid: *Metamorphoses*, 7–8, 10, 12–14, 24–26; allegories of in medieval literature, 24–25; introduction in Russian literature, 25–26; in the poetry of Shelley, 43; in the poetry of Verlaine, 66; in the poetry of Briusov, 105–8, 111; in the poetry of Crane, 142
Ovide Moralisé, 24–25

Pan, 4–11, 20–23, 148–50; as Arcadian figure, 7–11, 28, 37, 64; as Dionysian god, 8–11, 20, 22–23, 29; as Orphic figure, 8–11, 22–23, 25, 28; as faun and satyr, 8, 28; derivation of name, 9; as prefiguration of Christ, 11, 27; in medieval literature, 23–25; introduction into Russian literature, 25–26; as demonic figure, 27; and the modern clown, 40, 50, 54–55, 60; in the poetry of Gautier, 55–57; in the poetry of Laforgue, 60–63; in the poetry of Mallarmé, 68, 71–79; in the poetry of Briusov, 91, 113–16, 118; in the poetry of Stevens, 120–24; in the poetry of Crane, 120, 138–39, 141, 144
Pan-pipe, 7–8, 10–11, 20–21, 43, 61–62
Pasternak, Boris: "Hamlet," 166 (n.15)
Paul, Sherman, 136
Persona. *See* Masks, poetic
Peyre, Henri, 23, 26, 160 (n.26)
Phanocles: *Erotes*, 14, 156 (n.24)
Pharmakos, 54–55
Philostratus, 156 (n.24)

Picasso, Pablo, 51, 53
Pierrot, 5, 50–55; in the poetry of Laforgue, 57–61; in the poetry of Verlaine, 63–66; in the poetry of Stevens, 119–20, 124–25; in the poetry of Crane, 119–20, 134–35
Pirandello, Luigi, 104
Piselli, Francesco, 68–69, 71
Pitre: defined, 69; poet as, 5–6, 40–41, 50, 52–56; in the poetry of Verlaine, 65–66; in the poetry of Mallarmé, 68–71; in the poetry of Blok, 90–91, 94–104, 117; in the poetry of Crane, 119–20, 131–34, 136–37; in the poetry of Stevens, 119–21
Poe, Edgar Allan, 67, 90, 144
Poetry, self-reflexive: definition of, 3–4, 37; in modern poetry, 3–6, 37–39, 48–49; transition from discursive to mimetic mode, 37–39
Poggioli, Renato, 159 (n.65), 165 (n.1)
Pseudo-Eratosthenes, 157 (n.24)
Pushkin, Aleksandr: *Ruslan and Liudmila*, 40
Py, Albert, 41

Rabelais, François: *Le Quart Livre*, 27
Ramsey, Warren, 57, 101, 119, 121, 167 (n.1)
Rand, Edward K., 158 (n.46)
Reichel, Edward, 39
Riddel, Joseph, 121, 126, 127, 167 (n.11)
Ridge, George R., 38, 48
Ronsard, Pierre de: *Hymne des Daimons*, 27; "Première Ode à la Fontaine Bellerie," 30; "L'Orphée," 33–34

Roscher, W. H., 8, 11, 159 (n.8)
Rouault, Georges, 51, 53

Sachs, Curt, 20–21
Sand, George, 52
Sand, Maurice, 162 (n.6), 166 (n.11)
Senior, John, 164 (n.46)
Seznec, Jean, 158 (n.60)
Shakespeare, William: *Henry VIII*, 35–36
Shelley, Mary: *Midas*, 43
Shelley, Percy Bysshe: "Orpheus," 42–43, 47; "Hymn of Pan," 43–44
Shroder, Maurice Z., 37–38
Sidney, Phillip: "Apology for Poetry," 36
Sir Orfeo, 24, 35–36
Smith, Harold, 68, 70, 72, 74, 75, 77
Spears, Monroe K., 38–39, 119
Spenser, Edmund, *Shepheardes Calender*, 27–28, 30–32; *Faerie Queene*, 32; "The Ruines of Time," 36
Starobinski, Jean, 2, 53, 67
Stevens, Wallace: and French Symbolism, 119–22, 124–25; "The Comedian as the Letter C," 119–21, 124–27; "The Weeping Burgher," 119–22; "Peter Quince at the Clavier," 119–24; "Pierrot," 122
Storey, Robert, 119, 124–25, 162 (n.6), 167 (n.11)
Strannik. See *Iurodivyi*
Strauss, Walter, 86–87, 164 (n.41)
Struk, Danylo, 104
Symbala et Emblemata, 26
Syrinx, 7, 61–63, 75

Taupin, René, 121, 125, 167 (n.1)
Theocritus, 7

Thompson, Ewa M., 91–94, 165 (nn.5, 7)

Unterecker, John, 168 (n.17)

Valery, Paul, 49
Vengerova, Zinaida, 89
Verlaine, Paul, 53, 55; "Pierrot," 63–64, 66, 97; "Pierrot Gamin," 64–66; "Caprice," 65–66; *Fêtes galantes*, 66–67
Villon, François: "Double Ballade," 32
Virgil: *Georgics*, 12–14, 18, 22, 24–25, 35, 44–45; *Aeneid*, 24; *Eclogues*, 24; allegories in medieval literature, 24–25
Vogel, Lucy, 91, 103

Wasserman, Earl, 161 (n.49)
Weber, Alfred, 3–4
Weber, Brom, 128
Wellek, René, 37
Welsford, Enid, 94, 162 (n.13), 166 (n.9)
Wheat, Linda R., 167 (n.1)
Wilson, Milton, 161 (n.49)

Yeats, William Butler: "Song of the Happy Shepherd," 28
Yur'eva, Zoia, 26

OHIO UNIVERSITY LIBRARY

Please return this book as soon as you have finished with it. In order to avoid a fine it must be returned by the latest date stamped below.

RETURN BY

APR 24 1987

RETURN BY

MAY 16 1991

APR 29 1991

JAN 4 1993

Quarter Loan

RETURNED BY:

NOV 29 199

FEB 10 1995

RETURN BY 1995

MAR 15 1995

APR 0 5 1995

SEP 1 1 2003

OCT 2 9 2008 RECEIVED

JUL 0 9 1986